# IN DEFENSE OF THE ALIEN

## Volume XXIII

*Reform of the 1996 Immigration Laws – Employment Migration into the United States – INS Restructuring – INS Processing, Entry, Applications, and Citizenship – Human Rights of Migrants: Refugee Protection, Gender-Based Violence and Trafficking – Integration of Immigrants and their Children*

# IN DEFENSE OF THE ALIEN

# Volume XXIII

*Reform of the 1996 Immigration Laws – Employment Migration into the United States – INS Restructuring – INS Processing, Entry, Applications, and Citizenship – Human Rights of Migrants: Refugee Protection, Gender-Based Violence and Trafficking – Integration of Immigrants and their Children*

Proceedings of the 2000 Annual National Legal Conference on Immigration and Refugee Policy

**Edited by Lydio F. Tomasi**

2001

Center for Migration Studies

New York

CMS is an educational non-profit institute founded in New York in 1964 committed to encourage and facilitate the study of the sociodemographic, economic, historical, political, legislative and pastoral aspects of human migration and refugee movements. CMS organizes an annual national legal conference on immigration and refugee policy, the proceedings of which are published in a volume series entitled **IN DEFENSE OF THE ALIEN**. This text represents the Twenty-Third Volume of that series.

*IN DEFENSE OF THE ALIEN*
*VOLUME XXIII*

*Reform of the 1996 Immigration Laws – Employment Migration into the United States – INS Restructuring – INS Processing, Entry, Applications, and Citizenship – Human Rights of Migrants: Refugee Protection, Gender-Based Violence and Trafficking – Integration of Immigrants and their Children*

*First Edition*



*The Center for Migration Studies of New York, Inc.*
*209 Flagg Place*
*Staten Island, New York 10304-1122*

ISSN 0275-634X; v.23
ISBN 1-57703-014-1

Printed in the United States of America

# CONTENTS

# Introduction

The 23rd edition of the National Conference was again convened against the backdrop of the ever-changing debate on U.S. immigration. With the economy in good shape, the GOP's anti-immigrant fever of the mid-1990s had subsided. Population control zealots were seeking in vain to restrict immigration by stoking anti-immigration rage with the absurd notion that foreign workers were taking American jobs. In February, the AFL-CIO Executive Council, in an unprecedented change of policy, approved a resolution calling for an amnesty allowing the 5 to 6 million illegal immigrants to apply for legal residency and for full workplace rights for immigrant workers. Such amnesty was welcome by many as responsible statesmanship acknowledging the implications of globalization for both developed and developing countries. Old legislation passed by Congress (such as the Illegal Immigration Reform and Immigrant Responsibility Act leading to automatic detention and removal for legal immigrants convicted of certain crimes), was back on the table together with a long agenda of immigration legislation pending in the 106th Congress that included INS restructuring and budget; the admission of legal temporary workers; refugees; alien eligibility for public assistance; and Central American and Haitian adjustment.

Many of these items were discussed at the six sessions of the twenty-third National Legal Conference on Immigration and Refugee Policy and form the six parts of this volume of the conference proceedings.

Reform of the 1996 immigration laws is the topic of Part I. Numerous legal challenges have been brought attacking various provisions of 1996 legislation which severely limited procedural due process rights of aliens as well as expanding grounds for removal while contracting available relief. Several important bills have been introduced to deal with key issues. Part I considers pending legislation and lawsuits as well as reasonable models for revision of these laws.

Part II deals with high-skilled migration to the United States. The issue of the migration of high-skilled labor to the U.S. continues to be controversial. Intracompany transfers are frustrated by issues like spousal work authorization. H-1B visas are limited in number, a ceiling that will be reached well before the end of the fiscal year. Critics claim H-1B policy hurts U.S. workers. Employment related permanent immigration is below authorized levels due, critics claim, to INS inefficiency in the application process. Part II reviews policy and proposals affecting substance and process.

The issue of INS restructuring remains on the table. The failure of the 1999 session of Congress to pass a bill is leading to reconsideration by many players and the probability of reopening of negotiations. Part III reviews proposals and positions at the early stages of the 2000 session of Congress.

A basic strategy of immigration regulation is controlled entry at the border. For noncitizens this sometimes means delay in processing at entry. Frustration often does not end there. Long delays for citizenship are the norm in a system apparently incapable of handling its workload. Part IV focuses on INS processing issues and its effects on visitors, permanent residents, and citizenship applicants.

Part V addresses the critiques about erosion of protection for refugees and asylum seekers. It specifically addresses asylum seekers from gender-based violence and legislative remedies. Finally, Part V addresses the issue of trafficking, its effects on asylum seekers and the human rights of trafficked migrants.

Much has been written about the integration of immigrants entering the U.S. over the last three decades. The major focus has been on economic integration. Attention recently has focused on second and succeeding generations and their experiences in American society and to the claim by some elite critics who once again predict that today's newcomers to America will never become real Americans. Part VI presents information from new studies of immigrants and second generation immigrants and pays particular attention to non-economic integration including health, language use and religion.

An exceptional group of panelists from Congress as well as members of the bar, the academy and the private sector make these proceedings enlightening and challenging. To all of them our sincere thanks. We are also deeply thankful to the Conference Program Organizing Committee and to all the members of the Conference Advisory Committee as well as to the following institutions and organizations for their financial support: The State Education Department/SUNY; The Migration Health Program, DHHS; the USCC Migration and Refugee Services; The Hebrew Immigrant Aid Society; Church World Service, Immigration and Refugee Program; The Lutheran Immigration and Refugee Service; and the New York Association for New Americans.

*Lydio F. Tomasi*
*Center for Migration Studies*

# PART I

# REFORM OF THE 1996 IMMIGRATION LAWS

# 1

# Understanding the Impact of the 1996 Deportation Laws and the Limited Scope of Proposed Reforms

NANCY MORAWETZ
*New York University School of Law*

## *INTRODUCTION*

In 1996, Congress enacted two laws – the Antiterrorism and Effective Death Penalty Act[1] (AEDPA) and the Illegal Immigration Reform and Immigrant Responsibility Act[2] (IIRIRA) – that drastically changed the consequences of criminal convictions for lawful permanent residents. Although lawful per-

[1]Pub. L. No. 104-132, 110 Stat. 1214 (1996) (codified in scattered sections of 8, 18, 22, 28, 40, and 42 U.S.C.).
[2]Pub. L. No. 104-208, div. C, 110 Stat. 3009-546 (1996) (codified in scattered sections of 8 and 18 U.S.C.).

manent residents had long been subject to deportation[3] for criminal convictions, the 1996 laws make such deportation mandatory in large classes of cases.[4] Furthermore, the new laws provide that permanent residents convicted of a wide array of crimes are automatically placed in detention following the completion of any criminal sentence.[5]

Much of the initial commentary on the 1996 laws focused on the unfairness of applying these laws retroactively.[6] The first cases to come before the courts involved persons who had committed crimes prior to the enactment of the new laws and who faced new deportation consequences for their conduct.[7] Retroactive application provided an important doctrinal hook for challenging the severity of the laws as they applied to this group. Established legal precedent against reading statutes to apply retroactively,[8] together with constitutional limitations on applying new rules to old facts,[9] offered a ready basis for questioning the application of the laws to people who committed crimes prior to the 1996 enactments. But even outside the courts, retroactivity served as a magnet for commentary, particularly in newspapers and other media.[10] Indeed, changing the rules is contrary to

[3]Under IIRIRA, deportation is now termed "removal." I continue to use the term "deportation" because I believe it better reflects the real impact of the laws.

[4]*See infra* Part II. *See generally* Nancy Morawetz, *Rethinking Retroactive Deportation Laws and the Due Process Clause,* 73 N.Y.U. L. Rev. 97, 107-14 (1998) (describing changes in the deportation laws that resulted from the enactment of AEDPA and IIRIRA).

[5]*See* Immigration and Naturalization Act (INA) § 236(c)(1), 8 U.S.C. § 1226(c)(1) (Supp. II 1996).

[6]*See, e.g.,* U.S. Comm'n on Immigration Reform, 1997 Report to Congress: Becoming an American: Immigration and Immigrant Policy 143-45 (1997); Morawetz, *supra* note 4; Peter H. Schuck & John Williams, *Removing Criminal Aliens: The Pitfalls and Promises of Federalism,* 22 Harv. J.L. & Pub. Pol'y 367, 372 (1999) (observing that opponents of the 1996 laws focus on their retroactive effect); Paige Krasker, Note, *Crimes of the Past Revisited: Legal Aliens Deported for Past Crimes Under the Retroactive Application of the Antiterrorism and Effective Death Penalty Act,* 22 Suffolk Transnat'l Rev. 109 (1998); Bruce R. Marley, Comment, *Exiling the New Felons: The Consequences of the Retroactive Application of Aggravated Felony Convictions to Lawful Permanent Residents,* 35 San Diego L. Rev. 855 (1998); Sara A. Martin, Note, *Postcards from the Border: A Result-Oriented Analysis of Immigration Reform Under AEDPA and IIRIRA,* 19 B.C. Third World L.J. 683, 694 (1999); Anjali Parekh Prakash, Note, *Changing the Rules: Arguing Against Retroactive Application of Deportation Statutes,* 72 N.Y.U. L. Rev. 1420 (1997).

[7]*See, e.g.,* cases cited *infra* note 67.

[8]*See, e.g.,* Martin v. Hadix, 119 S. Ct. 1998, 2004 (1999); Landgraf v. USI Film Prods., 511 U.S. 244, 265 (1994).

[9]*See* Morawetz, *supra* note 4, at 131-43.

[10]*See, e.g.,* Pamela Hartman, *Law Ships Vietnam Vet Back to Mexico,* Tucson Citizen, Apr. 24, 1999, at A1; Anthony Lewis, *Punishing the Past,* N.Y. Times, Mar. 30, 1998, at A17; Mirta Ojito, *Old Crime Returns to Haunt an Immigrant,* N.Y. Times, Oct. 15, 1997, at B1; Bob Ray Sanders, *INS Threatens to Send Man, 27, Back to Laos over Teen Mistake,* Fort Worth Star-Telegram, Aug. 11, 1999, at 1.

well-entrenched conceptions of justice. It is also simply irrational to ignore rehabilitation shown through years of work and family life.

Strong as the challenges to retroactivity may be, they run the risk of distorting the debate about the new laws. Although the first cases involved people with past convictions, the laws permanently change the position of legal residents who are already in this country or who will immigrate in the future. The new immigration laws increase the likelihood that a permanent resident will face mandatory deportation for any criminal conviction. In addition, changes in criminal justice policies, Immigration and Naturalization Service (INS) enforcement policies, and the new mandatory detention system render the new laws far more unforgiving in practice than is apparent from their texts. As a result, the new deportation regime greatly increases the risk that a conviction for a crime will result not only in criminal punishment, but also in exile and family separation.[11]

The 1996 laws, together with most proposals for their reform, have assumed that Congress should develop a one-size-fits-all test that will determine which permanent residents with convictions should be deported. Whether through the label of certain classes of crimes or through the length of the person's sentence, Congress has mandated the deportation of persons whose family members may all reside in this country, who may have grown up here, who may be needed for the emotional and financial support of minor children or elderly parents, or who may present other compelling equities that counsel against deportation.

This essay argues that the effort to develop a per se list of offenses or sentences that mandate deportation is fundamentally misguided. Because of the immense consequences of detention and deportation – both for the permanent resident and for the family members who will be left behind – the deportation system should reflect a fair evaluation of each case. The system cannot be just if it depends solely on the label of the crime or the sentence imposed.

[11]Several commentators argue that the prospective application of the new laws is unfair and illegal. *See, e.g.*, Terry Coonan, *Dolphins Caught in Congressional Fishnets – Immigration Law's New Aggravated Felons*, 12 Geo. Immigr. L.J. 589 (1998) (criticizing the aggravated felony definition in the new immigration laws); Kathleen M. Keller, *A Comparative and International Law Perspective on the United States (Non)Compliance with Its Duty of Non-Refoulement*, 2 Yale Hum. Rts. & Dev. L.J. 183 (1999) (contending that the 1996 laws violate the Convention Relating to Refugees); Iris Bennett, Note, *The Unconstitutionality of Nonuniform Immigration Consequences of "Aggravated Felony" Convictions*, 74 N.Y.U. L. Rev. 1696 (1999) (arguing that the aggravated felony provisions result in nonuniform immigration consequences and are thus unconstitutional).

Part II of this essay outlines the major features of the new laws that mandate deportation of legal permanent residents with criminal convictions. Part III outlines how changes in the criminal justice system, mandatory detention, and INS enforcement of the new laws magnify the impact of the new deportation rules. Part IV discusses how the new laws are inconsistent with core immigration policies as well as with other laws and policies that protect the integrity of families. Finally, Part V argues that legislative reform efforts, at a minimum, should endeavor to restore the basic discretion of immigration judges to review each individual case, rather than to develop a new set of rules that rely solely on the label of the crime or the sentence imposed.

## *II. THE 1996 DEPORTATION PROVISIONS*

Prior to 1996, the deportation laws relating to long-term legal permanent residents convicted of crimes operated as a two-step process. The first step was to determine whether a person was deportable. The second step was to determine whether the person should be deported, based on all the facts and circumstances of the case. This second step offered an opportunity to consider such issues as whether the person had shown rehabilitation, whether deportation would hurt family members, and whether the person had strong ties to his or her country of origin. When the balance of equities counseled against deportation, a permanent resident could be granted relief from deportation.[12] The new deportation laws have greatly increased the number of permanent residents who are deportable under the first step, while virtually eliminating the second step – the individualized assessment of the appropriateness of deportation. As a result, it is now much more likely that a lawful permanent resident with only one conviction will be subject to deportation and that anyone subject to deportation will be barred from relief.

### *A. "Aggravated Felonies"*

With regard to deportability and eligibility for relief, the most publicized aspect of the new laws is their Alice-in-Wonderland-like definition of the term "aggravated felony."[13] This term plays a central role because it is one of the triggers for mandatory detention and deportation. As the term

[12]*See, e.g., In re* Marin, 16 I. & N. Dec. 581, 584-85 (B.I.A. Aug. 4, 1978).
[13]*See* Coonan, *supra* note 11, at 594-95; Bennett, *supra* note 11, at 1698-703; Anthony Lewis, *Mr. Smith Tells a Tale,* N.Y. Times, Mar. 10, 1997, at A15.

is defined, a crime need not be either aggravated or a felony. For example, a conviction for simple battery[14] or for shoplifting[15] with a one-year suspended sentence – either of which would be a misdemeanor or a violation in most states – can be deemed an aggravated felony.[16]

The most significant changes in the aggravated felony categories consist of modifications in the length of sentence requirements for a crime of theft or violence to qualify as an aggravated felony. Under the 1996 laws, a sentence of one year is sufficient to receive the aggravated felony status.[17] For example, the Third Circuit has held that a conviction for the misdemeanor crime of petty theft under New York law with a one-year sentence constitutes an aggravated felony under the immigration laws.[18] Many of the crimes added to the aggravated felony definition fit within the broad immigration law category of "crimes involving moral turpitude."[19] For example, any crime with an element of fraud falls into this category.[20] The importance of the aggravated felony designation for these convictions is that a single conviction triggers deportability and bars relief from deportation. For instance, under the old law, a person convicted of shoplifting and given a suspended sentence was not deportable unless he or she had two convictions,[21] and such an individual was not barred from relief.[22] Under the new laws, the conviction results in mandatory deportation.

[14]*See* Susan Levine, *On the Verge of Exile: For Children Adopted from Abroad, Lawbreaking Brings Deportation,* Wash. Post, Mar. 5, 2000, at A1 (discussing the case of Mary Anne Gehris). Publicity about the Gehris case led to an unusual pardon from the Georgia Board of Pardons and Parole. *See id.* For a discussion of Gehris's case, *see infra* p. 1943.

[15]*See* Patrick Smikle, *Immigrants Face Deportation for Minor Offenses,* Inter Press Service, Apr. 29, 1999, 1999 WL 5948369 (discussing the case of Olufolake Olaleye, who faces deportation for shoplifting).

[16]Many aspects of the new immigration regime face challenges in light of the penalties imposed by IIRIRA. As a result, the precise contours of the current law are not clear. One argument is that a crime prosecuted as a misdemeanor cannot be an aggravated felony. This argument has met resistance in the courts. *See, e.g.,* United States v. Graham, 169 F.3d 787, 791 (3d Cir. 1999).

[17]*See* INA § 101(a)(43)(F)-(G), 8 U.S.C. § 1101(a)(43)(F)-(G) (Supp. II 1996). Prior to 1996, these crimes were not denominated aggravated felonies unless the sentence imposed was at least five years. *See* INA § 101(a)(43)(F)-(G), 8 U.S.C. 1101(a)(43)(F)-(G) (1994) (amended 1996).

[18]*See Graham,* 169 F.3d at 793.

[19]*See* Dan Kesselbrenner & Lory D. Rosenberg, Immigration Law and Crimes § 6.2(a) (Norton Tooby, updating ed., 1999) (describing crimes that courts have treated as "crimes involving moral turpitude").

[20]*See* Jordan v. DeGeorge, 341 U.S. 223, 227-31 (1951).

[21]*See* INA § 241(a)(2), 8 U.S.C. § 1251(a)(2) (1994) (amended 1996).

[22]*See* INA § 212(c), 8 U.S.C. § 1182(c)(1994) (amended 1996).

For crimes that had previously been considered aggravated felonies, the new laws bar relief regardless of the length of the prison sentence or whether the person received any prison sentence at all.[23] This dramatically changes the consequences of the aggravated felony label.[24] For example, it had long been the case that the lowest level conviction for possession of a controlled substance with intent to distribute was called an aggravated felony.[25] Now, a person with such a conviction who has never served a day in prison is subject to mandatory deportation. José Velasquez, for example, was at a party when a friend approached him looking to buy drugs.[26] Velasquez told the person that he did not sell drugs, but he identified someone else who might.[27] He was arrested and later pled guilty to drug conspiracy, even though he had no financial connection to the person that he had suspected was selling drugs.[28] The court imposed a fine and placed Velasquez on probation.[29] Velasquez's conviction is treated as an aggravated felony, and Velasquez, who has lived in the United States for thirty-nine years as a legal resident, now faces mandatory deportation.[30] Similarly, a person with two drug possession convictions may be treated as an aggravated felon even if the convictions were misdemeanors under state law.[31]

### *B. Crimes Committed Within the First Five or Seven Years of Residence*

For legal permanent residents who are convicted of a crime within their first five or seven years of legal residence, the law is even less forgiving. During an immigrant's first seven years of residence, any crime that makes the person deportable stops the clock for counting continuous residence and therefore bars the person from relief from deportation, even if

[23]*See* INA § 240A(a)(3), 8 U.S.C. § 1229b(a)(3) (Supp. II 1996).

[24]Some commentators assume that the aggravated felony label accurately "conjure[d] up images of hardened, deviant criminals" when it was first introduced into law. Coonan, *supra* note 11, at 590. But the breadth of the label as applied to drug crimes dates back to 1990. *See, e.g., In re* Davis, 20 I & N. Dec. 536 (B.I.A. May 28, 1992) (discussing the scope of the drug trafficking definition).

[25]*See In re* L-G-, 21 I. & N. Dec. 89, 93-96 (B.I.A. Sept. 27, 1995) (interpreting INA § 101(a)(43), 8 U.S.C. § 1101(a)(43) (1994) (amended 1996)).

[26]*See* Velasquez v. Reno, 37 F. Supp. 2d 663, 665 (D.N.J. 1999).

[27]*See id.*

[28]*See id.*

[29]*See id.*

[30]*See id.* at 664 (noting that the INS charged Velasquez with removal as an alien who conspired in illicit trafficking).

[31]*See In re* L-G-, 21 I. & N. Dec. 89, 94-95 (B.I.A. Sept. 27, 1995).

the conviction is for a crime that would not otherwise bar relief.[32] Thus, a crime such as simple possession of drugs will lead to mandatory deportation.[33] In addition, during an immigrant's first five years of legal residence, any crime involving moral turpitude that *could* be punished by a sentence of one year is grounds for mandatory deportation, even if the person is sentenced to only probation or a fine.[34] In New York, for example, the crime of theft of services is a Class A misdemeanor that carries a possible sentence of one year in prison.[35] A person could receive such a conviction for jumping a turnstile or using unauthorized cable service.

The new mandatory deportation rules for legal permanent residents with fewer than five or seven years of residence have not received much attention. Perhaps the group affected by them is assumed to have more tenuous ties to the United States and therefore engenders less sympathy. It is also possible that there has not yet been full enforcement of these provisions because those immigrants who do not receive prison sentences are less likely to be identified by the INS immediately following their convictions.[36] But the provisions can be devastating for immigrant families because almost any infraction that occurs during the period of adjustment to life in the United States makes a legal permanent resident subject to mandatory deportation. For immigrants who come to this country as a family unit, these provisions mandate that a teenager who gets into relatively minor trouble – such as shoplifting or hooking into a cable wire without authorization – must be ordered back to the country that the fam-

[32]*See* INA § 240A(d)(1), 8 U.S.C. § 1229b(d)(1) (Supp. II 1996). Under the old law, the clock for evaluating whether the person had seven years of residence continued to run during the period when the INS did not seek deportation and during any deportation proceedings. *See* Morawetz, *supra* note 4, at 108 & n. 54. Although some legislators criticized this rule as creating an incentive for delay, *see, e.g.,* S. Rep. No. 104-249, at 15 (1996), the rule also allowed for more flexibility in cases where the person had strong ties to the United States but did not have the magic seven years. For example, in many families, the person with the conviction is a young person who came to the United States as a child or teenager. A single drug possession conviction at the age of seventeen could result in permanent exile for this person.

[33]*See* INA § 237(a)(2)(B), 8 U.S.C. § 1227(a)(2)(B) (Supp. II 1996).

[34]*See* INA § 237(a)(2)(A)(i), 8 U.S.C. § 1227(a)(A)(i) (Supp. II 1996). A person found to be deportable under this provision will also be ineligible for relief because that person will not have accumulated the required seven years of continuous residence prior to the commission of the crime. *See* INA § 240A(d), 8 U.S.C. § 1229b(d) (Supp. II 1996). Under the old law, a single conviction for a crime involving moral turpitude was not a ground of deportability unless the individual was sentenced to at least one year of incarceration. *See* INA § 241(a)(2)(i), 8 U.S.C. § 1251(a)(2)(i) (1994) (amended 1996).

[35]*See* N.Y. PENAL LAW § 155.25 (McKinney 1999).

[36]*See* Schuck & Williams, *supra* note 6, at 402.

ily has left behind. Moreover, if the INS does not identify the teenager soon after the conviction, he or she will live under the threat of deportation for the rest of his or her life. Because there is no statute of limitations on deportation proceedings, it will not matter when the INS chooses to enforce the law or how much time the person will have lived in this country since the crime. All that will matter is that the person has a conviction that is a ground for deportability and that the crime occurred within the person's first five or seven years of residence.

## C. *New Definitions of Conviction and Sentence*

The 1996 laws also changed the definitions of "conviction" and "sentence."[37] First, as interpreted by the Board of Immigration Appeals (BIA), the term conviction now includes dispositions that are not treated as convictions by state law, such as expunged convictions.[38] Second, the laws provide that any reference to a term of imprisonment shall include any period of time that the sentence is suspended.[39] Thus, the immigration laws treat a suspended sentence of one year, which for all practical purposes is the same as one year of probation, as a one-year prison term.[40]

The case of Nathan Jones illustrates the impact of the new definition of conviction.[41] Jones received a youthful offender disposition for a crime that he allegedly committed at the age of seventeen. Under the relevant state law, Jones should receive a second chance, and his youthful offender disposition should be sealed. But under recent decisions interpreting the new definition of conviction,[42] the youthful offender disposition is no different from a conviction in the eyes of the immigration law. Jones now faces deportation from the country that has been his home since childhood and separation from his family.

The case of Mary Ann Gehris demonstrates the effect of the new sentence definition. Gehris was convicted in Georgia for battery arising from

[37]*See* INA § 101(a)(48), 8 U.S.C. § 1101(a)(48) (Supp. II 1996).
[38]*See In re* Roldan-Santoyo, Int. Dec. No. 3377, at 12, 19 Immig. Rep. (MB) B1-437, B1-444 to B1-445 (B.I.A. Mar. 3, 1999).
[39]*See* INA § 101(a)(48)(B), 8 U.S.C. § 1101(a)(48)(B) (Supp. II 1996).
[40]*See id.*
[41]Jones is a pseudonym. The facts presented here are from a real case, but because one of the purposes of youthful offender adjudications is to protect the young person from the stigma of a conviction, I have not used his real name.
[42]*See, e.g. In re* P (B.I.A. Sept. 10, 1999) (unpublished decision) (on file with the Harvard Law School Library).

an incident in which she pulled the hair of another woman.[43] She received a one-year suspended sentence.[44] Under the new definition of sentence, her crime is a "crime of violence" with a sentence of one year, classifying her as an aggravated felon who is both deportable and barred from relief.[45]

As Gehris's case illustrates, the various provisions of the new laws interact in ways that compound the problems with each provision. Gehris would not have faced deportation if suspended sentences did not receive the same treatment as actual incarceration or if Congress had not changed the aggravated felony definition. She also would not have been in this position if Georgia, the state where she was convicted, decided to achieve its penal objectives through the use of probation instead of a suspended sentence. But together, the result of the new aggravated felony and sentence provisions is that this woman faced mandatory deportation for pulling someone's hair.

## *III. HOW CONTEXT MAGNIFIES THE CONSEQUENCES OF THE NEW DEPORTATION CATEGORIES*

The impact of the 1996 laws is only partially revealed in the statute books. These statutes identify who is subject to deportation and who is potentially eligible for relief from deportation. But added to these legal changes regarding the right to remain in the United States are several practical changes in the situation of legal permanent residents charged with committing crimes. First, these immigrants, like other defendants, face a criminal justice system that is meting out higher penalties and doing so in ways that disproportionately affect certain communities. Second, most noncitizens with any criminal record, even those eligible for relief from deportation, are now subject to mandatory detention. The result is that they must pursue their legal claims from detention facilities that may be thousands of miles away from their homes and families. Third, legal permanent residents face an immigration enforcement system that has greatly increased resources and that is subject to reduced judicial review. Any one of these changes would have significantly altered the consequences of being a legal permanent resident charged with a crime. Together, they dramatically reshape the rights of these individuals.

[43] *See* Levine, *supra* note 14.
[44] *See id.*
[45] *See id.*

## A. *The Criminal Justice Context*

Changes in criminal laws and criminal justice practices have magnified the impact of the 1996 deportation provisions. The restructuring of the immigration law comes at a time when the criminal justice system is imposing higher penalties under an increasing number of mandatory sentencing and "truth in sentencing" schemes.[46] It is now more likely than ever that a person convicted of a crime will serve a prison sentence, and that sentence will probably be longer than sentences have been in the past. To the extent that the immigration law bases its assessment of the seriousness of the crime on the length of the sentence, it is simply more likely that the same crime committed today will carry a sentence that meets the old immigration law's requirements for deportability and exclusion from relief. When the new immigration provisions are added to the mix, the likelihood that criminal conduct will be punished by banishment significantly increases.

Indeed, the advent of mandatory sentencing and stricter sentencing practices has probably contributed to the perceived problem of the "criminal alien" population. When Congress passed the 1996 laws, it was in part responding to statistics showing a growth in the number of criminal aliens in the nation's prisons.[47] Part of this increase, however, was attributable to the overall rise in incarceration. Nationwide, incarceration rates increased fivefold between 1972 and 1997.[48] It should not come as a surprise that the incarceration of noncitizens increased as well.[49]

Changes in criminal justice policies with respect to crimes that do not lead to incarceration have also affected the practical meaning of the new deportation laws. Several jurisdictions have embarked on criminal justice

[46]*See* Mark Mauer, *Race to Incarcerate* 32 (1999); Michael Tonry, *Rethinking Unthinkable Punishment Policies in America,* 46 UCLA L. Rev. 1751, 1787 (1999).
[47]*See, e.g.,* H.R. Rep. No. 104-469, pt. 1, at 118 (1996); 142 Cong. Rec. H2361 (1996) (statement of Rep. Solomon); 142 Cong. Rec. S3347 (1996) (statement of Sen. Kyl).
[48]*See* Mauer, *supra* note 46, at 19.
[49]Discussions in Congress about the "criminal alien" problem focused on the large percentage of foreign-born people in the federal prison population and apparent increases in the population of noncitizens who are incarcerated. *See* sources cited *supra* note 47. These statistics are misleading as a picture of the rate of crime by noncitizens. Available data indicate that foreign-born residents make up a disproportionately small percentage of the state prison population and a disproportionately large percentage of the federal prison population. In July 1998, for example, foreign-born residents made up 7.6% of the state prison population, *see* Schuck & Williams, *supra* note 6, at 379, whereas that month, they made up 9.3% of the general population, *see* Population Estimates Program, U.S. Census Bureau, Quarter-

programs that target low-level crimes.[50] In New York City, for example, new police practices resulted in a fifty percent increase in misdemeanor arrests between 1993 and 1996.[51] Under these practices, it is far more likely today that the police will arrest and the city will prosecute a person who jumps a turnstile in a subway station.[52] If convicted of theft of services, that person could face mandatory deportation.[53]

The likelihood of deportation is greater in communities that are subject to elevated levels of police activity and in which people are more likely to be arrested and prosecuted. For example, a person of color who is

ly Estimates of United States Foreign-Born and Native Resident Populations; April 1, 1990 to July 1, 1999, http://www.census.gov/ population/estimates/nation/nativity/ fbtab001.txt (Apr. 11, 2000). In contrast, foreign-born persons made up 29% of federal prisoners in September, 1998. *See* Schuck & Williams, *supra* note 6, at 379. If the state and federal prison populations are combined, the percentage of foreign-born prisoners at the end of 1998 was 9.3% - a number equivalent to the general population statistics on the percentage of foreign-born residents. Of those incarcerated in federal prisons for drug crimes, the available evidence indicates that non-citizens are actually less likely than citizens to have played a serious role in the crime. *See* John Scalia, Bureau of Justice Statistics, U.S. Dep't of Justice, Noncitizens in the Federal Criminal Justice System, 1984-94, at 7 (1996).

The state prison statistics indicate an increase in the percentage of the prison population that is foreign-born. *See* Department of Corrections, State of N.Y., The Impact of Foreign-Born Inmates on the New York State Department of Correctional Services (1998) [hereinafter Impact]; Schuck & Williams, *supra* note 6, at 380-81. Some of this apparent growth may in fact be a result of more accurate statistics. *See id.* at 377-78 (noting that states have only been required to report statistics on foreign-born residents since 1992). The statistical increase may also reflect a growth in the overall percentage of the general population that is foreign-born. *See, e.g.*, U.S. Census Bureau, U.S. Dep't of Commerce, Profile of the Foreign-Born Population in the United States: 1997, at 2 [hereinafter Foreign-Born] (reporting that the population of foreign-born persons grew by 30% between 1990 and 1997). But the overall levels of incarceration for foreign-born persons in state prisons remain below the rate for the native population. *Compare* Impact, *supra* (reporting that, in 1997, 13% of New York inmates were foreign-born), *with* Foreign-Born, *supra*, at 2 (reporting that, in 1997, 20% of the population of New York was foreign-born).

The federal statistics also reflect immigration crimes, such as convictions for illegal reentry, which only affect noncitizens. Persons convicted of illegal reentry are subject to substantial prison sentences. *See* INA § 276(b)(2), 8 U.S.C. § 1326(b)(2) (Supp. II 1996) (imposing a 20-year term of imprisonment for persons who reenter the country after being deported for an aggravated felony conviction). Over time, they can be expected to make up a growing portion of the federal prison population.

[50]*See generally* Dan M. Kahan & Tracey L. Meares, *Foreword: The Coming Crisis of Criminal Procedure*, 86 Geo. L.J. 1153, 1160-61 (1998).

[51]*See* Bernard E. Harcourt, *Reflecting on the Subject: A Critique of the Social Influence Conception of Deterrence, the Broken Windows Theory, and Order-Maintenance Policing New York Style*, 97 Mich. L. Rev. 291, 198-99 (1998).

[52]*See* David Rohde, *A Brush with the Law Increasingly Ends with a Night in Jail*, N.Y. Times, Feb. 6, 2000, at A29.

[53]*See supra* pp. 1939, 1941.

more likely to be stopped while driving[54] is also more likely to be saddled with a drug possession conviction if someone in the car is carrying drugs. That conviction, even if it involves only a small amount of drugs, could mean mandatory deportation.[55]

We probably have not yet felt the full impact of the interplay between these changes to the criminal justice system and the new deportation laws. Petty offenses that lead to minor criminal sanctions are less likely to be identified at the time of the conviction through current immigration enforcement practices.[56] But stricter enforcement of laws against petty crime is creating a new class of deportable legal permanent residents, many of whom, under the new laws, will have no relief from deportation.[57]

## *B. The Detention Context*

The 1996 laws also changed the rules for detention.[58] Under these laws, a person convicted of any one of a wide range of crimes, including sim-

[54]*See* Angela J. Davis, *Race, Cops and Traffic Stops,* 51 U. Miami L. Rev. 425, 425 (1997); David A. Harris, *The Stories, the Statistics and the Law: Why "Driving While Black" Matters,* 84 Minn. L. Rev. 265, 265 (1999); Anthony C. Thompson, *Stopping the Usual Suspects: Race and the Fourth Amendment,* 74 N.Y.U. L. Rev. 956, 957-60 (1999).

[55]For example, one legal permanent resident was convicted under these circumstances in 1978, approximately three years after he came to the United States. *See* Telephone Interview with James A. O'Malley, Attorney, O'Malley & Associates (May 1, 2000). He was not placed into removal proceedings until 1997. *See id.* Although he received a sentence of probation, he is ineligible for relief under the government's reading of the law because his crime took place less than seven years after his arrival. *See id.*

[56]*See* Schuck & Williams, *supra* note 6, at 408 (describing how permanent residents not sentenced to prison are less likely to be identified immediately after their convictions through regular INS screening practices). Those permanent residents who are not identified through initial screening efforts may find themselves placed in proceedings years later if they apply for citizenship or a new permanent residency card or if they take a trip outside the country. They may also be picked up as a result of later efforts to ferret out "criminal aliens." *Id.* at 385.

[57]Young people who have been legal permanent residents for less than seven years are particularly vulnerable. *See supra* p. 1942.

[58]Mandatory detention policies stem in part from claims that detention is needed to enforce the deportation laws. For example, a 1989 GAO report indicated that many people released on bond failed to appear for their deportation hearings. *See* General Accounting Office, GAO/GGD-90-18, Immigration Control: Deporting and Excluding Aliens from the United States 3 (1989) (noting that about 27% of those on bond had not appeared at their hearings). This study does not, however, support current detention rules. First, the study indicated that nonappearance was principally a problem with people who had entered the country illegally. *See id.* at 23. In addition, problems with the INS address system were responsible for some

ple drug possession, is subject to mandatory detention.[59] Mandatory detention applies even to classes of legal permanent residents who remain eligible for relief from deportation,[60] and it applies while the permanent resident pursues administrative appeals.

Mandatory detention imposes extreme costs on permanent residents who wish to contest their deportation. It means that a person who has already served his or her sentence or has never before set foot in a prison[61] must in effect agree to incarceration, for an indefinite period of time, while he or she pursues claims of nondeportability or eligibility for relief. The permanent resident must do so knowing that many claims, such as constitutional claims or claims that the agency has misread the statute, will not be adjudicated until after the administrative process is complete. Indeed, substantive adjudication of claims asserted in court will only occur once the claims have cleared many hurdles, including jurisdictional issues. The permanent resident must also accept the fact that the period of incarceration may take place in facilities that are thousands of miles from his or her home and family.

Not surprisingly, these residents often conclude that the costs of pursuing legal claims – years in detention and uncertain success – are simply too high. Advocates who work with permanent residents facing deportation report that many legal permanent residents with solid legal claims for relief give up their day in court.[62]

of the failures to appear. *See* General Accounting Office, GAO/GGD-92-20, Immigration Control: The Central Address File Needs to be More Accurate 8 (1992) (finding a 22% error rate in address information for aliens). No one has studied why it is necessary to require detention of permanent residents who are identified as neither dangerous to the community nor flight risks.

[59]*See* INA § 236(c)(1), 8 U.S.C. § 1226(c)(1) (Supp. II 1996).

[60]For example, a person who is deportable for a single simple drug possession is subject to mandatory detention, *see* INA § 236(c)(1)(B), 8 U.S.C. § 1226(c)(1)(B) (Supp. II 1996), but generally is not barred from relief.

[61]The INS reads the mandatory detention law to apply to people who never serve any time in prison. *See* Immigration & Naturalization Serv., U.S. Dep't of Justice, Policy Statement, Mandatory Custody of Criminal Aliens in Proceedings (July 13, 1999) (on file with the Harvard Law School Library). There is a good textual argument against this reading. The relevant statutory language provides for detention when the person "is released." INA § 236(c)(1), 8 U.S.C. § 1226(c)(1) (Supp. II 1996). A person who has not been incarcerated has not been "released."

[62]*See* Telephone Interview with Andrea Black, Attorney, Florence Immigrant and Refugee Rights Project (Mar. 9, 2000); Telephone Interview with Laurie Kozuba, Founder and Director, Citizens and Immigrants for Equal Justice (Mar. 9, 2000).

The result of the mandatory detention scheme and its coercive impact on those placed in deportation proceedings is that the practical effects of the new immigration laws are more severe than is apparent from a reading of their texts. A person with a single drug possession conviction, who is technically not subject to mandatory deportation, may find detention so unbearable that he or she abandons the right to remain in this country as a legal permanent resident. In addition, the outer edges of the aggravated felony definition, which in theory can be challenged through the agency and in court, are in practice determined by INS enforcement officers who draft charging documents and thereby wield the power to impose mandatory detention.[63]

## C. *The Immigration Enforcement Context*

The practical scope of the new laws is also a function of INS interpretation and enforcement. Along with changing the substance of the old law, Congress authorized significant increases in the budget for enforcement.[64] Congress also continues to place considerable pressure on the INS to increase deportations. Specifically, Congress audits INS enforcement efforts and treats any failure to deport expeditiously a person who fits the criminal alien label as evidence of the INS's failure.[65]

In response, the INS has adopted a take-no-prisoners approach with regard to the deportation of criminal aliens. For example, the INS uses its considerable interpretive power to construe the provisions of the 1996 laws in ways that render more legal permanent residents both deportable

[63]In deciding whether an individual is subject to mandatory detention, the standard is whether the INA is "substantially unlikely to prevail" on its claim that the legal permanent resident is subject to mandatory detention. *In re* Joseph, Int. Dec. No. 3398, at 3, 14, 20 Immig. Rep. (MB) B1-217, B1-224 (B.I.A. May 28, 1999) (reporting that a permanent resident had been detained for over five months despite prevailing before both the immigration judge and the BIA on his claim that he was not subject to mandatory detention). Even when a legal permanent resident is granted bond, the INS can appeal and invoke an automatic stay of release from detention. *See In re* Joseph, Int. Dec. No. 3387, at 16-17, 20 Immig. Rep. (MB) B1-1, B1-11 (B.I.A. Apr. 23, 1999).

[64]*See* Schuck & Williams, *supra* note 6, at 454.

[65]*See, e.g.*, General Accounting Office, GAO/T-GGD-99-47, Criminal Aliens: INS' Efforts to Identify and Remove Imprisoned Aliens Continue to Need Improvement 2 (1999); General Accounting Office, GAO/T-GGD-97-154, Criminal Aliens: INS' Efforts to Identify and Remove Imprisoned Aliens Need to be Improved 1, 5-7 (1997); General Accounting Office GAO/GGD-99-3, Criminal Aliens: INS' Efforts to Remove Imprisoned Aliens Continue to Need Improvement (1998).

and ineligible for relief from deportation. One of the first interpretive questions regarding the 1996 laws was whether to read the new bars to relief to apply retroactively. The INS assumed an aggressive posture on this issue, not only arguing for full retroactivity to the BIA, but also taking the unusual step of asking the Attorney General to overturn the BIA's conclusion that only partial retroactivity was permissible.[66] The INS continues to litigate this issue in the courts despite subsequent case law casting doubt on the Attorney General's decision that the statutes were retroactive.[67] Similarly, when mandatory detention provisions went into effect in October 1998, the INS chose to read the statute to extend mandatory detention to people who had been released from prison long before mandatory detention existed.[68] Only after the courts rejected this position did the INS revise its reading.[69] The INS continues to read mandatory detention to apply to permanent residents who never served time in prison.[70] The INS also pursues expansive interpretations of the terms "aggravated felony"[71] and "conviction"[72] and restrictive readings of the new provisions for relief.[73] Finally, once the INS successfully litigates its

[66]*See In re* Soriano, 21 I. & N. Dec. 516, 534 (B.I.A. June 27, 1996, Att'y Gen. Feb. 21, 1997).
[67]The courts have generally held that the new rules cannot be applied in cases that were pending when AEDPA was enacted. *See, e.g.,* Pak v. Reno, 196 F.3d 666, 675-76 (6th Cir. 1999); Shah v. Reno, 184 F.3d 719, 724 (8th Cir. 1999); Mayers v. INS, 175 F.3d 1289, 1302-03 (11th Cir. 1999); Goncalves v. Reno, 144 F.3d 110, 134 (1st Cir. 1998), *cert. denied,* 526 U.S. 1004 (1999). *But see, e.g.,* Turkhan v. Perryman, 1888 F.3d 814, 827 (7th Cir. 1999). The courts are divided on whether AEDPA's bars to relief can be applied to persons who were not in INS proceedings at the time that AEDPA was enacted. *Compare* Tasios v. Reno, No. 99-6061, 2000 WL 223333, at *9 (4th Cir. Feb. 28, 2000), *with* Sandoval v. Reno, 166 F.3d 225, 241 (3d Cir. 1999). The Fourth Circuit concluded that the *Soriano* decision is not supportable in light of subsequent decisions of the Supreme Court. *See Tasios,* 2000 WL 223333, at *6.
[68]*See, e.g.,* Velasquez v. Reno, 37 F. Supp. 2d 663, 665 (D.N.J. 1999).
[69]*See In re* Adeniji, Int. Dec. No. 3417, 20 Immig. Rep. (MB) B1-425, B1-428 (B.I.A. Nov. 3, 1999). The INS changed its position after its interpretation of the scope of mandatory detention was rejected in numerous court decisions. *See, e.g.,* Aguilar v. Lewis, 50 F. Supp. 2d 539, 544 (E.D. Va. 1999); Alwaday v. Beebe, 43 F. Supp. 2d 1130, 1133 (D. Or. 1999); Velasquez, 37 F. Supp. 2d at 672.
[70]*See supra* note 61.
[71]*See In re* Magallanes-Garcia, Int. Dec. No. 3341, at 2, 18 Immig. Rep. (MB) B1-222, B1-225 (B.I.A. Mar. 19, 1998) (upholding the argument that driving under the influence is an aggravated felony).
[72]*See In re* Roldan-Santoyo, Int. Dec. No. 3377, 19 Immig. Rep. (MB) B1-437, B1-447 (B.I.A. Mar. 3, 1999).
[73]*See In re* Perez, Int. Dec. No. 3389, 20 Immig. Rep. (MB) B1-79, B1-82 to B1-83 (B.I.A. May 12, 1999) (upholding a broad application of the clock-stopping rule).

interpretive claims in agency courts, it aggressively defends against judicial oversight.[74]

The INS enforcement effort also takes surprisingly aggressive forms at the local level. In 1998, a local enforcement initiative in Texas led to the arrests of 500 legal permanent residents with old convictions for driving under the influence.[75] More recently, the INS office in Atlanta has begun to train local district attorneys to seek criminal dispositions in cases involving noncitizens that allow for speedy deportations. The training materials teach prosecutors how to manipulate the immigration laws to subject noncitizens to mandatory deportation.[76] For example, the materials encourage prosecutors to seek one-year suspended sentences, which lead to mandatory deportation.[77]

Overall, the INS's approach to enforcement suggests an agency mentality in which the principal goal is to demonstrate increased numbers of criminal alien deportations. Indeed, the INS Commissioner's reports to

[74]For the last four years, the INS has argued that the courts have no jurisdiction to review any issues other than constitutional questions. However, the courts have overwhelmingly ruled that habeas jurisdiction over basic issues such as statutory interpretation questions remains. *See* cases cited *supra* note 67. And the Supreme Court has rebuffed the government's efforts to obtain review of these rulings. *See, e.g.,* Navas v. Reno, 526 U.S. 1004 (1999) (denying petition for writ of certiorari). We are now entering a new phase of litigation as the government argues that the permanent jurisdictional rules under IIRIRA prohibit judicial review. *See generally* Gerald L. Neuman, *Jurisdiction and the Rule of Law After the 1996 Immigration Act,* 113 Harv. L. Rev. 1963 (2000). The uneasy status of judicial review has led one commentator to suggest that 1996 was the year that "the rule of immigration law died." Daniel Kanstroom, *Surrounding the Hole in the Doughnut: Discretion and Deference in U.S. Immigration Law,* 71 Tul. L. Rev. 703, 704 (1997).

[75]*See 500 to Be Deported for Drunk Driving Convictions,* Chi. Trib., Sept. 4, 1998, at 25.

[76]*See* Atlanta Dist. Office, Immigration & Naturalization Serv., U.S. Dep't of Justice, Immigration & Naturalization Service Update: Removal of Criminal Aliens (on file with the Harvard Law School Library).

[77]*See id.*

[78]*See, e.g., Departments of Commerce, Justice, and State, The Judiciary, and Related Agencies Appropriations for 2000: Hearings Before the Subcomm. on Commerce, Justice, State, the Judiciary, and Related Agencies of the House Comm. On Appropriations,* 106th Cong. 577 (1999) (statement of Doris Meissner, Commissioner, Immigration and Naturalization Service) (reporting a 10% increase in the deportation of "criminal aliens"); *Proposals to Reform the Immigration and Naturalization Service. Focusing on Its Ability to Provide Services to Immigrants, Visitors, and Prospective Citizens: Hearings Before the Subcomm. on Immigration of the Senate Comm. on the Judiciary,* 105th Cong. 104 (1998) (statement of Doris Meissner, Commissioner, Immigration and Naturalization Service) (stating that, during the first 10 months of fiscal year 1998, the INS "removed criminal aliens at a rate of more than 1,000 per week, putting [it] on track to remove more criminal aliens [in 1998] than the total number of criminal and non-criminal aliens removed in fiscal year 1995"); *see also* Immigration & Naturalization Serv., U.S. Dep't

Congress express pride over the high numbers of criminal aliens who have been deported.[78] In this atmosphere, there is little attention paid to the human casualties of the new deportation regime.[79]

## *IV. THE IMPACT OF THE NEW LAWS ON FAMILIES*

The combined impact of the new immigration legislation, tougher criminal justice policies, mandatory detention rules, and vigorous INS enforcement has not fallen solely on legal permanent residents convicted of crimes. These laws directly affect the families of legal permanent residents. By eliminating (in most cases) the system of relief hearings that allowed family members to testify about the consequences of family separation, the laws operate as a statement that the effects of deportation on family members do not matter. This result is highly incongruous with both existing immigration laws and general values that permeate our legal system.

For the most part, our immigration law, like our family law, endeavors to keep families together.[80] The majority of the immigrant visas awarded each year for persons to immigrate as lawful permanent residents are based on family relationships.[81] The immigration system reflects the law's assumption that family unity is an important value. We

of Justice, INS Sets New Removals Record; Fiscal Year 1999 Removals Reach 176,990 (Nov. 12, 1999) [hereinafter Removals Record] (on file with the Harvard Law School Library). There is no effort in these reports to distinguish between legal residents and persons without legal immigration status. Thus, although the gross number of "criminal aliens" removed from the United States has increased from 7,000 per year, *see* Schuck & Williams, *supra* note 6, at 384-85, to 62,000 per year, *see* Removals Record, *supra*, not all of the people reflected in these numbers are legal permanent residents.

[79]Recent suggestions that prosecutorial discretion can ameliorate the severe consequences of the 1996 laws, *see, e.g.*, Anthony Lewis, *'Cases that Cry Out'*, N.Y. Times, Mar. 18, 2000, at A25, ignore this evidence that the agency is a partisan player in a campaign to achieve high deportation statistics. But even if a system of prosecutorial discretion were established, it would be problematic. First, there is no statute of limitations on deportation proceedings. As a result, the beneficiary of such discretion lives in permanent limbo. *See* Letter from Robert Raben, Assistant Attorney General, to Hon. Barney Frank, U.S. House of Representatives (Jan. 19, 2000) (on file with the Harvard Law School Library). Furthermore, prosecutorial discretion depends on a prosecutor who will play the roles of judge and jury and who will assume these multiple roles without the benefit of a hearing in which the evidence can be tested.

[80]*See generally* Peggy Cooper Davis, Neglected Stories: The Constitution and Family Values (1997) (discussing constitutional jurisprudence protecting family interests).

[81]*See* Immigration & Naturalization Serv., U.S. Dep't of Justice, Annual Report: Legal Immigration, Fiscal Year 1998, at 7 (1999).

value allowing husbands and wives to live together; we value allowing parents and children to live together.[82] Although some aspects of our family immigration policy have been controversial – in particular, providing visas based on sibling relationships – no one seriously questions the importance of maintaining the integrity of the nuclear family by permitting the members of a family to live in the same country.[83]

The current system of mandatory detention and mandatory deportation seriously undermines these family values. Families are in crisis from the moment that the INS places a family member in detention. The family may now be without a breadwinner; the family members left behind may face eviction due to their inability to make mortgage or rent payments. The family suffers from the emotional toll of having a loved one in detention, often thousands of miles from home.[84] When the deportation order becomes final, the system forces many of these families to separate permanently.[85] As a legal matter, family members who are United States citizens may not be able, under the laws of their loved one's former country, to immigrate to that country. The United States is hardly unique in its regulation of when and how noncitizen family members who are outside the country may immigrate to join family members who are within the country.[86] Furthermore, it may be impractical and extremely difficult for the family to leave the United States. Family members may have jobs, go to school, or have other strong ties to this country. They may have dependent elderly relatives who cannot leave. They may have paid into pension schemes and Social Security. They may have built a business in the United States or may be unable to begin a new career in a new country. Even if they are able to leave and immigrate to the native country of the deported family member, they would in effect experience

[82]The importance of family ties has been stressed by the INS and the family law bar in the debate over the fate of Elian Gonzalez. *See, e.g.,* Tony Doris, *Family Lawyers Debate Cuban Boy's Fate,* TEX. LAW, Jan. 17, 2000, at 35 (quoting INS Commissioner Doris Meissner's statement that Elian Gonzalez belongs with his father).

[83]*See, e.g.,* H.R. Rep. No. 104-469, pt. 1, at 134 (1996) (explaining proposals to change the rules regarding sibling visas but stating that "[t]he preservation of the nuclear family ... should continue to be a cornerstone of U.S. immigration policy").

[84]*See* Telephone interview with Andrea Black, *supra* note 62.

[85]People who are deported as aggravated felons are permanently barred from reentry into the United States. *See* INA § 212(a)(9)(A)(ii), 8 U.S.C. § 1182(a)(9)(A)(ii) (Supp. II 1996).

[86]*See, e.g.,* Hiroshi Motomura, *The Family and Immigration: A Roadmap for the Ruritanian Lawmaker,* 43 Am. J. Comp. L. 511 (1995) (comparing United States and German family immigration law).

deportation as well -they would be removed from the country that they consider their home and sent to another country to which they may have only attenuated connections or no connections at all.

The new deportation laws deny immigration judges the opportunity to take family integrity into consideration. John Gaul, for example, was adopted from Thailand when he was three years old.[87] His adoptive parents are United States citizens and raised him in Florida; because they had adopted him, Gaul's parents mistakenly believed that he was a citizen.[88] His family eventually filed a petition for citizenship.[89] However, Gaul turned eighteen before the government processed his application, and he became ineligible for automatic citizenship as the adopted child of United States citizens.[90] Meanwhile, Gaul had taken part in stealing a car and forging checks, was convicted, served twenty months, and was placed in deportation proceedings.[91] In 1999, Gaul was deported to Thailand.[92]

Gaul's case illustrates the serious threat to family integrity posed by the new laws. Gaul's adoptive parents brought him to the United States, and he grew up as the child of Americans. Over 15,000 children from all over the world come to the United States each year under like circumstances.[93] No one imagines that any of these children will engage in crimes, but crime is a statistical certainty with any group. For the immigration laws to treat Gaul as a stranger because of his criminal convictions disrespects the fundamental commitment that Gaul's parents and other American parents make each year to their foreign-born adopted children.[94]

Other families immigrate as families. Nathan Jones,[95] for example, immigrated with his entire nuclear family. The family joined Jones's aunts and uncles already living in this country. There is now no one in his former country to whom he could return. Moreover, Jones is currently in college

[87]*See* Jim Sloan, *Adoptee Faces Deportation,* Tampa Trib., July 18, 1998, at 1.
[88]*See id.*
[89]*See id.*
[90]*See id.*
[91]*See id.*
[92]*See* Amy Herdy, *Son Returned to Unfamiliar Land,* St. Petersburg Times, Feb. 23, 1999, at 1A.
[93]The most recent State Department figures show that 15,774 orphaned children entered the United States on immigration visas in fiscal year 1998. *See Immigrant Visas Issued to Orphans Coming to the U.S.: Top Countries of Origin,* http://travel.state.gov/orphan_numbers.html.
[94]Many adoptive parents understand the procedures and file the appropriate naturalization papers for their children. But Gaul's case is hardly an isolated occurrence. *See* Levine, *supra* note 14 (describing cases of adoptees from Brazil, Germany, Japan, and Canada who have faced deportation).
[95]*See supra* p. 1942.

and helps care for his younger sisters while his parents work night shifts. If he is deported, his parents and siblings will lose his daily presence and support.

In other cases, lawful permanent residents who have lived in the United States since childhood have married citizens and started their own families.[96] Contrary to popular belief, these permanent residents do not automatically become citizens upon marrying a citizen. Now their spouses face the new dual system of criminal justice in which the consequences of a conviction for a legal permanent resident are far different from those facing a citizen. The new laws provide no forum in which these spouses can speak to the specific harm they will face – emotionally and financially – as a result of their permanent separation from their lawful permanent resident spouses or their own exile to a foreign land.

Deportation that results in the separation of parents from their minor children – many of whom are United States citizens – raises further concerns. Our legal system generally observes the principle that children should be brought up by their parents,[97] and it separates parents from their children only in cases of abuse or neglect. Otherwise, the law recognizes that the parental bond is unique and deserves close protection.[98] But with mandatory deportation, children may face permanent separation from parents who have fully served a criminal sentence, often on the basis of conduct that the criminal justice system treated as not warranting serious punishment.

The consequences of such separation can be severe. For example, when his father was detained, Tino Corso's son had to drop out of school to take care of his siblings while his mother worked.[99] Ian Chapman's family resorted to welfare.[100] Gerardo Mosquera's son committed suicide, in part over despondence at the deportation of his father.[101] These stories should

[96]*See, e.g.,* Velasquez v. Reno, 37 F. Supp. 2d 663, 664 (D.N.J. 1999) (describing how José Velasquez became a legal permanent resident at age 13 and later married a United States citizen and raised three United States citizen children).

[97]*See, e.g.,* Meyer v. Nebraska, 262 U.S. 390, 399 (1923).

[98]*See, e.g.,* M.L.B. v. S.L.J., 519 U.S. 102, 116-19, 124, 128 (1996) (requiring the provision of an adequate record for an indigent parent appealing the termination of parental rights); Santosky v. Kramer, 455 U.S. 745, 768 (1982) (requiring clear and convincing evidence for the termination of parental rights).

[99]*See* Leslie Casimir, *Deportation Law Stings Immigrants, Rips Families,* N.Y. Daily News, Jan. 13, 2000, at 3; Telephone Interview with Laurie Kozuba, *supra* note 62.

[100]*See* Casimir, *supra* note 99.

[101]*See* Patrick J. McDonnell, *Deportation Shatters Family,* L.A. Times, Mar. 14, 1998, at B1 (discussing Gerardo Mosquera Jr.'s suicide as a "[t]ragedy" in which a "[t]eenager kills himself after his father – a legal U.S. resident for 29 years – is sent to Colombia because of [a] $10 marijuana sale in 1989").

not come as a surprise. The cornerstone of this country's family law is the concept that parents are fundamentally important in the lives of their children. When children are deprived of their parents – and particularly when they are deprived of their parents in ways that seem arbitrary and unjustifiable – we should expect the children to suffer harm.

Of course, the criminal justice system has long made decisions that separate families, including separating parents from their minor children. But even current sentencing laws do not routinely cause permanent separation of families. In addition, when judges have discretion, they can structure sentences to reflect the impact that separation will have on families. When judges do not have discretion, sentences with a definite end date at least provide the family with a fixed day by which they may reunite. The new detention and deportation system, in contrast, imposes permanent separation. It fails to consider the impact of separation on families, ignores the best interests of children, and provides no certain end date other than permanent separation through deportation.

## *V. THE MISGUIDED QUEST FOR A NEW SYSTEM OF DEPORTATION-BY-LABEL*

Given the multiple ways in which the new deportation system separates American families, solutions must be multifaceted. It will not be enough, for example, to change the rules that determine who is eligible for a waiver of deportation. As long as enforcement and detention policies remain on their current track, even those permanent residents facing deportation who are given the possibility of relief will continue to face pressure to leave their families.[102] Similarly, independent changes in criminal justice policies will continue to alter the impact of the immigration laws, even as the laws existed prior to 1996.[103] Reforming the new mandatory deportation rules, however, is central to any solution. Unless individuals are provided with a forum to present their cases to remain in this country, it will be difficult to control governmental efforts to maximize the yield of "criminal aliens" deported.

Congress has begun to consider reforms to mandatory deportation. A common feature of the bills pending in Congress is an effort to distinguish criminal records that should allow for a consideration of factors that weigh against deportation from criminal records that should serve as

[102]*See supra* section III.B.
[103]*See supra* Section III.A.

grounds for mandatory deportation. Although these bills would alleviate some of the hardships imposed by the 1996 laws, they err in assuming that the government should take a step as serious as deportation based solely on the label of the crime or the sentence imposed.

Two bills, Senate Bill 173[104] and House Bill 1485,[105] are largely designed to return the law to the proposals that passed the two houses in 1996.[106] These bills would restore relief from deportation for long-term permanent residents convicted of aggravated felonies for which the sentence of incarceration was less than five years.[107]

Another bill, House Bill 2999,[108] parses through the 1996 changes in the definition of an aggravated felony and provides some relief from deportation based on the label of the crime.[109] A legal permanent resident who was convicted of receiving stolen property and received a two-year sentence, for example, would now be eligible for relief, provided the person met all of the other criteria in H.R. 2999.[110] In contrast, a legal permanent resident convicted of other crimes labeled "aggravated felonies" would endure the same fate as under current law. A conviction for "sexual abuse of a minor," for instance, or for any "drug trafficking" crime

[104]S. 173, 106th Cong. (1999).

[105]H.R. 1485, 106th Cong. (1999).

[106]Both the House and the Senate versions of IIRIRA would have permitted legal permanent residents with seven years of lawful residence to seek a waiver unless they had been convicted of an aggravated felony for which they had been sentenced to at least five years in prison. *See* H.R. 2202, 104th Cong. § 240A(a) (1996) (*reprinted in* H.R. Rep. No. 104-469, pt. 1, at 23 (1996)); S. 1664, 104th Cong. § 150(b) (1996) (*reprinted in* S. Rep. No. 104-249, at 125 (1996)). The final version of the law, as it emerged from a midnight conference committee, omitted the five-year sentence requirement, thereby barring relief for anyone convicted of an aggravated felony. *See* H.R. Conf. Ref. No. 104-828, at 213 (1996). Congress rolled this version into the budget bill, making its passage inevitable. *See* All Things Considered: Reporters Give Their Impressions of the 104th Congress (NPR radio broadcast, Sept. 27, 1996), http://search.npr.org/cf/cmn/cmnpd01fm.cfm?Prg Date=09%2F27%2F27%2F1996&PrglD=2 (comments by Peter Kenyon) (observing that "both sides are trying to avoid another government shutdown").

[107]H.R. 1485 also would establish a new form of waiver that is not restricted according to the number of years of a sentence. *See* H.R. 1485 § 4(a) 106th Cong. (1999). This bill would allow relief "on a case-by-case basis for urgent humanitarian reasons, significant public benefit (including assuring family unity), or any other sufficiently compelling reason." *Id.* It is unclear who would be provided with relief or what procedures would be used to determine eligibility.

[108]H.R. 2999, 106th Cong. (1999).

[109]*See id.* § 2.

[110]These criteria include having no other felony conviction and having maintained a good moral character during all periods of residence in the United States. *See id.*

would continue to require automatic deportation irrespective of the sentence imposed.[111]

There are two principal problems with the approach of these bills. First, like the 1996 laws, these bills attempt to identify a label that will fairly describe the seriousness of the criminal offense. This task is extremely difficult in a national immigration system that must apply a single definition to convictions originating in a wide range of state criminal justice systems. Second, these bills mostly assume that a criminal record alone should resolve the question whether to deport a person.[112]

The immigration law's provisions for the deportation of legal permanent residents who have been convicted of crimes depend on the conviction records from the criminal justice systems of the fifty states as well as the federal system.[113] The provisions depend, therefore, on the enforcement policies and sentencing schemes of the states and the specific police practices of different communities. Because the states define crimes differently, the consequences of committing certain crimes can vary dramatically.[114] In theory, the adoption of a federal definition of crimes that mandate deportation could mitigate such disparate consequences.[115] But federal definitions applied to state criminal justice schemes are also problematic. For example, the immigration law's aggravated felony definition for drug trafficking borrows from federal criminal law. Under this definition, a drug sale or two drug possession convictions may constitute an aggravated felony.[116] When this federal definition is applied to state convictions, it reaches crimes that states may prosecute only as violations or misdemeanors.[117] Simply put, using federal definitions in the context of the kinds of crimes prosecuted by U.S. Attorneys is very different from

[111]*See* INA §§ 101(a)(43)(A)-(B), 240A(a)(3), 8 U.S.C. §§ 1101(a)(43)(A)-(B), 1229b(a)(3) (1994 & Supp. II 1996).

[112]To the extent that H.R. 1485 permits cancellation of removal upon showing of hardship or other factors counseling against deportation, *see supra* note 107, it is not subject to this criticism.

[113]*See* Bennett, *supra* note 11, at 1700; Christina LaBrie, Note, *Lack of Uniformity in the Deportation of Criminal Aliens,* 25 N.Y.U. Rev. L. & Soc. Change (forthcoming 2000) (manuscript at 12-24, on file with the Harvard Law School Library).

[114]*See* Bennett, *supra* note 11, at 1720-29 (describing disparate immigration consequences for offenses of statutory rape and assault crimes).

[115]*See id.* at 1730-32 (proposing that aggravated felonies be defined as a matter of federal law); LaBrie, supra note 113 (manuscript at 25) (arguing for increased federal definition of crimes).

[116]*See In re* L-G-, 21 I. & N. Dec. 89, 94-95 (B.I.A. Sept. 27, 1995).

[117]*See supra* pp. 1940-41.

using federal definitions in the context of the kinds of crimes prosecuted by state and local prosecutors. This distinction is especially true today when "quality of life" campaigns lead local prosecutors to pursue more of the lowest level offenses.[118]

Before 1996, the application of federal definitions to state criminal statutes meant that, as between two permanent residents who had participated in the same conduct but in different states with different laws, one might face deportation proceedings while the other would not. But at the same time, the ability of people facing deportation to apply for a waiver of deportation[119] mitigated the injustice that resulted when the enforcement practices in one jurisdiction were more onerous than those in another. Although the person with the deportable conviction could face deportation proceedings, deportation was not mandatory. The deportation hearing process was a forum in which immigration judges considered the seriousness of the crime, the person's rehabilitation, and the many additional factors – such as the impact on the person's family – that were relevant to the deportation decision. Today, however, the disparities between state criminal justice practices can mean the difference between staying with one's family and facing permanent deportation to a country with which one may have no connection.

In addition, the labels that the 1996 laws use to identify crimes that necessitate deportation can be highly misleading. Each label has a technical meaning in immigration law jurisprudence that can be very different from the meaning typically associated with that label.[120] Misleading labels, however, are only symptomatic of the underlying categorization problem. Any attempt to single out a certain category of crime – even if only to label it as "serious" – is likely to include cases in which people who have been convicted of the crime should not be subject to mandatory deportation.

Consider, for example, the label "drug trafficking," which most people probably associate with serious crimes. The current definition of drug trafficking in immigration law, however, refers to any transfer or attempted transfer of a drug, no matter how small the amount and no matter how insignificant the individual's role in the alleged transfer.[121] José

[118]*See supra* p. 1945.
[119]*See supra* p. 1939.
[120]*See generally* Anthony G. Amsterdam & Jerome Bruner, Minding the Law: Cognition, Culture, and the Court (forthcoming 2000) (manuscript at ch. 2, on file with the Harvard Law School Library) (discussing categories and categorization).
[121]*See, e.g., In re* Davis, 20 I. & N. Dec. 536, 542-43 (B.I.A. May 28, 1992) (stating that the law classifies a state misdemeanor drug conspiracy conviction as an aggravated felony).

Velasquez, for example, pled guilty to a fairly minor drug charge and was sentenced to probation and a $5000 fine.[122] Yet the immigration laws do not look beyond the surface of his conviction. They deem Velasquez to be a drug trafficker and thus an aggravated felon.

Consider also the label "sexual abuse of a minor," which Congress added in 1996 to the list of aggravated felonies that subject immigrants to mandatory deportation. This label includes some very serious crimes, but the INS also argues that it includes any prosecution that is based on the age of one party in a sexual relationship, with the relevant age depending on the varied policies of the fifty states.[123] Because such statutory rape laws are strict liability offenses, a person can be convicted of the offense regardless of whether the victim consented or whether there were other mitigating factors.

For example, Chue Xiong emigrated with his family from Laos in 1987 to escape persecution from the Laotian government.[124] In 1994, when he was eighteen years old, Xiong had what the Seventh Circuit later described as a consensual sexual relationship with his then-fifteen-year-old girlfriend.[125] Xiong was convicted of statutory rape and was subsequently ordered deported.[126] On appeal, the Seventh Circuit held that Xiong's crime was not a crime of violence and, therefore, did not fit into the aggravated felony category for violent crimes.[127] Following remand, however, the INS recharged Xiong under the new aggravated felony category of sexual abuse of a minor.[128] From the INS's perspective, the consensual nature of the relationship and the closeness in age between Xiong and his girlfriend apparently were irrelevant.[129]

Xiong's case illustrates the dangers of using a simple label to determine consequences as serious as deportation. Statutory rape laws encompass a broad array of conduct, including conduct that is pervasive in American society. Regardless of whether it is desirable, the fact is that a majority of girls in this country engage in sexual intercourse before they turn eighteen.[130] In some states, their partner's conduct is per se illegal.[131]

[122]*See* Velasquez v. Reno, 37 F. Supp. 2d 663, 665 (D.N.J. 1999); *see also supra* p. 1940.
[123]*See* Bennett, *supra* note 11, at 1720-24.
[124]*See* Xiong v. INS, 173 F.3d 601, 603 (7th Cir. 1999).
[125]*See id.* at 607.
[126]*See id.* at 604.
[127]*See id.* at 604-07.
[128]*See* Telephone Interview with Lisa Palumbo, Attorney for Chue Xiong, Legal Assistance Foundation of Chicago (Jan. 25, 2000).
[129]*See Xiong*, 173 F.3d at 607.
[130]*See* Susan Moore & Doreen Rosenthal, Sexuality in Adolescence 1 (1993).
[131]*See, e.g.*, Cal. Penal Code § 261(a)-(d) (West 1999).

The offenders may be substantially older men but in most cases are young men or boys.[132] The circumstances may or may not indicate genuine consent. Given the breadth of conduct covered by the definition of sexual abuse of a minor, it is difficult to justify an across-the-board assumption that deportation should automatically follow any such conviction.[133] Xiong has not had the chance to exhibit twenty years of good behavior since his conviction. But his crime hardly provides a reasonable basis for automatic deportation and separation from his family.

Even the aggravated felony label that almost all would agree identifies the most serious felons – a conviction of murder – can apply in surprising ways. Brenda Loftus was convicted in 1994 of voluntary manslaughter after she killed her abusive husband, and the trial judge sentenced her to ten years probation.[134] According to news reports, Loftus killed her husband after he threatened to kill their daughter, a threat that she took seriously after her years of abuse.[135] She did not succeed in persuading a jury to acquit her, but the sentence of probation suggests that the judge did not see her as an ongoing threat to society. An immigration judge has now ordered Loftus deported. The law did not permit this judge to consider the mitigating circumstances of Loftus' crime or the effect of deportation on her teenaged daughter.[136]

These examples illustrate the difficulty of identifying a list of crimes that will always justify deportation. Crime labels are rarely an accurate reflection of the range of conduct covered by the label, and no label can possibly incorporate the many different ways that criminal law is applied in practice, especially across state criminal justice systems. The label of the conviction also provides a simple snapshot of the person's life: it does not reveal the ties to this country, the person's record of rehabilitation, the risk

[132]*See* Elizabeth Hollenberg, Note, *The Criminalization of Teenage Sex: Statutory Rape and the Politics of Teenage Motherhood,* 10 Stan. L. & Pol'y Rev. 267, 270-71 (1999).

[133]Indeed, it was a case similar to Xiong's that first captured the media's attention regarding the 1996 laws. Jesus Collado, like Xiong, was a teenager who was convicted of statutory rape for having a sexual relationship with his girlfriend. *See* Pamela Constable & William Brantigan, *Thousands Confront Deportation Dragnet's Longer Reach,* Wash. Post, Oct. 26, 1997, at A3; Anthony Lewis, *When It Is Unjust,* N.Y. Times, Dec. 26, 1997, at A39; Ojito, *supra* note 10; Frank Trejo, *The Long, Long Arm of Immigration Law,* Dallas Morning News, Nov. 18, 1997, at 1A. The Alliance for Justice featured Collado's story in a 1997 video. *See* Videotape: With Liberty and Justice for All? (Alliance for Justice 1997). Although much of the media attention in Collado's case focused on the time that had passed since his conviction, the press and commentators also noted that the crime was not that serious. *See* sources cited *supra.*

[134]*See* Frank Trejo, *Judge Orders Deportation for Woman in '92 Slaying,* Dallas Morning News, June 3, 1999, at 29A.

[135]*See id.*

[136]*See id.*

of future criminal activity, or the consequences that deportation would have for the individual's family. Yet under the new immigration laws, the sanction of deportation is regularly and automatically meted out on the presumption that the label of a crime is all we need to know about a person before entering an order of banishment.

Legislative approaches that look to the length of a sentence are somewhat better, but also problematic.[137] Chue Xiong, for example, received a five-year prison sentence and served less than two years.[138] The sentence was severe given the underlying facts of the case: similar conduct is not a crime in many states,[139] and not all prosecutors would prosecute such a case. Yet Xiong's sentence would place him outside the reach of congressional proposals that would bar deportation relief for those with five-year sentences.

More generally, a mandatory deportation rule that depends on the length of a sentence relies too much on the sentencing and parole policies of different states. One state may sentence a person to a two-year definite term, whereas another may sentence the person to a ten-year term with the understanding that the person would be released after two years. In practice, the sentences are the same, but because the states use different sentencing formulations, only the person in the first state could seek relief from deportation.

Indeed, even the law in effect from 1990 to 1996, which barred relief for those who had served five years in prison, made unwarranted assumptions about the appropriateness of applying the extreme sanction of deportation. With mandatory sentencing, a five-year sentence is not unusual and may be applied to first-time offenders. For example, Franklin Henderson, who successfully persuaded the Second Circuit not to apply the new bars to relief to his case retroactively, served within a few days of five years.[140] In his case, which fell under the old law, an immigration judge examined all of the mitigating factors. She wrote:

[137]*See, e.g.*, Coonan, *supra* note 11, at 614-17 (proposing that the bar to relief be based on the length of sentence).

[138]*See* Xiong v. INS, 173 F.3d 601, 603 (7th Cir. 1999).

[139]*See* Bennett, *supra* note 11, at 1722-24 (describing state variations in the age of consent and the relevance of the age gap between the minor and the accused).

[140]In Henderson's case, there was a dispute over how to calculate the five years. The government contended that Henderson had served slightly more than five years; Henderson's attorney argued that he had served slightly less than five years. Because the immigration judge found that the crime was not an aggravated felony under the law of the Second Circuit, she never resolved the question whether Henderson had served five years. *See* Opinion of Hon. Sarah M. Burr, Immigration Judge, *reprinted in* Appendix to Petitioner's Brief, Henderson v. INS, 157 F.3d 106 (2d Cir. 1998) (No. 97-4050).

> Based on the record before me I will simply state that the negative factor in this case is the respondent's one drug arrest and one drug conviction. There are a number of favorable factors, including the fact that he has been a lawful permanent resident for 28 years, that all his immediate family resides in the United States, including his wife, his children, and his grandchildren who are all either lawful permanent residents or citizens of the United States. Additionally, the respondent has a consistent history of employment with the same employer from 1975 until the present, with the exception of his period of incarceration. He has documented the payment of taxes from 1980 until the present, he has a record of excellent adjustment to parole supervision, as well as an exceptionally positive prison record. Clearly the balancing of the equities in this case falls in respondent's favor.[141]

Henderson's case reminds us of what is lost if no judge can look at the full record. It may or may not be a good rule of thumb that a person who serves a five-year sentence should be deported. Nevertheless, some people will be like Henderson. They will have committed a crime but will also have many strong equities to show. Because of the serious impact that deportation has on both individuals and families, the law should not be blind to these facts.

Ultimately, proposals that apply a rule of deportation-by-label reflect an assumption that the law will fall on "criminal aliens" for whom there is no duty to determine if the label is accurate or to evaluate whether there are mitigating circumstances. But the cases demonstrate that labels can mislead and that there may be individual facts that militate against deportation. These cases show that people facing deportation include members of our communities who have often grown up in this country. In many cases, these people have no ties to the country to which they will return, and their deportation will cause hardship to United States citizen parents, spouses, and children left behind.

In 1953, a Presidential Commission charged with reviewing the deportation laws suggested that some legal permanent residents are so integrated into American society that they should be shielded from deportation based on a criminal conviction.[142] After describing several cases of perma-

[141] *Id.*

[142] *See* President's Commission on Immigration and Naturalization, *Whom We Shall Welcome,* 193-216 (1953) [hereinafter President's Comm'n]. I am indebted to Renee Redman for first bringing the work of this Commission to my attention. The 1953 Commission provided the first critique of the 1952 laws on national origin quotas and serves as the early legislative history of the 1965 amendments that abandoned those quotas. *See generally* Gabriel J. Chin, *The Civil Rights Revolution Comes to Immigration Law: A New Look at the Immigration and Nationality Act of 1965,* 75 N.C. L. Rev. 273, 275-80 (1996). One can only hope that the approach of the 1953 Commission will inspire a rethinking of the deportation laws as they apply to legal permanent residents convicted of crimes.

nent residents who were ordered deported, the Commission observed:

> Each of the aliens is a product of our society. Their formative years were spent in the United States, which is the only home they have ever known. The countries of their origin which they left – in two cases during infancy, in another, at the age of 5 years – certainly are not responsible for their criminal ways. . . . If such a person offends against our laws, he should be punished in the same manner as other citizens and residents of the United States and should not be subject to banishment from this country.[143]

The Commission proposed that any person who was lawfully admitted before the age of sixteen or who had resided in the United States for twenty years should not be subject to deportation based on any criminal conviction.[144]

Such a proposal falls far outside of the current congressional debate. But it demonstrates the modesty of even the most radical congressional efforts to mitigate the effects of the 1996 laws. As the 1953 Commission observed, there comes a point at which we must treat a person as a part of American society. To insist that we closely examine each person's case before entering a deportation order and that we refrain from making gross generalizations based on the label of the crime or the sentence imposed is to ask very little indeed.

## *VI. CONCLUSION*

The impact of the 1996 deportation laws goes far beyond their retroactive reach. By imposing mandatory deportation for vast new categories of criminal convictions, the laws permanently change the rights of legal permanent residents in the United States. No longer does the immigration system provide a forum for families to testify about the consequences of deportation; no longer is there any opportunity to show rehabilitation or to present evidence that the crime was not as serious as the statutory label might suggest. Even many who should fall outside the reach of the law are giving up their right to remain in this country as a result of the coercive effects of mandatory detention.

Reform must begin by recognizing the interests at stake – both of legal permanent residents and of their family members. With policy concerns such as family integrity in the balance, reform efforts should aim to restore a system that at least is able to evaluate the individual facts of

[143]President's Comm'n, *supra* note 142, at 202.
[144]*See id.*

each case. This country should no longer hide behind gross assumptions about the categories of crimes that should mandate deportation. True reform will only come with America's willingness to respect fair treatment for those whom we can hardly call strangers.

# PART II

## EMPLOYMENT MIGRATION INTO THE UNITED STATES

2

# Temporary Workers and Evolution of the Specialty H-1B Visa

B. LINDSAY LOWELL
*Georgetown University*

Evolution of the Specialty H-1B visa presages a new regime of global temporary workers. In the United States, the information technology (IT) sector is growing rapidly and Congress is considering increasing the number of H-1Bs. This paper argues that the various players all are correct in their basic assertions: employers have a real need for the best and the brightest, the H-1B workers are all too often found in exploited conditions, and the proposed increase in the H-1B cap has serious consequences for the individual H-1B visaholder and the permanent system. Balancing these facts suggests that the broken permanent system be fixed first and that the temporary system then be reformed.

The myriad complexities of the U.S. system of immigration are often misunderstood. It is particularly difficult for many observers to keep in mind that permanent immigrants and temporary migrants are truly different classes of admission. The distinction is mostly kept clear in the case of tourists or businesses travelers, but it is increasingly blurred in the case of work authorized migrants. This blurring is most evident in today's debates over the class of work-authorized visas.

Permanent immigrants are individuals and families whom we affirmatively admit as residents of the United States and who, under ideal conditions, ultimately become naturalized citizens. Legal permanent residents recreate the best of the American tradition and reaffirm our commitment to long-held values as a nation of immigrants. In the best of that tradition these citizens-in-waiting are accorded, or should be accorded, most of the rights and responsibilities enjoyed by natives.

Temporary migrants are individuals whom we conditionally admit, often along with their families, for limited periods of time for the purpose of carrying out specific endeavors. Again, it takes little explanation to see how this is the case for tourists or even most foreign students. Work authorized individuals also have clearly constrained rights: they may work, but only under certain restrictions, and they may not ever expect, for example, eligibility for U.S. welfare. Until the past decade, they could not expect to stay as permanent residents.

However, today's skilled Specialty worker visa (H-1B) conflates temporary and permanent status, while proposals for revisions of the agricultural visa (H-2A) flirt with creating a direct connection.[1] If we live in an increasingly global economy and, by obvious extension, a *de facto* if not state-sanctioned global labor market, then it is reasonable to forecast increasing demand for temporary workers who are both skilled and unskilled.[2] In this and other aspects of international mobility the past is an imperfect guide to what is clearly a dynamically evolving and growing class of international migrants. The resolution of today's debates over the Specialty H working visa may well set in motion the future system we use to admit "temporary" workers. It appears as if conflation is likely to be the order of the day.

## *TODAY'S TEMPORARY MOVEMENT IS SOMETHING NEW*

Consider that permanent immigration has gone through booms and busts, while temporary migration has grown steadily throughout the past centu-

[1]Proposals on the H-2A would make the foreign worker eligible for permanent residency status after a short period of work as a temporary H-2A.

[2]In a parallel fashion there is reason to expect increased pressure on the permanent system, but at least there already exists a consensus on the basic structure and principles that determine who and how many we admit.

ry. During the first decade of the century just under 9 million immigrants were admitted, more by far than in the preceding or following decades. Following the long hiatus of the depression years through the 1960s, immigration began to grow again, reaching about 10 million in the last decade of the twentieth century. It is fair to say that the level of international mobility for permanent residency is now repeating levels seen before even if it were one hundred years ago.

Movement for purely temporary reasons, at today's levels, is a purely new phenomenon. Temporary "admission numbers" count each and every entry into the United States and hence are often a multiple count of the same individual. Nonetheless, only 770,000 temporary admissions were counted in the first decade of the twentieth century, a number that increased to 7 million in the 1950s. By the last decade of the century there were some 230 million temporary admissions.[3] Because these are multiple counts they reflect both a stupendous increase in the number of individuals involved, as well as a significant increase in back-and-forth mobility. Revolutions in transportation, tourism, and the global economy are driving a level of temporary international mobility not prefigured by past experience. To be sure, a substantial fraction of the supposedly "permanent" international flows of yesteryear were actually temporary migrants or "birds of passage" (Piore, 1979). But that dynamic exists today as well. A large share of "permanent" immigrants circulate regularly to their original homeland and more than 20 percent of immigrants end up returning home for good sooner or later. The temporary movement that exists today is fundamentally different because it is not a by-product of otherwise permanent visaholders. More precisely, policy mechanisms explicitly define it as temporary at the outset.

The class of thus-defined temporary movement has reached levels that easily surpass the past or present return movements of legal permanent residents, and exceed the level of permanent immigration itself. Note that in 1994 the United States counted the admission of 804,000 permanent legal residents. In that same year, 5.6 million individual temporary visas were issued and 22 million entries and exits of temporary visaholders were tallied. Lest the skeptic note that many of these were transitory tourists or businessmen, the only available estimate of "person years" sug-

[3]Figures for 1900-1909 and 1950-1959 are from the Immigration and Naturalization Service. The estimate for the 1990s is made by the author assuming constant growth rates between 1990 and 1996 (after which official counts are not available).

gests that this temporary flow generated a year-round presence equivalent to at least 1.4 million persons in 1994.[4] Even the temporary *worker* classes have grown significantly and exceed the number of employment-based permanent admissions.

There are a number of temporary visas for work purposes in the United States and the reader is encouraged to study that alphabet soup in any of a number of publications (INS, 1997; Lowell, 1999b). The balance of this paper will focus on the so-called H-1B visa because it is the key bone of contention in Congressional debate at this time. Resolution of that debate will set in play the shape of the temporary program and, by default, future changes in the permanent program. It is the single largest work-authorization class with 137,000 visas issued to principals alone last year. It has immense implications for employers, domestic workers, and this nation's sense of fair play.

## *EVOLUTION OF THE SPECIALTY WORKER H-1B VISA*

Skilled workers have long been admitted under an H-1 visa that was created in the early 1950s. Originally, the visa required that the job filled by a foreign worker be temporary and that the foreigner establish an intent to return home. Since then, the double temporary provisions of this nonimmigrant visa have been removed. Employers have been able to hire for permanent positions since 1970 and, with the introduction of the H-1B visa in 1990, the worker may have the dual intent to stay either temporarily or permanently. As one might expect, these changes are associated with expectations of permanency on the part of many employers and foreign workers.

As the number of visas issued was increasing in the late 1980s, Congress imposed restrictions intended to protect the domestic worker. Originally, the visa had no numerical limitations and few labor protections. That changed in 1990 when a numerical cap of 65,000 new H-1Bs per year was imposed. A numerical cap is intended to damp down escalating demand for foreign workers and encourage internal market adjustments that are in the best long-term competitive interests of the U.S. economy (*e.g.*, increased training, better wages and working conditions, new technologies, or innovative production strategies).

[4]For technical reasons, this person-year figure is likely to be substantially too low (Lowell, 1999b). Of course, things run both ways. Another way to look at it is that 40 percent of the permanent illegal migrants, about 300,000 yearly and in addition to the 804 thousand legal permanent admissions mentioned in the text, are estimated to have first entered as temporary migrants.

Demand for the H-1B has indeed continued to grow. Today, this largely reflects demand for the visa by the rapidly expanding information technology (IT) sector. It reflects, too, the growth in supply of foreign-born IT graduates from U.S. colleges, the changed nature and appeal of the visa, and procedural backlogs faced by those who would prefer admission via the permanent system that make the H-1B an easier alternative. In recent years, employer demand for H-1Bs has been such that the numerical cap was exceeded before the year ran out. In response, Congress raised the cap in 1999 for a three-year period and is once again considering raising the cap to meet the apparent demand for H-1Bs.

Primarily as the result of lobbying by the information technology industry, in the closing months of 1998 the U.S. Congress passed the "American Competitiveness and Work Force Improvement Act." That legislation, beginning in October of 1998, provides an increase in the number of available H-1B visas from 65,000 per year to 115,000 per year in 1999 and 2000, and 107,500 in 2001. Unless new levels are legislated, the numerical limit is to return to 65,000 in the year 2002. As a trade-off to those who opposed increased numerical limits, the Bill includes new worker protections for so-called H-1B-dependent firms, *e.g.*, those most likely to unfairly exploit the specialty worker at the expense of U.S. workers. Dependent firms are defined as those with a certain percentage (ca. 15 percent) of their workforce who are H-1Bs. To date, however, these regulations have not been codified and implemented.

The new law also has a requirement that H-1B workers receive the same fringe benefits as U.S. workers. The Act requires an additional $500 fee for petitions filed and provides for new investigative procedures and new penalties for violations. The bulk of the fee will go toward training of displaced workers and scholarships for low-income students. Employers such as universities, federally-funded research institutes, etc., are exempt from the fee. A report by the National Science Foundation is to address the impact of H-1Bs on the information technology labor market, including purported discrimination against older workers in the information technology industry that may be abetted by the supply of H-1Bs.

While employers welcomed the increase in the H-1B cap, even that will not be sufficient, given backlogs carried over from prior fiscal years and ever growing demand. Already, by the end of December 1998, 59,108 of the 115,000 H-1B visas available for Fiscal Year 1999 had been used, 19,431 of the visas were issued to migrants whose applications were held over from the last fiscal year and 39,677 were new cases. Indeed, available visas under the cap ran out before year's end in 1999. Already in fiscal year 2000, the available visas are running out and the INS will process no new applications by midyear.

With the demand for H-1B workers exceeding even the expanded cap, Congress is once again being lobbied to increase the permitted H-1B workers. Several bills have been considered that variously increase the numbers by at least 40 to 75 percent, introduce an unlimited H-1 for foreign graduates of U.S. schools, impose new fees for training, and enforce the dependent-employer safeguards. A bipartisan Senate bill, the American Competitiveness in the Twenty-First Century Act (ACTFCA), would raise the annual H-1B visa cap to 195,000 for three years. It would also create a class of unlimited visas for certain foreign workers with graduate degrees from U.S. colleges and universities. A bipartisan bill in the House of Representatives would increase the cap to 200,000 for three years while doubling the application fee to $1,000. Yet another bill in the House would increase the application fee and introduce significantly new worker protections while removing the numerical cap altogether for a two-year period.

## *ARGUMENTS FOR AND AGAINST MORE H-1BS*

Because it was already evident at the outset of this year that the H-1B cap for fiscal year 2000 would be exceeded in the spring, it seemed certain that there would be passage of a bill increasing the number of H-1B workers by mid-year. Despite amendments to the Senate bill that threaten to drag it down, it still looks likely to pass before year's end.[5] While there are many political machinations that are slowing its passage, there are substantive disagreements that are holding up votes for the significant increases being called for. The facts in the matter are, as usual, contested by opposing camps who make strong claims to imperfect facts.

Business interests clamor for more H-1Bs with a few often compelling arguments. These tend to boil down to the information technology sector's hold on the national imagination. With only 8 percent of the U.S. labor force, this sector is estimated to generate about one-third of the recent strong productivity gains in the New Economy (DOC, 2000). The core IT sector alone has grown 47 percent from 1.5 to 2.2 million between

[5]Amendments being considered include campaign finance reform, as well as amnesty programs for unauthorized residents and certain classes of Central Americans whose temporary protected status is ending.

mid-decade in 1995 and today, comprising over one-third of all scientific and engineering jobs. Some point to a survey of IT employers suggesting that as many as 800,000 IT jobs are unfilled because of shortages. When even casual observers note a tight labor market in *all* sectors of the economy, coupled with the sector's aura, calls for more H-1Bs seem irresistible.

A variety of parties oppose any increase at all or at least increases that fail to incorporate substantial labor protections or training. Traditional opponents to any further increases come from advocates for U.S. labor, as well as careful observers who see no strong analytic evidence for shortages in the IT sector. The former point to prevalent anecdotes about the exploitation of H-1Bs and claim that they undercut domestic wages. The latter point out that despite well-known complaints from employers, average wage growth in IT has not been spectacular. Unemployment in IT has risen slightly in the past year, although it remains about half the national average. And debate rages over whether or not domestic supplies of IT workers are or will be enough; after all, economists argue, supply would meet demand if wages were raised.

Thus, these core contestants in the debate primarily use economic arguments. Without an increased supply of foreign H-1Bs business interests claim that domestic workers will be unavailable at any cost, thus hurting the industry's legendary productivity. They also say they will have to get the work done abroad if they do not get more H-1Bs. Those opposed note the soft nature of the shortage estimates and would welcome increased wages for domestic workers, while arguing that going offshore is in fact an impractical threat.

A third set of actors to the debate is motivated not by economic arguments *per se*, but by the implications for the system of permanent admissions. Pro-increase actors of this stripe castigate opponents of more H-1Bs as restrictionists who, they claim, do not like immigrants.[6] This suggests that those making the claim make no distinction between the rights and obligations given to temporary versus permanent visaholders. In fact, actors of this stripe who oppose more H-1Bs would preferentially admit most foreign workers as permanent residents. They call for fixing the permanent system before meddling with the temporary; last year inefficient

[6]As if temporary "nonimmigrant" workers and permanent citizen-track "immigrants" were the same thing. One suspects that these actors at some level either really make no distinction or trivialize it. And they are mindful that the proposed numbers, coupled with the nature of the H-1B, will likely lead to calls for increasing the cap on permanent admissions which helps accomplish a goal of increased numbers overall (*see* discussion in next section).

U.S. agencies processed only 61,000 for permanent admission out of the legal cap of 140,000. There is clearly room in the permanent system for expansion.

## *BALANCING EVIDENCE*

Each actor in the debate has some truth. What is lacking is a balancing of the truths with an eye toward the national interest that, for my purposes here, can be reduced to the successful management of a very large-scale temporary work program. I will define success as meeting employers' legitimate needs while protecting domestic workers, along with administrative efficiency and transparency. My own research leads me to believe that employers by and large are good actors and their need for highly-skilled foreign workers is legitimate. Yet current worker protections are exposing too many to abuse. And while the H-1B program is efficient in meeting employer demand, numerical increases threaten to greatly disrupt the system of permanent admissions. Transparency is increasingly being forfeited in the H-1B visa program.

Business actors in the information technology sector are correct in saying that aliens meet a need for the best and the brightest. As mentioned above, the IT sector has grown significantly and almost all of that growth has come in the highly-trained occupations of computer scientists and engineers, not programmers (Ellis and Lowell, 1999). At the same time, U.S. enrollments and graduates in computer sciences dipped in the early to mid-1990s and enrollments only began to climb in the last part of that decade. More graduates are a couple of years off. In the meantime, the supply of foreign (and domestically) trained alien workers offers an alternative.[7] Just over one-third of natives in the core IT occupations do not have even a college degree, while four tenths of foreign IT workers have a Master's degree or better compared with one-seventh of natives who have such degrees. With unemployment rates running around 2 percent in IT, and with demand escalating, foreign workers are a quick solution to production bottlenecks at the upper end.

[7]Twenty percent of H-1Bs are graduates of U.S. institutions of higher education. Forty percent of H-1Bs have Masters degrees or better. In fact, the higher average education of immigrants in IT translates into higher average earnings compared with natives. After controlling for human capital differences between IT immigrants and natives, there are no wage differentials (Lowell and Taylor, 2000). This implies that immigrants are paid fairly and that most adverse H-1B effects work through their disproportionate concentration in the contingent segment of IT (*see* next paragraph).

Labor advocates are correct in saying that the many anecdotes about abuses of H-1Bs add up to realistic concerns. Consider contingent jobs (undesired and/or temporary) in the IT industry broadly defined (Lowell and Taylor, 2000). Using Bureau of Labor Statistics measures that tend to understate the situation, it can be shown that 5 percent of IT jobs are contingent. This is often out-contracted work bereft of benefits, and earnings are an astounding 46 percent less than for otherwise similar core (permanent) IT workers. What is more, while wages increased roughly 15 percent for core IT workers during this period, there was absolutely no wage growth in the contingent sector. The H-1B policy appears to contribute to this phenomenon with a disproportionately high share (20%) of recently-arrived foreign IT workers holding contingent jobs.[8] In today's truly sizable IT labor force, unscrupulous parties at the periphery exploit too many H-1Bs and undercut mainstream employers.

Immigrant advocates correctly insist that increases in the number of H-1Bs pose serious challenges. Estimates indicate that there are currently 420,000 in the H-1B workforce and about half are working in the core IT industry (Lowell, 2000). Indeed, fully one-quarter of yearly growth in the IT workforce has come from H-1Bs in the prior half decade. The estimates also indicate that at least half and possibly as many as two-thirds of H-1Bs intend to stay in the United States. But given the overall and per-country caps on the permanent system, it is likely that it can absorb no more than 25,000 H-1Bs. Clearly, if we are admitting 115,000 H-1Bs this year, or 200,000 and more under Congressional proposals, most H-1Bs and their employers will not be able to realize the implicit offer of permanent residency. The proposed higher H-1B cap will produce H-1B working populations of more than 710,000, increasing the number exposed to exploitation and leaving more to face the unanticipated decision to return home at the end of their visa stay.

The evidence suggests that there is a real need for the highly trained foreign H-1B workers (exceptional bachelor degree holders or at least a Masters degree). But it is unclear that the best way to meet this need is by expanding the H-1B program as it and the permanent system are currently configured. Doing so risks putting ever larger numbers of H-1Bs in exploitive conditions which undercuts domestic workers, as well as the majority of employers who compete fairly. More H-1Bs also means that

[8]All immigrants comprise one-seventh of the IT labor force. Recently arrived immigrants, those in the country five years or less, are predominantly H-1B temporary workers (Lowell, 2000).

transparency is sacrificed, *i.e.*, for a large number of H-1Bs, the promise of permanent residency will be rescinded at the end of their visa stay.

## *CONCLUSIONS*

Temporary migration is not what it was in the past. The numbers involved are very significant and the pressures that drive them are likely to continue in the near future. This is not simply an IT thing. Global transformations have been behind the wave and the New Economy, with its rapacious demand for labor, is already generating calls from several other sectors in the U.S. economy for more guestworkers and immigrants. It remains to be seen, however, whether or not Congress and the Administration will see the big picture or continue to muddle through with *ad hoc* responses to episodic economic and political demands.

The first lasting reform that Congress should undertake is reform of the permanent system. With only 61,000 out of 140,000 permanent employment slots being used, it should be obvious that something is amiss. When employers are asked, they report that they would prefer to sponsor permanent resident visaholders (Lowell, 1999a). Straightening out the system would create that possibility for many.[9] It would also be reasonable to lift the per country cap on employment-based admissions for an interim period, at least for highly qualified petitioners (*i.e.*, Masters degree or better). The permanent class is preferable from the vantage of domestic safeguards because the immigrant is a free agent able to freely negotiate and leave an employer if he so chooses. And permanent admission is central to the American tradition of successful integration; supplementing that tradition with large populations of floating temporary visaholders runs serious risks.

After reforming the permanent system Congress should give serious attention to the thorough revisions required for a successful temporary program of the future. The so-called dependent employer clause would screen out potentially abusive employers and offer one simple protection. It or similar, simple provisions should be implemented. What is more, the H-1B remains a transitional visa, *i.e.*, the worker may intend to stay per-

[9]The Department of Labor is in the process of streamlining its paperwork processing of permanent visas (certification) which should help. However, the INS is also involved and their processing times are now very slow. Serious consideration should be given to improved, simpler labor protections and user fees that are directly plowed back into administration of the program.

manently and the stay is essentially for six years, hardly a length of time that even the most casual observer would think of as temporary. It would be best to be honest with foreign workers and employers by requiring that the visaholder demonstrate an intent to return home at the end of his visa stay, and to make the duration of that stay no more than three years.[10] Structured in this way there is room for generous numbers that should be subject to change based upon some agreed-upon labor market indicators. Under these conditions, a large scale temporary program would retain transparency and operate without causing disequilibrium and inequities.

## *REFERENCES*

DOC (U.S. Department of Congress)
2000 *Digital Economy, 2000.* Washington, DC., http://www.ecommerce.gov

Ellis, R. and B. Lindsay Lowell
1999 Foreign-Origin Persons in the U.S. Information Technology Workforce, Report III of the IT Workforce Data Project, the United Engineering Foundation, www.uefoundation.org

INS (U.S. Immigration and Naturalization Service)
1997 *Statistical Yearbook of the Immigration and Naturalization Service,* 1996. Washington, DC: U.S. Government Printing Office.

Lowell, B. Lindsay
1999a "Information Technology Companies and U.S. Immigration Policy: Hiring Foreign Workers." In *Research on Immigration and Integration in the Metropolis.* http://riim.metropolis.net/Virtual%20Library/2000/wp00S4.pdf

———
1999b Skilled Temporary and Permanent Immigration to the United States. In *Research on Immigration and Integration in the Metropolis.* http://riim.metropolis.net/Virtual20/Library/1999/wp99S2.pdf

[10]Such requirements would not disbar an H-1B from ultimately applying for a permanent slot, but they would be transparent insofar as they would not promise what cannot be assured. The argument that dual intent was given to permit employers to screen H-1Bs makes sense only if the program were the small program that it once was (and one not dominated by one or two national origin groups). Today's large scale temporary program outstrips the capacity of the permanent system to absorb temporary visaholders.

3

# Temporary Workers at the Top and Bottom of the Labor Market

PHILIP MARTIN
*University of California, Davis*

Guest or foreign worker programs aim to add workers to the labor force without adding permanent residents to the population. They have failed to achieve this goal in every country and in every time period in which they were tried. Some guest workers invariably settled, the number of guest workers often rose to greater than expected levels, and the rationale for the guest worker program changed. All the industrial democracies have guest worker programs, but none has found "best practice" ways to keep guest worker programs true to their goals.

The U.S. admits nonimmigrant foreigner guest workers with at least 19 different visas that range from A for ambassadors to TN for NAFTA professionals, although only 14 of these visas result in the foreign worker being considered a U.S. employee. About 395,000 foreign workers were admitted as U.S. workers with nonimmigrant visas in FY96, the most recent data available (these INS data double-count individuals entering the U.S. several times in one year). Another 640,000 foreigners were admitted as students or exchange visitors and a large but unknown number of foreign students were also employed at least part time by U.S. employers for wages. Many of these nonimmigrants remain in the U.S. for more than one year, so the number of legal nonimmigrant workers is probably well over one million in a labor force of 138 million in 1998, including 132 million employed workers.

The U.S. in the 1990s debated the admission of two types of temporary foreign workers: H-1Bs, or foreign professionals with a BA or more admitted to the U.S. with renewable three year visas to fill vacant jobs that require a BA or more, and H-2As, temporary foreign farm workers admitted to fill temporary U.S. farm jobs. These programs differ in many respects, including admission criteria that employers must satisfy, the number of foreign workers admitted, and the prospects for increasing the number of admissions.

There are similarities and differences in the debate over temporary foreign workers at the top and bottom of the U.S. labor market. In both cases, U.S. employers initiate the admissions process by requesting permission to employ foreign workers. However, employer requests and the debate over them use words that have political but not economic meaning, such as "shortage." Shortage is not a term found in economics texts. Instead, the economically meaningful concept is how demand and supply respond to wage changes that bring supply and demand into balance. In many discussions of labor shortages, demand is forgotten.

## *GUEST WORKERS*

Almost all nonimmigrant or guest worker programs include the word "temporary" in their statement of purpose, which suggests that the presence of the foreign worker as well as the need for foreign workers should be limited in time. Experience proves the aphorism that "there is nothing more permanent than temporary workers," largely because the incentives of both employers and foreign workers tend to expand the programs and extend the stay of workers.

In the 1990s, the U.S. added more guest worker programs, with each aiming to fill a narrow range of vacancies in a particular labor market, such as programs that admit foreign nurses for inner city hospitals. At the same time, the capacity of the public Employment Services and other regulatory bodies to credibly determine whether there is a genuine need for foreign workers, and to ensure that employers keep their promises to pay prevailing or other wages, has eroded.

Employers who request permission to employ guest workers currently pay for the privilege in the form of 1) fees to lobbyists to get the regulatory hurdles between the foreign worker and the U.S. job as low as possible, 2) fees to lawyers to navigate the regulatory labyrinth, and 3) lost production due to the time that a position remains unfilled until regulatory requirements are met. The result is often perverse: once employers have learned to negotiate the regulatory system, anticipating administrative fees of up to several thousand dollars per worker and waiting times that are sometimes measured in months, they tend to avoid serious searches for alternative ways to get work done and become ever more reliant on foreign workers.

A better way to regulate the admission of foreign workers for niche labor markets would be to impose taxes or fees on employers in exchange for giving them easier access to foreign workers. A fee system represents a tradeoff between two competing goods: easy access to foreign workers on the one hand, and protection for U.S. workers on the other. Under a fee system, employers would prove that they made a good faith effort to recruit foreign workers by paying fees, and the fees collected from employers would be used to cover the cost of enforcement of labor laws in affected industries, to train and retrain U.S. workers, and to develop productivity-increasing technologies. Fees could be adjusted up or down as the national interest changes.

Employer-paid fees could be spent in a manner that might reduce the litigation and controversy that currently accompanies the admission and employment of foreign workers. If the employer-paid fee consisted of 1) an upfront fee and 2) a percentage payroll tax equivalent to the pension and unemployment taxes that most guest workers will not derive benefits from, and was administered on the same narrow labor market basis that the guest worker program was targeting (by industry, occupation, and/or area), then occupational, industry, or regional funds could be established and administered by representatives of employers, workers, and government, with each fund having the responsibility to spend the fees paid by employers who hire foreign workers in a manner that ends reliance on foreign workers in the industry, occupation, and/or area. Such a fee system permits those closest to the labor market in which foreign workers are present to decide on the optimal way to end dependence, with the side benefit that making decisions on how to spend employer fees should also reduce the often adversarial nature of foreign worker admissions and employment.

## *H-1B FOREIGN PROFESSIONALS*

The H-1B program, created in 1990 by modifying another program, permits foreigners with BA degrees or more to enter the U.S. or up to six years to fill U.S. jobs that require a BA or more. In exchange for making it easier for employers to obtain foreign professionals, an annual cap of 65,000 was imposed on the program. Each H-1B was permitted to remain in the U.S. for up to six years, for a maximum 390,000 H-1B workers employed in the U.S. at any time.

In 1997, employers used all available H-1B visas before the end of 12 months, and they persuaded Congress to approve an increase in the annual ceiling to 115,000 in FY99 and FY00 and 107,500 in FY01. However, even this higher number of H-1B visas was used up in mid-June 1999, three months before the end of the federal fiscal year, and the FY00 allocation was used up by March 2000, generating pressures to raise the annual ceiling again. Thus, Congress in 2000 is debating raising the H-1B ceiling again.

The leading Senate bill, the American Competitiveness in the Twenty-First Century Act (S. 2045), would raise the cap on the number of H-1B visas that can be issued to foreign professionals to 195,000 through 2005. S. 2045 was approved in March 2000 by the Senate Judiciary Committee on a 16-2 vote. In the House, a bipartisan bill would increase the number of H-1B visas from the current 115,000 to 200,000, and to double the employer-paid training fee from $500 to $1,000; training fees are used to provide scholarships for U.S. students to encourage them to study computer programming and engineering. The proposal would also set aside 10,000 foreign student visas for universities and colleges to attract the best high-tech students.

The Clinton administration supports raising the H-1B visa ceiling, but has not decided which bill to back. The White House issued a statement: "We are ready to support a reasonable increase in the number of H-1B visas as long as it reflects a balanced approach that protects and prepares the U.S. work force." Both Vice-President Gore and Governor Bush have endorsed raising the H-1B cap.

The H-1B program is controversial. Much of the debate involved in raising the annual ceiling on H-1B visas centered on changes to program regulations, with the Senate bill not counting against the higher annual limit foreigners with an MS or more from a U.S. university or those being paid $60,000 a year or more. The House bill changes the DOL bureaucracy in a manner that would allow employers to file their attestations by computer. Critics argue that the H-1B program allows U.S. employers to hire young foreign professionals who are willing to work long hours, and thus avoid hiring older U.S. programmers who might need retraining and may be less likely to put in 16-hour days.

Many H-1B workers come to the U.S. in the expectation that their U.S. employers will sponsor them for immigrant status, which means that the H-1B workers hope their U.S. employers will prepare an application to the U.S. Department of Labor to obtain certification that no American worker is available to fill the job for which the employer is sponsoring the foreigner. There are 140,000 employment/economic green cards available each year for foreign workers and their families, but no more than 9,800 or seven percent can be given to nationals of any one country. Over 40 percent of H-1B workers are from India, and this per-country limit means that many Indians whose U.S. employers want to sponsor them for immigrant status must wait until a green card becomes available. Most H-1Bs stay with the employer who brought them into the U.S. only until they become immigrants, then leave for other U.S. jobs.

### *H-2A FARM WORKERS*

The H-1B program permits employers to have foreign professionals admitted by attestation, which means that a U.S. employer opens the door to foreign workers by attesting that it tried in good faith but failed to find U.S. workers, and it will pay the H- 1B worker prevailing wages. The H-2A program, by contrast, is a certification program, which means that a U.S. employer seeking foreign workers to fill vacant U.S. jobs must first attempt to recruit U.S. workers by offering them at least DOL-determined wages and working conditions. DOL supervises the employer's recruitment of U.S. workers, and can deny certification if, *e.g.*, the employer does not offer adequate free housing to U.S. (and foreign) workers.

Labor certification includes what many U.S. farmers consider disadvantages:

- Certification exposes them to union referrals of U.S. workers who must be hired, even if the employer is convinced they are not "adequate workers."
- Certification imposes requirements that many farm employers cannot

and do not want to meet, including the provision of free housing for U.S. and foreign workers.

Farmers have since the early 1980s advocated a non-certification guest worker program. They succeeded in getting the U.S. House of Representatives to approve the Panetta-Morrison program in 1984, the U.S. Senate to approve the Wilson program in 1985, Congress to approve the Replenishment Agricultural Worker program in 1986, and the U.S. Senate to approve a revision of the H-2A program, AgJOBS, in 1998 (CAW, 1992, GAO, 1997, Rural Migration News, 1998-99). However, none of these programs became law.

The major agricultural guest worker proposal pending in Congress: S. 1814, the Agricultural Job Opportunity Benefits And Security Act of 1999 (AgJOBS), would make some unauthorized farm workers quasi legal, allowing them to earn a legal immigrant status if they continued to do farm work. More importantly, AgJOBS would change the system for admitting foreign farm workers in the future.

Under AgJOBS, unauthorized workers in the U.S. who could prove that they did at least 150 days or 880 hours of farm work in the 12 months ending October 27, 1999 could apply for new nonimmigrant status. These "quasi-legal" farm workers (called adjusted nonimmigrant aliens) could maintain their nonimmigrant status, and eventually earn an immigrant status, by doing at least 180 days of farm work each year for five of the next seven years, and were out of the U.S. at least 65 days a year. (S. 1815, The Farmworker Adjustment Act of 1999, includes only quasi-legalization).

More important, AgJOBS would change admissions procedures for foreign workers. One key change is the substitution of a registry run by the Employment Service for labor certification by DOL, thus accomplishing a key grower goal - to avoid having the DOL operate a certification process in which the government regulates the border gate. AgJOBS would require each state Employment Service to create a farm worker registry that would allow, but not require, farm workers - including those quasi-legalized under S. 1814 - to register for farm jobs. ES offices would verify the right to work of those who register, *i.e.*, complete I-9 forms on them, before workers could be registered. Farm employers seeking H-2A workers under AgJOBS would be allowed to reject workers who ask for jobs directly, rather than apply for jobs through the registry. Workers may only register in the state where they reside; quasi-legalized workers may only be referred to farm jobs in that state or contiguous states - other registered workers may be referred to farm jobs throughout the U.S.

Employers would submit job offers to the ES registry in their state at least 28 days before workers are needed. After the ES verifies that the job offers submitted paid prevailing wages, they would be listed in the registry, that is, each state registry would assume responsibility for: 1) verifying the legal status of workers seeking to register by checking the documents and data they provide with INS and SSA; 2) verifying that employer job offers satisfied requirements of any new program; and 3) contacting registered workers to determine if they wanted to accept jobs offered by employers. Workers who did not accept referral to a job within 12 months would be purged from the registry.

Employers seeking registry workers would complete a form very similar to the current H-2A application, providing information on the number of workers requested, the beginning and end dates of the work, wages and any benefits, and "bona fide occupational qualifications that must be possessed by a worker to be employed in the job opportunity in question." Admissions would work as follows: if an employer made a request for 100 workers at least 28 days before they were needed, and ES had only 40 registered workers willing to go to the requesting employer seven days before the need date, the grower would receive a "shortage report" from the registry that would grant him permission to bring 60 foreign farm workers into the U.S. The ES would be responsible for advertising and making both workers and farm employers aware of the registry.

AgJOBS would change several aspects of the current H-2A program, including ending the requirement that growers provide free housing after three or four years. It would also change minimum wage rules. Under the current H-2A program, a grower seeking certification to employ H-2A workers must pay the higher of three wage rates: the federal or state minimum wage; the Adverse Effect Wage Rate (the average hourly earnings of field and livestock workers in a USDA survey of farm employers); or the prevailing wage as determined by the ES. Under AgJOBS, employers would have to pay the higher of the prevailing wage or the AEWR, and both terms are redefined in AgJOBS. The prevailing wage is that determined by a state ES or another wage survey, including "an employer-generated prevailing wage survey." In a radical departure from current wage regulation, which protects individuals, an employer could pay a "piece rate or task rate or use any other incentive payment method, including a group rate [and] . . . shall be considered to be in compliance . . . if the average of the hourly earnings of the workers, taken as a group" is the minimum wage or more.

To offset charges that the AgJOBS program would be farm employers' field of dreams, AgJOBS includes a provision that allows anyone to file a complaint that an employer is violating labor laws. DOL would be required to investigate "serious child labor, wage, and housing violations" within 10 days. However, AgJOBS does not provide additional funds for labor law enforcement.

Several commissions and studies are required. A 12-member Commission on Housing Migrant Agricultural Workers is to be established, as well as a "bilateral commission between the United States and each country" sending 10,000 or more H-2A workers to the U.S. to "discuss matters of mutual concern." Required studies include: 1) the relationship between child care and child labor, by the Secretaries of Labor, Agriculture, and Health; 2) current field sanitation standards in agriculture, by the Secretaries of Labor and Agriculture; and 3) coordinated and targeted labor standards enforcement, by the Secretary of Labor in consultation with the Secretary of Agriculture.

After four years of AgJOBS, the General Accounting Office is to do a comprehensive report, with an eight-person advisory board, that answers eight questions, beginning with "whether the program has ensured an adequate and timely supply of qualified, eligible workers at the time and place needed by employers;" as well as whether the H-2A workers are employed only in authorized farm work and are departing the U.S. as required; whether employers are complying with program requirements; whether there is any displacement of U.S. workers by H-2A workers; and how U.S. workers' wages and working conditions were affected by AgJOBS. The GAO report is to conclude with recommendations on whether to continue AgJOBS.

Employer associations are urging members to contribute the higher of $1 an acre or $1 a worker to support enactment of AgJOBS. One farm employer organization, Agricultural Producers, which represents citrus producers in Arizona and California, announced in January 2000 that it would revive an affiliate organization, Farmers Harvest, to obtain H-2A workers for citrus employers and packinghouses if AgJOBS becomes law.

The Commission on Immigration Reform in 1995, on the other hand, concluded that: "a large scale agricultural guest worker program . . . is not in the national interest . . . such a program would be a grievous mistake." President Clinton agreed in a June 1995 statement that asserted that a guest worker program would increase illegal immigration, displace U.S. workers, and depress wages and working conditions. Most farm-worker advocates oppose AgJOBS, arguing that it would simply provide agricultural employers with more foreign workers when there are already farm labor surpluses. Some 180 interest and advocacy groups circulated a letter to members of Congress opposing AgJOBS.

## *CONCLUSIONS*

Immigration raises important tradeoffs, tradeoffs between goods that do not yield "correct" answers. Nonimmigrant workers illustrate some of these immigration tradeoffs. Making it easy for U.S. employers to obtain foreign workers can help to increase the level of economic activity, but also make it harder to achieve the competing good of maximizing wages and opportunities for U.S. workers, especially if the foreign worker is tied to one U.S. employer or if the foreign worker hopes to be sponsored by the employer for immigrant status.

At the unskilled end of the job ladder, the competing good is lower prices for consumers of goods produced in industries with significant shares of foreign workers who help hold down costs and prices, versus the competing good of adequate wages and working conditions for all U.S. workers. However, public policymaking would be enhanced by a clearer understanding of these tradeoffs.

Look at food. Americans spent about 11 percent of their $6 trillion in disposable income on food in 1998, including 6.6 percent on food eaten at home and 4.4 percent on food eaten away from home. "Food Check-Out Day" was February 9, meaning that the average U.S. household earned enough in the first 40 days of 2000 to pay its food bill for the year. To put food spending in perspective, Americans spent more on medical care in 1998, $888 billion, than they spent on food and alcoholic beverages, $848 billion. U.S. consumers also buy non-food items produced on farms, including cotton and other fibers as well as ornamental plants and flowers. Americans spent about $55 billion on ornamental plants and flowers in 1998, or about $200 a person.

Fresh fruits and vegetables illustrate how small the relationship is between cheap farm workers and cheap food. About 2.5 million individuals do farm work for wages sometime during a typical year, so that farm workers represent less than two percent of the 140 million persons with work experience in the U.S. each year. Almost 70 percent, or 1.7 million of these farm workers, are immigrants, and an estimated 50 percent were unauthorized in 1998-99.

What would happen to U.S. food prices if legal and unauthorized farm workers were not readily available? According to the U.S. Bureau of Labor Statistics, there were about 106 million "consumer units" in the U.S. in 1997, with an average of 2.5 persons each, and they spent an average of $35,000 during the year, including $4,800 for food. These food expenditures included $2,900 for food eaten at home, or about $55 a week, including $6 weekly for fresh fruits and vegetables.

Farmers got 18 percent of each retail dollar spent on fresh fruit in 1997 and 20 percent of each retail dollar spent on fresh vegetables. Wages and benefits paid to farm workers by fresh fruit and vegetable workers average a third of the farmer's costs, which means that farmers get about $0.19 for a $1 head of lettuce, and farm worker wages and benefits represent about six percent or $0.06 of the $1 retail price.

It is hard to determine how much farm wages would increase if foreign workers were not available. In 1966, one year after the end of the Bracero program, the fledgling United Farm Workers union won a 40 percent wage increase for grape harvesters. Average hourly farm worker earnings were about $7 in 1998, according to USDA, and a 40 percent increase would bring them to about $10 hourly. If a 40 percent farm worker wage increase were fully passed on to consumers, and if there were no farm productivity improvements, the $0.06 farm labor cost in a head of lettuce would rise to $0.08, and the retail price would rise from $1 to $1.02. A 40 percent increase in farm labor costs thus translates into a two percent increase at the retail level because: 1) farm labor is a fraction of farm prices; and 2) farmers receive only a fraction of the retail price of food.

For a typical 2.5-person consumer unit, a 40 percent increase in farm worker wages would increase annual spending on fresh fruits and vegetables by two percent or $6, or from $293 to $299 in 1997, about the cost of a movie ticket. Cheap farm workers are not the reason for cheap food-farm labor costs are typically about less than 10 percent of the retail price of fresh fruits and vegetables – the farmer's 20 percent share of retail times labor's 33 percent share of farmer costs means that farm labor represents an average 7 percent of retail prices.

U.S. consumers do not save much money because of low farm wages, but there still may be arguments for guest workers in some situations. However, experience teaches that three principles should guide the development of any new guest worker policies:

- Illegal immigration must be under control. Migrants may prefer to be unauthorized if they have to pay fees to get visas, or if they are tied to one employer. Employers can avoid wage and housing regulations, as well as the scrutiny of government agents, if they hire unauthorized workers outside the program.

- Employers must have a continued incentive to seek alternatives. Under the current H-2A program, once an employer satisfies program requirements, he pays only administrative fees. Employers who have adapted to guest worker rules do not actively seek U.S. workers or labor-saving alternatives. For example, the Florida sugar cane industry began importing Caribbean workers to hand-cut cane in 1943, and maintained that cane harvesting could not be mechanized because unique muck soils would bog down machines. But after a lawsuit was filed in the early 1990s that alleged that workers guaranteed $5.30 an hour and required to cut one ton of cane per hour should be paid $5.30 a ton, rather than the $3.70 a ton they were paid, cane companies mechanized the harvest within three years.
- Bilateral agreements should govern recruitment, remittances, and returns. The H-2A program gives U.S. employers complete discretion in where and how to recruit workers – employers can and do select the "best and brawniest" of foreign work forces; migrants often pay hundreds of dollars to get selected for U.S. farm jobs. The workers' home country should be involved in the guest worker program so that recruitment can be regulated, remittances used to foster job-creating growth, and worker returns facilitated.

The AgJOBS proposal does not satisfy these criteria. Instead, it hands a major new task to state ES offices that they are unlikely to be able to fulfill; the ES failure to register and have available to farmers legal workers will help to divert blame for "labor shortages" from farmers to the government. The complex legalization program, with its requirements for continued farm work, is likely to foster both exploitation and fraud. Workers wanting to satisfy the five years requirement to become immigrants are not likely to complain and risk firing. Farm labor contractors, on the other hand, could develop a lucrative sideline issuing real and false letters of employment to probationary AgJOBS workers.

## *REFERENCES*

Commission on Agricultural Workers (CAW)
1992 Report of the Commission on Agricultural Workers. Washington, DC: U.S. Government Printing Office. November.

California Rural Legal Assistance Foundation. Clearinghouse on Agricultural Guestworker Legislation. www.crlaf.org/gworkers.htm

Migration News Monthly. http://migration.ucdavis.edu

Rural Migration News. Quarterly. http://migration.ucdavis.edu or rural@primal.ucdavis.edu

# 4

# Proposed Framework for Consideration of Fundamental Reform of the Agricultural Labor System in the United States

RICK SWARTZ
*Rick Swartz and Associates*

This paper is premised on a judgment that 1999 may present an historic opportunity for Congress, the President and the nation to reform in fundamental ways the agricultural labor system in the United States. During recent weeks, there have been informal exchanges among private interests about possibilities for common ground on agricultural labor issues generally. Based upon these conversations and a sample of congressional offices, outlined below is a proposed framework for consideration of fundamental reforms of the agricultural labor system.

It should be understood that no interested party has yet endorsed any of these proposals. It also must be acknowledged that farmworker issues have for years been fraught with conflict, accusation, litigation, injustice and distrust.

Despite the challenges and suspicions, the framework proposed represents a good faith effort to invite all parties to consider whether at this time there is a "package of reforms" which would represent a dramatic improvement for farmer and farmworker alike. No one in this debate can or even attempts to defend the status quo. The challenge to the political system is to find the will to overcome past injustices and conflicts in order to address, for the future, the legitimate needs of all of those involved in agricultural labor.

## *PROPOSED FRAMEWORK*

Reform issues related to farm labor are many and complex. A framework to encourage a search for common ground and consensus among all major public and private interests is daunting, and could be approached differently by others. The approach taken here is to suggest six "baskets" of major issues, to break these down into more discrete subissues, and then to identify a menu of two or more reform ideas on each.

The hope is that such a menu, briefly explained and simply presented, may enable parties on all sides to identify one or more options which they can "work with" for each of the issues discussed. If there is sufficient interest, then perhaps over the next week or two the various parties can discuss informally whether despite past differences they can see the possibility of a reform package that would be worth serious consideration. If substantive dialogue can proceed there may be some promise of success. At the least, good faith efforts, even if they fail, would show respect for the urgency and opportunity to reform a farm labor system in America which no one defends.

The six proposed "baskets" of issues are:

- Legal status
- Access to housing, health care, education and essential human services
- Employment registry, rights and working conditions
- Targeted enforcement against exploitation, smuggling and dangerous conditions

- Temporary foreign worker programs and international considerations
- Assistance to state and local governments

## *A. ISSUES RELATED TO LEGAL STATUS*

The U.S. agricultural industry, particularly the labor-intensive fruit, vegetable and horticultural sector, for decades has employed a high proportion of foreign workers. Heavy reliance on foreign workers is indeed the norm in agriculture in virtually all industrialized nations. It is estimated that in recent years approximately 2.5 million persons are hired annually to do farm work. About one third work fewer than 25 days a year, a third between 25 and 150 days a year, and a third work more than 150 days at hired farm work.

Of the approximately 800,000 persons engaged in farm work more than 150 days a year and of the approximately 800,000 who work between 25 and 150 days a year, a significant proportion are undocumented immigrants not authorized to work in the United States. Although precise statistics are not available, experts and government agencies have estimated that between 30 and 60 percent of this work force is comprised of undocumented immigrants. That is, perhaps 480,000 to 960,000 of the *current* farm labor work force is undocumented.

Any possible consensus package of farmworker reforms must address the issue of legal status. Consultations to date suggest that many interested parties agree that it would be devastating to the entire U.S. agriculture economy if the current undocumented work force were suddenly to disappear.

It makes sense to consider options to provide the right to work and somehow legalize the status of undocumented workers already here. This would assure employers that much of their current work force would be brought within the law, and would enable the INS and other authorities to establish and appropriately regulate their presence. For workers, legal status would eliminate the fears and risks of a covert existence, and provide hope for a more secure future under the protection of the law.

*Options* related to legal status include:

1. *Accord H-2A status to current undocumented agricultural workers, with an opportunity to secure permanent legal residence under prescribed conditions.* The Senate approved such a concept in 1998, and the Congress adopted such a legalization program for undocumented farmworkers as part of the Immigration Reform and Control Act of 1986. However, consultations suggest

that the specific requirements and provisions of both the 1998 Senate proposal and the 1986 law would not attract widespread support in 1999. A compromise, however, may be possible.

For example, current undocumented agricultural workers could be offered an opportunity to apply from within the United States to become "legal" H-2A workers. If they abide by all legal requirements of H-2A workers and continue to work for a prescribed number of years and/or total months in agriculture, they would earn the right to adjust their status to legal permanent residence. If this general concept provides a basis for consensus, the challenge will be to find consensus on the specific terms to be met to establish eligibility for such a program. Such a program could also apply to persons not currently in the United States who may in the future be lawfully admitted under a reformed H-2A program upon documented shortages of legal workers.

2. *Strengthen the capacity of community-based groups and employers to assist the current undocumented agricultural work force and future H-2A admissions to acquire legal status.* Implementation of the type of program outlined above will require close cooperation between employers, government agencies and community-based groups which work with migrant workers. Public and private resources would be required to educate, counsel and otherwise assist farmworkers, determine whether they may be eligible, decide whether to apply and to navigate successfully and lawfully the application process. Application fees paid by the employer and/or worker could subsidize such assistance, together with direct government and philanthropic grants. The role of employers and private institutions would not only assist workers, but dramatically reduce risk of fraud in the application process. This institutional infrastructure will also be key to the worker registry, discussed in Section C.

3. *Provide a waiver of relevant provisions of the 1996 Immigration Act which bar lawful reentry to the U.S. of undocumented persons who have resided unlawfully in the U.S. for more than 180 days since January of 1997.* The Senate adopted such a provision in 1998 to enable members of the current undocumented agricultural work force to qualify for participation in a modified H-2A program.

## *B. ACCESS TO HOUSING, HEALTH CARE, EDUCATION AND ESSENTIAL HUMAN SERVICES*

In April of 1997, the U.S. Department of Labor published a "Profile of U.S.

Farmworkers." Regarding farmworker income and poverty, it found:

- Farmworkers had low individual earnings from farm work; the median income from farm work was between $2,500 and $5,000. Three fourths earned less than $10,000 annually.
- Only one-fourth of the farmworkers had non-farm work earnings. The median personal income from farm work and other work source combined was between $5,000 and $7,500.
- Few farmworkers had assets. About half (49%) owned a vehicle and about one third owned or were buying a house or trailer in the United States.
- Farmworker households also had low family incomes. The median was between $7,400 and $10,000, and over three fifths of farmworker households were in poverty.
- Despite pervasive poverty among farm workers, few used social insurance or social service programs.

Employers, farmworkers advocates, experts and government officials agree that seasonal migrant farmworkers, whether U.S. citizens, legal immigrants or undocumented, need decent, affordable housing in order to make the journey required to perform their work. There is general agreement that throughout the United States, there are severe shortages of decent, affordable or even habitable housing for farmworkers.

There also is general consensus that migrant workers generally do not earn enough to pay for health care and seldom have health insurance. The U.S. Public Health Service funds some migrant health centers, but available resources are inadequate to meet the need. Mobile units can be effective but few exist.

Although many farmworkers fit the income eligibility profile for Medicaid, Social Security insurance, and other federal or local assistance programs, many do not obtain benefits. Undocumented workers and some legal immigrants are ineligible. Many farmworkers who are eligible may not understand that they are eligible or lack assistance in seeking needed programs. Current use is remarkably low.

The lives of farmworker children, now as in the past, are difficult, poignant and all too often mired in poverty, poor health and inadequate educational opportunities. Child labor in the fields remains an issue. Children feel economic pressure to drop out of school in order to work. Some migrant children are U.S. citizens born of undocumented immigrants, and the fear of deportation of their parents often means children do not secure benefits or services for which they are eligible. The Migrant Head Start program and other initiatives can be beneficial, but as is the case regarding housing and health care, available resources are inadequate to meet the need.

Consultations suggest there is widespread consensus among employers and farmworker advocates that there is great need to reform and adequately fund initiatives related to the access of farmworkers to housing, health care, education and other essential human services, and that such efforts are in the public interest.

Options to address these needs include:

## *1. Housing*

- Provide new federal funding to states, local governments and private institutions to address farmworker housing shortages nationwide.

  Several states, including Florida and Washington, are now developing initiatives. For example, Florida Governor Bush is seeking $30 million in federal funds to initiate a statewide network of affordable housing for migrant and seasonal farmworkers. Components of this initiative included rental housing, inmate-modular produced homes, grants to non-profit groups to help develop and manage such programs and related assistance. Governor Locke of Washington has proposed significant housing initiatives as well, including $6 million of state funding.

  Employers and farmworker advocates alike might consider whether initiatives underway in Florida, Washington and other states are worthy of support and provide a model to help meet farmworker housing shortages in other parts of the country.
- Provide adequate funding to support existing USDA, HUD and related federal, state and local farmworker housing programs.

  Existing federal programs such as USDA Section 514-516 farm labor housing programs, community development block grant housing rehabilitation, and similar state and local programs require greater funding to meet significant housing needs across the country. It is beyond the scope of this paper to identify what levels may be required. If farmers and farmworker advocates alike agree they have a common interest in the availability of more and better farmworker housing, a comprehensive analysis can be undertaken to determine which programs require what level of funding to meet the need. Questions of eligibility are also very important.

- Provide tax credits or other incentives such as matching grants for agricultural employers, housing developers, or non-profit housing organizations to help meet the need for housing, and consider federal preemption of local regulations which unreasonably restrict farmworker access to housing.
- Providing housing for workers who may be in the area only for weeks has proven an intractable problem in many areas. As discussed in section E, employers who use H-2A temporary workers must provide some access to housing, but even if consensus on how to do this can be reached many other farmworkers have severe housing needs. And in some locales zoning laws and political opposition prevent the construction of farmworker housing even when the employer is willing to pay for it.

  If there is general consensus on the need, then interested parties might consider tax credits, grants and other concrete reforms to fairly enable both public and private institutions to greatly expand their efforts to meet the need.

## *2. Health Care, Education and Other Services*

- Create private insurance pools, perhaps with tax credits, to encourage private health and disability insurance.

  It is difficult to insure workers who sojourn for short periods among multiple employers. An option is to consolidate or pool employer/ employee premium payments and coverage. Some programs to this effect exist or are under consideration. Tax credits or other incentives to fund private insurance could significantly expand coverage. Such initiatives could reduce cost often borne by local hospitals for emergency care. Prevention programs can reduce overall costs as well.
- Provide eligibility and facilitate access of legal immigrant and citizen farmworkers to publicly funded health and other human services programs.

  Senator Moynihan is proposing legislation to restore federal benefit eligibility for some programs to certain legal immigrants, including some who are farmworkers. The Administration has made similar proposals. Outreach and assistance from community-based groups needs expanded public and/or private funding to assist those who are eligible to actually access services. Migrant education, Head Start, job training, and similar programs could similarly be reviewed to identify eligibility issues and access and barriers to access which may warrant appropriate reforms.

- Provide adequate funding for health, education and human services programs which target farmworkers.

  If there is sufficient interest from farmers and farmworker advocates, a comprehensive review can be undertaken to determine funding requirements for appropriate federal and/or state and local programs. For example, a $50 million increase for migrant education programs would reach an additional 75,000 – 100,000 migrant children. A $50 million increase in USDA's Community Facilities Program would allow significant expansion of child care among farmworkers in underserved rural communities.

  Some experts believe that one reason why the agricultural labor supply may be constricting is that recently enacted restrictions on legal immigrant access to human services has made it very difficult for some farmworkers to stay in agriculture. This is because either new restrictions on eligibility and/or fear of immigration consequences make it impossible for them to provide for their families, given the seasonal nature of the work and associated low incomes. Accordingly, issues related to access to essential services may be relevant to issues of domestic labor supply of legal workers.

## *C. EMPLOYMENT REGISTRY, RIGHTS AND WORKING CONDITIONS*

Regardless of conflicting opinions about a shortage of farmworkers, whether today or in the future, in the aggregate or on a spot basis, there may be consensus that there is a need for great improvement in matching available citizen and legal immigrant workers with available jobs. There may also be a general consensus that it is important to more effectively uphold and enforce the rights and duties of workers and employers alike to the full extent the law prescribes. Law-abiding employers are undercut competitively by those who violate the law. Upholding rights and obligations is important not only to the wellbeing of workers but also in encouraging them to stay within the agricultural sector. And despite disagreements about whether there are or may be labor shortages and how this should be documented before the admission of temporary foreign workers is authorized, there is agreement that foreign workers should not be admitted if there are enough U.S. citizens and legal immigrant workers to fill the available jobs.

Options to address these considerations include:

1. Establish an effective agricultural worker registry.

   Although there are sharp disagreements as to whether a "worker registry" mechanism should substitute for the "labor certification" requirement under current law before a temporary foreign worker can be admitted, there may be agreement that an effective farmworker registry is a good idea. The challenge is to construct the registry so that it works effectively to in fact match available workers with available jobs.

   The Department of Labor's FY 2000 budget request includes $10 million to develop "Agnet," a farm work registry modeled on the computerized "America's Job Bank." Some are concerned that regardless of how any such registry is established, many if not most farmworkers will have difficulty accessing or using it. They will require assistance, and therefore community-based groups working with farmworkers will need expanded capacity to provide such assistance, which may be essential to enable a registry to work effectively on behalf of employer and worker alike.

   To achieve these goals, it would appear that employers, farmworker advocates, community-based groups and government officials will need to come together to construct it. The question is if there is sufficient will on all sides to cooperate for this purpose. Any effort to secure broad support for comprehensive reform of our agriculture labor system must include basic agreement on how to construct and implement an effective agricultural worker registry, regardless of whether employer reliance on such a registry should substitute for the labor certification requirement of the current H-2A law.

2. Affirm and clarify the employment rights of all farmworkers and strengthen respect for such rights as a matter of employer practice and social norms.

   Under federal, state and/or local laws, farmworkers, like other workers, have a range of rights related to wages, safe working conditions, discrimination, child labor, collective bargaining, etc. Many farmworkers may not understand their rights or are afraid to assert them, especially the undocumented. Many employers do obey the law or wish to do so but some do not. Government agencies have the authority to monitor and enforce, but sometimes lack adequate resources or arguably misallocate available resources.

For decades there have been disputes over what rights farmworkers enjoy and the extent to which these rights are honored. If employers and farmworker advocates are willing to come together to seek consensus on fundamental farmworker reforms, it would seem appropriate that together they should attempt to achieve a new consensus regarding appropriate rights and how to uphold them more effectively.

This paper will not attempt such a review which would best be undertaken by individuals and groups more expert and directly responsible. Topics which such an effort might address could include child labor, safe working conditions, field sanitation, reform of outmoded provisions of the Migrant and Seasonal Agricultural Worker Protection Act and strengthening programs to educate employer and worker alike and to maximize voluntary compliance as a matter of norm and practice.

## *D. TARGETED ENFORCEMENT AGAINST EXPLOITATION, SMUGGLING AND DANGEROUS CONDITIONS*

Leaders of both the agriculture industry and farmworker advocates agree that today, as in the past, there are certain employers and farm labor contractors who persistently exploit, violate the law, perpetuate unsafe working conditions and actively recruit undocumented workers because these workers live in fear, have fewer rights and are more vulnerable to threats and reprisal. There also is agreement that strengthened INS border enforcement has led to a dramatic increase in organized smuggling of undocumented immigrants at higher cost and greater danger.

Consultations suggest that law-abiding employers and farmworkers have a shared interest in much greater enforcement efforts targeted at such actors. Options include:

1. Establish and adequately fund "swat teams" at DOL, INS and other relevant federal agencies with the sole and exclusive mandate of targeting all who engage in such notorious practices. Consultations among experts might produce specific targeting guidelines and effective enforcement practices for these purposes. Such initiatives might also provide federal funding and/or expand cooperation with state and local authorities to the same end.
2. Dramatically increase penalties against those convicted of multiple offenses, patterns and practices and otherwise punish the bad actors

as severely as possible while increasing their risks of being investigated, prosecuted and convicted.

3. Significantly expand cooperation with authorities in Mexico and other sending countries against abusive practices of farm labor contractors on foreign territory, coupled with continued expansion of international cooperation against alien smuggling rings.

Other initiatives might be developed if all parties work together to implement a renewed commitment to end the most egregious practices – practices which not only harm workers but which undermine the competitiveness of law-abiding employers.

## *E. TEMPORARY FOREIGN WORKER PROGRAMS AND INTERNATIONAL CONSIDERATIONS*

Agricultural employers agree with farmworker advocates that temporary foreign workers should not be admitted to the United States unless there are no legal immigrants or U.S. citizens willing and able to fill available jobs. They disagree, however, on whether such shortages now exist or might in the future, whether increased wages and improved conditions would attract a greater and sufficient number of domestic farmworkers to fill available jobs and about what specific requirements employers should have to fulfill before they are allowed to employ temporary foreign workers.

Agricultural employers have stated that the goal of a reformed temporary agricultural worker program should be "to facilitate increased U.S. economic activity and employment in agriculture and in its related "upstream" and "downstream" occupations, while not adversely affecting the wages, working conditions and employment opportunities of U.S. residents who do seasonal agricultural field work." (The Case for a New Temporary Alien Agriculture Program, NCAE, p. 17).

Consultations suggest that, thus stated, most interested parties would accept this as an appropriate public policy goal. Some have argued, however, that by definition temporary worker programs, and/or the changes in the H-2A program the Senate adopted in 1998, would adversely affect the wages and opportunities of U.S. residents.

It may well be impossible to resolve to the satisfaction of all fundamental conflicts over macroeconomic and normative considerations which inform conflicting opinions. It may be possible, however, to seek basic consensus on the key issues and options which must be resolved if there is to be any chance of employers and farmworker advocates to agree to a comprehensive package of reforms, including, but not limited to, reforms in the H-2A program. It is also important to address international considerations, and the interest and roles of foreign governments relating to temporary foreign workers. To this end, key issues include:

- Can a farmworker registry to match U.S. workers with jobs be effectively implemented, and if so, should employer participation in such a registry substitute for H-2A labor certification requirements under current law?
- What wages must be paid H-2A workers as a condition of their admission: the adverse effect wage rate which current law requires, the prevailing wage plus 5% provision the Senate approved in 1998, or some other standard?
- What housing, insurance, transportation, and other benefits must be provided H-2A workers as well as U.S. workers as a requirement of H-2A admissions?
- What incentives and/or requirements can best ensure that employers will have a strong preference to employ and retain U.S. citizens and legal residents, and will apply for H-2A workers only as a last resort when resident workers are not available?
- To the extent H-2A workers are admitted on a temporary basis, what requirements or provisions can fairly and best ensure that they return to their home country as may be required?
- Under what circumstances should H-2A workers who in the future may be admitted to the U.S. to work for the first time, become eligible to reside permanently?
- What role and programmatic initiatives are warranted regarding the involvement of foreign governments in the recruitment and protection of H-2A workers?
- To what extent, it any, should preference for H-2A participation be given nationals of certain countries, for example, Central Americans or Caribbeans from countries devastated by recent hurricanes?

There are a number of additional issues regarding proposed or possible changes in the H-2A program. But consultations suggest that the major issues identified above are the most important to resolve if there is any hope of achieving a broad-based, bipartisan consensus. Possible options to this end are identified below.

## *F. ASSISTANCE TO STATE AND LOCAL GOVERNMENTS*

Communities and counties where migrant and seasonal farmworkers live or sojourn often face strains on their local educational and service infrastructures. This is because of the seasonal nature of the work, high unemployment during the off-season and/or because of significant numbers of legal and unauthorized immigrant residents who often are not eligible for or cannot access federally funded programs. For these and related reasons, it may be appropriate to consider targeted federal assistance to such locales, given the importance of their vitality to the nation's agricultural production and economy, including the importance of agriculture to American exports.

There are precedents for federal impact aid or reimbursement to local governments related to special needs because of the presence of significant non-citizen populations. For example, the federal government reimburses for a period of time certain state and local government services provided to refugees fleeing persecution who are admitted to the U.S. Targeted assistance grants from HHS likewise help address local costs arising from refugees. In 1986, Congress provided impact aid to state and local governments related to a federal policy to provide legal status to certain undocumented immigrants.

In addition to proposals for federal funding for farmworker housing and other issues identified above, it may be appropriate to consider impact aid approaches to assist state and local governments related to farmworkers. If there is a general consensus to pursue this concept, specific proposals can be developed in consultation with appropriate state and local actors.

## *CONCLUSION*

As stated in the preface, the framework proposed herein represents a good faith effort to invite all parties concerned about the U.S. agricultural labor system to consider whether at this time in our history consensus can be achieved on a "package of reforms" which would represent a dramatic improvement for farmer and farmworker alike.

No one can defend the status quo. The ideas outlined above are not the only or necessarily best options. Hopefully this paper will stimulate better ideas, and help to activate the political will to overcome past conflicts and injustices to achieve reforms which in the future will well serve farmers, farmworkers and the public interest.

5

# Recent Temporary Worker Proposals in Agriculture

BRUCE GOLDSTEIN
*Farmworker Justice Fund, Inc.*

Temporary foreign worker programs – under which employers hire non-immigrant aliens to work inside the United States on a temporary visa – pose threats to our democratic traditions and to the economic status of working people. The deprivations of freedoms and the severe restrictions on economic activity that accompany most guest worker programs cannot be justified by dramatic changes in our economy, our population, computer technology, telecommunications, or expanding global trade. The model for hiring workers from outside the United States should be based *not* on non-immigrant, temporary visas, but rather on *immigration*.

Some observers have suggested that if America is to succeed in the worldwide competition to attract workers, it will have no choice but to offer the opportunity for immigration status and citizenship. Skilled workers, in other words, can exert some bargaining power. (Demetrios G. Papademetriou, *The Washington Post*, March 21, 2000, p. A25.) Unfortunately, workers with little education and technological know-how are unlikely to have the bargaining power to demand an offer of immigration status. In any event, the most fundamental problems with guest worker programs exist regardless of the workers' skill, education or socioeconomic levels.

## *THE GUEST WORKER'S ECONOMIC, LEGAL AND POLITICAL STATUS*

It doesn't really matter whether we're talking about an H-2A visa worker picking tobacco, cucumbers or sweet potatoes in North Carolina, an H-2B visa holder working in as a crab picker on the Eastern Shore of Maryland, or an H-1B worker from India who got his or her visa through a "body shop" and is working as a computer programmer for a high-flying technology company. All of these temporary visa holders are under similar pressures that immigrants and citizens do not face. A farm worker from Mexico working in North Carolina under the H-2A program aptly described it well during a recent focus group: the employers "take advantage. They help us. Right? But they also take advantage."

Employers of guest workers provide jobs to people who want jobs but often they do "take advantage." What do they take advantage of? They take advantage of the workers' anxiety and the opportunity to exert extraordinary control over the workers. This advantage for the employers stems from the legal status of guest workers.

As non-immigrant workers under our immigration law, guest workers generally have no right to remain in the United States except to work at the particular job for which an employer secured the visa. Many workers want to keep the job for the full length of the employment and would like to extend the job for an additional period if that is allowed under the particular program. When the job is seasonal, as in tourism or agriculture, many guest workers would like to receive an offer of a job and a visa from the same employer to return to the United States the following year. In some instances, the temporary worker hopes to be sponsored eventually by the employer for permanent labor certification so that he or she may obtain permanent resident immigration status.

In their restricted status as non-immigrants, the workers who hope for a future with the employers often believe that they must keep their employers satisfied. When such workers perceive themselves as lacking economic alternatives in their home country, their reluctance to take any measures that would jeopardize their job and visa often becomes very strong.

Moreover, as non-immigrants these workers have no political power. Frequently, the employers who use guest workers are well-organized and active politically. Few politicians seem able to withstand the employers' pressure. Indeed, political representatives and government agencies taking the "workers' side" of a guest worker program issue generally are seeking to promote the interests of the *United States* workers whose jobs and labor standards may be affected by the presence of guest workers.

The guest workers themselves have few defenders. Labor unions have often viewed guest workers as strike breakers or as low-wage competition used to undercut wages. Politicians are in the business of getting re-elected to Congress. Guest workers do not vote. They are not "constituents." Nor do they give campaign contributions, especially when they work at low-paid jobs. When members of Congress conduct oversight of the Department of Labor's handling of guest worker programs, employers' pressure is often successful at preventing guest workers from being protected. The Department of Labor and other agency officials often view guest worker programs as "no-win" situations. If the agency stands up for the rights of the guest workers, a few worker advocates may applaud the effort, but members of Congress may be delaying confirmation of Presidential nominations to the agency or threatening to limit federal appropriations for cherished programs. In this context, the agency often claims that its even-handedness is evidenced by the fact that both the workers' and growers' representatives criticize the agency. This agency attitude serves as an incentive for interest groups to mobilize their forces, but doesn't tend to protect guest workers' interests.

## *THE IMPACT ON WORKERS*

The fear that comes from this imbalance of economic and political power has a powerful effect on the workers' willingness and ability to demand better wages and working conditions, the manner in which they perform the job, and their willingness to challenge unlawful conduct.

The concept of applying for a job by selecting an attractive employer has been all but eliminated under the H-2A program. In North Carolina, where about one thousand employers use the H-2A and H-2B programs, most employers rely on a central processing entity operated by the North Carolina Growers Association (NCGA). As the *Charlotte Observer* noted in an impressive series, "Desperate Harvest" (Oct. 31, 1999), "H-2As can't choose their employer – they are assigned by the Growers Association. H-2A rules don't let them negotiate wages and hours."

Job performance is dramatically affected by guest worker status. Growers will sometimes candidly explain that they prefer one ethnic group, such as "the Mexicans," or "the Jamaicans," over another group, such as "Americans." A Georgia onion farmer quoted by the *Washington Times*, "INS upsets farmworkers' onion cart" (May 29, 1998, p. B9), says "The problems you have with American workers are endless." But the reality often is that the H-2A workers, by virtue of their non-immigrant status and economic situation, will work as hard as possible for the low wages offered. The Florida sugar cane growers used the H-2A program for over 50 years before mechanizing the harvest. The large corporate growers squeezed out of the sugar cane cutters an amazing average productivity level of 1.41 tons of cane *per hour*. Alec Wilkinson, *Big Sugar*, p. 104 (Vintage 1990 ed.).

The guest workers rarely complain. Making economic demands on employers constitutes a major risk, a risk that is generally not worth taking for most workers. As Leah Beth Ward correctly described it, "Workers who pay recruiters in Mexico up to $500 for H-2A visas rarely complain to the government or growers about living or working conditions because they fear losing their jobs." ("Desperate Harvest," *Charlotte Observer*, Nov. 1, 1999.) If they lose their jobs, they lose their visas.

The U.S. General Accounting Office found evidence of the H-2A workers' reluctance to attempt to enforce the law. In fiscal year 1996, the Department of Labor Wage and Hour Division (WHD) "received no complaints from workers employed by H-2A employers." This was not due to a lack of violations. As the GAO noted: "in 1997, [Western] ranchers employing sheepherders failed to pay them the proper wages under the three-quarter [minimum work] guarantee, but no complaint had been filed with WHD. WHD only became aware of the situation when one of the sheepherders was assaulted and a local newspaper publicized the attack. The employers admitted that they failed to pay the appropriate wages . . . ("U.S. General Accounting Office, H-2A Guestworker Program: Changes Could Improve Services to Employers and Better Protect Workers," Dec. 1997, No. GAO/HEHS-98-20, p. 61.) The GAO also questioned the legality of the North Carolina H-2A employers' denial of transportation cost payments and three-quarter guarantee wages to "almost 40 percent of their H-2A workers (1,763 workers) . . . ." *Id.*

U.S. workers – citizens and immigrants – often cannot compete for jobs held by guest workers. Millions of workers in other nations would be pleased to have the opportunity to work in the United States at almost any wage and under any productivity requirement. In agriculture, it has been very common for employers to stop employing U.S. workers altogether once they start hiring guest workers. American workers know that they will be replaced by foreign guest workers if they challenge their employers' conduct. The presence of guest workers also represents a major threat to any union organizing campaign. Indeed, the first real successes in organizing agricultural workers by the United Farm Workers of America did not occur until after 1964, when the *bracero* program ended. (Maralyn Edid, Farm Labor Organizing, Cornell Univ. ILR Press 1994, pp. 33-34.)

## *CONGRESS AND GUEST WORKER PROGRAMS*

Congress has recognized the need to prevent guest worker programs from causing "adverse effects" on U.S. workers and to prevent employers from exploiting the vulnerability of foreign workers. Under the old *bracero* program, as well as the H-1B, H-2A and H-2B programs, there have been labor protections, at least on paper. There were substantial labor protections written into the *bracero* program, which began as a temporary emergency program during World War II but which ran until 1964. Its notorious reputation for abuse of farm workers stems primarily from the lack of enforcement of the employers' obligations and the workers' rights. (*See* Kitty Calavita, *Inside the State: The Bracero Program, Immigration and the I.N.S.*, Routledge 1992; Ernesto Galarza, *Merchants of Labor: The Mexican Bracero Story*, McNally & Loftin, 1964.) Of course, the law's protections, as well as enforcement, should have been much stronger.

The H-2A program is much less well-known, but over time, as the exposés add up, the public is likely to recognize it, too, for its abusiveness. (*See, e.g.*, Alec Wilkinson, *Big Sugar: Seasons in the Cane Fields of Florida*, Knopf, 1989.) Farmworker advocates have sought reform of the Department of Labor's H-2A regulations and practices for many years. Efforts since 1994 to persuade the Clinton Administration to adopt pro-worker reforms have failed under two different Secretaries of Labor.

The employers who demand "reform" of the H-2A guest worker program frequently argue in favor for less "bureaucracy" and "red tape." The red tape for H-2A is not onerous and, for the most part, the government's role is fully justified. Employers who claim a labor shortage should be obligated to recruit inside the United States in a meaningful way and should be required to submit their job offer in advance to enable the government to ensure that U.S. labor standards are not being undercut. Such prerequisites to hiring foreign labor are not unnecessary red tape.

It is difficult to understand how the H-2A government bureaucracy could be so onerous when the Florida sugar cane growers used the H-2/H-2A program for over fifty years, and currently the Department of Labor approves 94% to 99% of all applications. (GAO Report (1997) at p. 44.) While there are some allegations under the H-2A program of delays of a matter of days in processing applications, a few more resources for the understaffed H-2A program and some improved management would quickly remedy those problems. But much more than procedural rules and government oversight is at stake. Some of the recent legislative proposals would effectively permit employers to bypass unemployed U.S. farmworkers. Unemployment rates in California's Central Valley, America's major agricultural production area, hover in the double digits. Such U.S. workers deserve first crack at any available jobs with an employer that seeks guest workers. H-2A recruitment requirements and efforts currently are too weak to attract workers to available jobs, especially compared to the massive recruitment campaigns for H-2A workers that occur in Mexico and Jamaica.

Employers who demand "reform" also contend that the "economics" of the program must change. For this reason, as explained in greater detail below, the proposals for a new agricultural guestworker program would lower wage rates, eliminate the housing requirement, kill the three quarter minimum work guarantee, reduce the Secretary of Labor's authority to enforce the workers' statutory and contract rights, and make many other changes that would lower workers' incomes and reduce still further their ability to protect themselves. Labor protections that existed under the *bracero* program would not exist under pending proposals (in the 106th Congress, they include H.R. 4056, H.R. 4548, S. 1814 and S. 1815).

Congress will soon address these issues but, not surprisingly, the quality of the debate over policy thus far has been unsatisfactory. Some basic choices must be made.

## *GUEST WORKERS V. UNDOCUMENTED WORKERS*

Employer lobbyists often argue that the "*status quo* is untenable." By this, they mean that, according to the Department of Labor National Agricultural Workers Survey (March 2000), 52 percent of crop workers in the United States lack authorization to work. Employers often proclaim that the rate is 70 percent or 80 percent. The employers essentially want to turn undocumented workers into guest workers, and argue that this would benefit the workers by making them "legal."

The Hobson's choice between being a guest worker and an undocumented worker should be rejected. The undocumented workers who have been performing farm work should be offered the opportunity to gain immigration status. The untenable *status quo* for the nation's farmworkers should be improved by adopting policies that empower farmworkers to secure decent wages, working conditions, benefits and housing.

A system of guest workers is not more desirable than a system of undocumented workers. Neither one is acceptable. In *Merchants of Labor: The Mexican Bracero Story* (McNally & Loftin, 1964), Ernesto Galarza compared the farmworker who had crossed the Rio Grande into the United States illegally (then often called a "Wetback") and the guest worker under the U.S.-Mexican contract labor agreement known as the *bracero* program:

> The Wetback himself as he gained experience was constantly shopping the black labor market, for he generally considered himself a 'libre' (free worker) in contrast with the bracero, who was restricted to a named employer. [p. 82]

Recently, three undocumented farmworkers from Mexico were profiled in a South Carolina newspaper article. (Ben Brazil, "Immigrants follow trail of money through Lowcountry," *Charleston (S.C.) Post and Courier*, July 9, 2000.) The three were picking tomatoes 12 hours per day, earning a piece rate, and sleeping on the concrete floor of a grower's barracks. When they learned about "better-paying, more stable jobs at a farm in another state," these unauthorized workers left to find the farmer with the better job. An exodus of undocumented workers can cause an employer to increase wage rates.

H-2A guest workers, by contrast, may not change employers to seek higher wages if they want to maintain their status. More importantly, if an H-2A worker does leave the job (called "jumping contract"), the employer immediately gets another guest worker at the same wages and working conditions. Thus, the departure of H-2A workers need not have any effect on job terms. Indeed, when H-2A sugar cane cutters at the Okeelanta Corporation went on strike in 1986 over low piece rates, the company called out the police and sheriff, including canine officers with dogs, and sent three hundred fifty cutters back home to Jamaica. (Big Sugar, pp. 227-28.) The inability of H-2A workers to "vote with their feet" by going to another employer puts them at an economic disadvantage.

The heavy presence of undocumented workers in agriculture is of the growers' own doing, and they should not be rewarded for it by transforming these workers into indentured servants under a guest worker program. Agricultural employers have been notorious for ignoring immigration policy for several generations. Undocumented workers have been crossing the border and obtaining these jobs from agricultural employers who have welcomed them. Some employers claim that the immigration law prevents them from inquiring into immigration status once an identification document that looks realistic is presented, even if it is fraudulent. But many employers have actively avoided even asking for identification.

A growing number of employers in all industries relies on labor contractors or "crew leaders" to supply workers, and expect the labor contractors to be responsible for compliance – or more accurately, liability for noncompliance – with the immigration laws.

In many instances, the labor standards are so poor and demeaning that only undocumented workers will accept the job. Again, low wages and bad conditions are associated with the employers' reliance on labor contractors. The employer pays so much to the labor contractor, who makes his or her profit by paying the workers as little as possible. ("Farm workers face hard times," *San Jose Mercury News*, July 9, p. 1A; Philip L. Martin and J. Edward Taylor, "Merchants of Labor: Farm Labor Contractors and Immigration Reform," Washington, D.C.: The Urban Institute 1995, p. 15.)

In agriculture, real wages have dropped over the last decade. Employee turnover has increased, with seasonal agricultural workers earning fewer days of employment each year than they did a decade ago. Poverty rates among farmworkers increased from less than one-half to three-fifths of that labor force. Benefits like vacation pay, sick leave, health insurance, and retirement plans continue to be rarities among agricultural workers, especially among those who work in the fields. (U.S. Department of Labor, Findings From the National Agricultural Workers Survey (NAWS) 1997-1998, A Demographic and Employment Profile of United States Farmworkers, Research Report No. 8, March 2000, pp. iv, 24-25, 33-37, 39.) Unemployment rates among citizen and legal-immigrant farmworkers are extraordinarily high. Double-digit unemployment persists in many of the nation's major agricultural production counties. The Congressional Research Service estimated unemployment among farmworkers at 11-13 percent from 1994 through 1998. (Linda Levine Congressional Research Service Report for Congress, Farm Labor Shortages and Immigration Policy (December 1999), p. 10.) California's official unemployment data for unemployment rates in major agricultural production area of 10 percent to 20 percent. In Fresno County, a huge producer of agricultural products, the unemployment rate in September 1999 was 9.5 percent, about double the state-wide average. (Mark Schacht and Kristina Rowe, Joblessness in the California Heartland, California Rural Legal Assistance Foundation, June 2000, pp. 3-6.) The labor surplus has produced the logical result: workers willing to accept low wages and poor conditions because they have little choice.

At the same time that farmworkers' conditions worsened, agricultural productivity dramatically increased and the labor-intensive fruit and vegetable sector substantially increased the value of its produce and the value of its exports. In the words of the chief lobbyist and the chief economist for the agribusiness groups' lobbying campaign, "During the last several decades, markets for labor intensive commodities have expanded dramatically in the United States and throughout the world." (Statement of Monte B. Lake and James S. Holt, on behalf of the National Council of Agricultural Employers, at U.S. Department of Agriculture, Agricultural Outlook Forum 2000, February 25, 2000.) The value of production of fruits, vegetables and horticulture – labor-intensive crops – grew by 52% to $15.1 billion between 1986 and 1995. Exports of these products, according to the USDA, grew from $4.0 billion in FY 1988 to $10.26 billion in FY 1999. (Data obtained from U.S. Department of Agriculture, Foreign Agricultural Service, U.S. Trade Data Collection, Horticultural Exports).

Farmworkers have not shared the benefits of these developments. Nor have farmworkers shared in the subsidies and bailouts that Congress has provided to the growers of capital-intensive major commodities, such as wheat, soybeans and livestock.

For almost one hundred years, government commissions have told agriculture how to stabilize its work force and stop the heavy dependency on new waves of exploitable foreign labor. (*See, e.g.*, President's Commission on Migratory Labor, Migratory Labor in American Agriculture (1951), p. 23; Commission on Agricultural Workers, Report of the Commission on Agricultural Workers (1992) p. 139.) Employers must improve wages and working conditions and modernize their labor practices to attract and retain workers. Many other jobs in this economy are seasonal (construction, tourism, education, child care, recreation, tax preparation) without dooming their participants to starvation-level wages and conditions. Agriculture can start to act like a modern employer too. Growers seem to cooperate on every aspect of their businesses – marketing, research and development, and lobbying – but rarely work cooperatively to modernize employment practices. For example, growers in different areas could put together a series of consecutive seasonal jobs that would increase each farmworker's annual earnings and encourage them to return each year. Rather than using fly-by-night labor contractors, the employers could work cooperatively on recruitment and transportation arrangements that include efficient use of safe vehicles. These and many other basic responses to the law of supply and demand should be encouraged.

In addition, the discriminatory labor laws that exclude agricultural workers and make farm labor unattractive must end. These discriminatory laws include denial of minimum wage to many farmworkers, exemption from overtime pay under federal law, discriminatory exceptions from health and safety protections, obstacles to securing workers' compensation for work-related injuries and illnesses, and denial of the right to organize labor unions free from retaliation. Such discriminatory laws push documented workers out of agriculture and allow exploitation of the undocumented workers.

## *GUEST WORKER STATUS V. IMMIGRANT STATUS*

One of the reasons that the employers may assert for choosing guest-worker status over immigration status is that *politically* it is impossible to increase our immigration quotas because Congress just won't do it. The employers argue that Congress will not approve of an "amnesty" or "legalization" of undocumented farmworkers, and that any legislation would have to be far different from the "special agricultural worker" legalization program in the Immigration Reform and Control Act of 1986. (*See* section 210 of the Immigration and Nationality Act, 8 U.S.C. § 1160.)

As far as agriculture is concerned, the employers certainly haven't tried. For the last five years, agribusiness has been lobbying strenuously for a new guestworker program or a revision to the H-2A program to lower wage rates, eliminate the housing requirement, reduce government oversight and make recruitment inside the U.S. so minimal as to be futile. Agricultural employers have *not* sought to join forces with farmworker groups, immigration, labor, religious, Hispanic and other organizations to seek an immigration program to legalize the status of several hundred thousand undocumented farmworkers. As explained below, some pieces of legislation have held out the prospect of immigration status for a few lucky farmworkers, but the legislation does not represent an effort to join forces with farmworker and immigration groups to craft a compromise.

I believe that Congress would not stand in the way of such a coalition of employers and farm workers, and neither would President Clinton or the current pesidential candidates, other than Mr. Buchanan. Of course, various immigration policy issues would need to be addressed in any such legislation (such as methods to reduce employers' hiring of undocumented workers), but those could be worked out while providing the employers with the willing work force they desire and ensuring farmworkers some reasonable protections under immigration and labor laws.

## *THE AGRICULTURAL EMPLOYERS' LATEST LEGISLATIVE EFFORTS*

The agricultural industry made serious efforts to pass guest worker legislation during the 104th Congress (1995-96) and 105th Congress (1997-98). The House defeated an effort led by Representative Richard Pombo (R.-Cal.) and Representative Saxby Chambliss (R.-Ga.) to append a guestworker program to immigration legislation during 1996 (Congressional Record, March, 1996). In July 1998, the Senate, with little debate, approved a guestworker program offered by Sen. Gordon Smith (R.-Ore.) and Sen. Ron Wyden (D.-Ore.) as an amendment to an appropriations bill. The House took no action in 1998 and the President's opposition prevented the Senate amendment from being added by the Speaker of the House to the conference committee's final version of the appropriations bill.

The American Farm Bureau Federation and the National Council of Agricultural Employers came forth with a new version of this legislation in the 106th Congress (1999-2000). The employers demanded "reforms" to the H-2A program and offered a new temporary, non-immigrant program under which some of the participating workers could eventually apply for immigration status.

Political maneuvers resulted in four guestworker bills being introduced. Two bills were introduced in the House, H.R. 4056 by Rep. Bishop (D.-Ga.) and H.R. 4548 by Rep. Pombo (R.-Cal.). Two bills were introduced in the Senate, S. 1814, which is the companion to H.R. 4056, and S. 1815.

The principal Senate sponsors of both Senate bills were Sen. Gordon Smith (R.-Ore.) and Sen. Bob Graham (D.-Fla.).

On July 27, 2000, the House immigration subcommittee approved H.R. 4548 after rejecting several amendments offered by Democratic members of the subcommittee and approving several amendments by Rep. Lamar Smith (R.-Tex.), an immigration restrictionist who is the subcommittee chair. The Senate immigration subcommittee has taken no action. As this article was being drafted, the agricultural industry lobbyists were pressing Congress to pass the legislation once it returned from its August recess.

The bill that the House immigration subcommittee approved, Rep. Pombo's H.R. 4548, would establish a three-year "pilot program" based on an unlimited number of new H-2C visas. The H-2A program would continue, but there would be little point in using it since the H-2C program would be so advantageous to employers. The H-2C program would contain virtually all of the "reforms" that the employers sought in the other bills regarding the H-2A program. The key differences between H.R. 4548 and the other bills is that, under pressure from Rep. Lamar Smith, the Pombo bill did not contain the proposal to create a new "adjustment" guest worker program. The table below outlines the various proposals:

| Bill Number | H.R. 4548 | H.R. 4056 | S. 1814 | S. 1815 |
|---|---|---|---|---|
| Title | Agricultural Opportunities Act | Agricultural Job Opportunity Benefits and Security Act of 1999 | Agricultural Job Opportunity Benefits and Security Act of 1999 | Farmworker Adjustment Act of 1999 |
| Principal Sponsors | Rep. Pombo | Rep. Bishop | Sen. Gordon Smith, Sen. Bob Graham, Sen. Larry Craig, Sen. Jesse Helms, *et al.* | Sen. Gordon Smith and Sen. Bob Graham |
| Main Provisions | Create 3-year H-2C Pilot Program. | Change H-2A Program (similar to H-2C proposal). Create new non-immigrant "adjustment" program. | Change H-2A Program (similar to H-2C proposal). Create new non-immigrant "adjustment" program. | Create new non-immigrant "adjustment" program. |

## *THE PROPOSED "ADJUSTMENT" PROGRAM*

The "adjustment" program in H.R. 4056, S. 1814, and S.1815, would create a new system of "non-immigrant" agricultural workers. They would be permitted to perform only temporary or seasonal jobs in agriculture. To enter the program, workers would need to apply within one year after enactment of the bill. They would have to show that they had worked at least 150 days in agricultural employment during the one year ending October 27, 1999 (the date the Senate bill was introduced). Then, they would form a pool of farmworkers who would need to work 180 days per year in agriculture to maintain their status. They would need to leave the United States each year for at least 65 days. To earn the right to apply for permanent resident alien status, these guestworkers would have to provide employment records to show that they worked 180 days per year in each of five years. They apparently would have seven years to complete this requirement, although it is unclear whether "good cause" would have to be shown for failing to acquire the full 180 days in a particular year and continuing in the program. For those who complete the work process and are otherwise eligible, the issuance of green cards will be staggered over 5 years. There will be a waiting list whose members will be given temporary resident status and the right to work at any job.

The adjustment program proposal was vigorously opposed by a wide variety of organizations for numerous reasons and was opposed by the Clinton Administration.

First, the bill contains no labor protections. Not even the minimal labor protections in the proposed "reform" of the H-2A program would be offered to the "adjustment" workers. Even the notoriously abusive *bracero* program had considerable labor protections in the law and in the workers' employment contracts. The *bracero* program, much like today's H-2A program, required recruitment of U.S. farmworkers, and required employers to provide housing, transportation benefits, minimal working conditions and protection against wage depression. This proposal lacks even the labor protections that were in the *bracero* program. Such workers would probably be ineligible for any government services, including publicly-funded legal assistance.

Second, many of the farmworkers who join the adjustment program as temporary non-immigrant workers will not secure enough work to retain their status. It will be very difficult for many farmworkers to obtain and prove the required 180 days of agricultural employment each year. The National Agricultural Workers Survey found that seasonal farmworkers average only 24 weeks of work and work is not available every day of the week. About one-fourth of farmworkers in this country survive by working in non-farm jobs for part of the year, but these guest workers would be forbidden to work outside agriculture.

Third, under that kind of pressure on guest workers to secure evidence of 180 work days, workers will lack the bargaining power to demand better wages and working conditions. Workers will be too afraid to challenge unlawful conduct, demand better conditions, join a labor union, or file a lawsuit, for fear of being unable to gain evidence of sufficient employment to qualify for continuing status and later adjustment to permanent residency. Some unscrupulous growers and labor contractors will refuse to provide proof of employment unless workers comply with unreasonable, even illegal, demands. The wages of all farmworkers, including citizens and permanent resident immigrants, will suffer harm from the presence of several hundred thousand guest workers desperate to take an agricultural job under any conditions.

Fourth, the promise of a green card will be a cruel hoax for many workers. As indicated above, many guest workers under this program will never acquire a green card due to their inability to secure 180 days of work in agriculture each year for five years. Some applications for green cards will be rejected due to confusion about the obligation to apply within the six-month window immediately after completing five years of work. Others will be denied immigration status because they have committed three misdemeanor violations or one felony crime. In addition, because the issuance of green cards will be staggered over a period of 4 to 5 years or more, some guest workers will complete their years of work only to find themselves placed on a waiting list.

Fifth, the legislation is anti-family. Some families are potentially going to be divided for about 16 years under this adjustment program. While the farmworkers are guestworkers for five to seven years, they have no right to get visas for family members. While on the waiting list from one to five years, as temporary resident aliens, the workers may not petition for their family members. Until the guestworkers get their green cards – six to twelve years after beginning the program – ordinarily they will not be permitted to apply for immigration visas for their family members. Once the application is filed, the waiting list for immigration visas for relatives in Mexico is often about six years. Under the 1996 immigration amendments, those relatives who have been found in the United States illegally before that time, can then be barred for an additional ten years.

A wide variety of organizations opposed the "adjustment" guest worker program for these and other reasons.

## *H-2A "REFORM"*

The proposals to change the H-2A program and create a new H-2C program would make a system that is already unfriendly to workers even worse.

Under current law, an agricultural employer that anticipates a labor shortage for seasonal jobs may apply for a labor certification from the Department of Labor. The employer must demonstrate that there is not an adequate number of qualified farmworkers at the place and time needed, and that the wages and working conditions being offered would not "adversely affect" the wages and working conditions of similarly employed farmworkers. (8 U.S.C. §§1101(a)(15)(H)(ii)(a), 1188(a)(1).) An H-2A labor certification entitles employers to obtain temporary visas for foreign workers who are tied to one employer and do not acquire immigration status.

*Avoiding Employment of U.S. Workers*: Under the current H-2A program's "50% rule job preference," employers must hire qualified U.S. workers who apply by the time one-half the season has elapsed. H-2A program employers must affirmatively recruit in the private marketplace (this is known as "positive recruitment") and use the federal-state Job Service to circulate job offers to areas where migrant workers may be located. No such recruitment or hiring would be required under the H-2A changes proposed in H.R. 4056/S. 1814 or under the proposed H-2C program in H.R. 4548. The new proposals are designed to fail U.S. workers and justify the hiring of exploitable guest workers.

Employers need only consider a U.S. workers' job application if it was submitted through a "job registry," a new government agency to be established in each state. The job registry could have as little as 14 days to recruit U.S. migrant workers before the employer would get access to guestworker visas. Yet, guest workers could be recruited for months. Employers could reject qualified U.S. workers who applied for a job directly to the employer, or through a nonprofit group, a union, or a labor contractor. Yet, employers could use labor contractors to hire foreign workers. While the growers claim that such obstacles to U.S. workers applying for jobs will help ensure that undocumented workers are not hired, nothing in the bill stops the growers from hiring undocumented workers.

*No Housing Required*: The current H-2A program requires employers to offer housing, and to provide it at no cost to the worker. The Senate bill would eliminate the housing obligation and authorize H-2A/H-2C employers to provide modest housing allowances (at least for three years).

Due to a severe housing shortage for farmworkers, and the inadequacy of their wages and the allowance, farmworkers will not be able to find housing or to finance its development. All burdens will fall on farmworkers themselves and local communities.

*No Minimum Work Promise*: Under the H-2A program employers have been required to offer the opportunity to work at least 3/4 of the workdays in the stated period of employment. If the employer does not offer this minimum amount of work, it must pay compensation to the worker for the shortfall. This "three-fourths guarantee" gives migrant workers some indication of their potential earnings should they decide to make the long trip for the job. It also discourages employers from over-recruiting to secure a labor surplus and drive down wages, since compensation would have to be paid if a large oversupply of workers is recruited. The new bill lacks any minimum work guarantee.

*Wage Provisions Would Lower H-2A Wage Rates:* Under the current H-2A program, employers must pay the highest of three minimum wages: the federal or state minimum wage; the local "prevailing wage" for particular crops, as determined by the Department of Labor using state agency wage surveys; and the H-2A "adverse effect wage rate" or "AEWR." The AEWR is supposed to compensate for the depression in wages caused by the presence of foreign workers. The Reagan administration changed the AEWR methodology, lowering the H-2A wage rates by an average of 20%. The H-2A AEWR is now defined as the regional average wage for field and livestock workers, as found in Department of Agriculture annual surveys. Often the AEWR is higher than the local prevailing wage and therefore many H-2A employers must pay workers at least the AEWR.

Under the new bill, farmworkers affected by the H-2A guestworker changes would suffer a pay cut in many instances. The bill redefines the term "adverse effect wage rate" (or "AEWR"). The AEWR would be the local "prevailing wage" plus five percent, up to a maximum of the regional average wage for field and livestock workers. In many instances, the local prevailing wage (plus five percent) is lower than the regional average wage for field and livestock workers. In addition, those workers whose local prevailing wage for a particular happens to be higher than the regional average wage, could have their wage rates lowered to the regional average wage. Under current law, if the prevailing wage is higher than the AEWR, then the prevailing wage must be paid.

Employers could easily evade the limited wage protections in the bills. First, the employers could increase productivity standards to overcome the effects of any potential increases in prevailing wage rates. Such "speed-ups" would no longer be regulated.

More importantly, no individual worker would be guaranteed the H-2A minimum required wage rate. The bill sets a minimum allowable wage of the local prevailing wage or the newly defined adverse effect wage rate. But the bill allows employers a way around such wage rates. The employer may offer an alternative, incentive wage system ("piece rate," "group rate," "task rate") and merely demonstrate that its employees, "taken as a group," on average earn the H-2A minimum wage rate. If the group as a whole earns the minimum rate, then some workers, by definition, are earning below that minimum rate. The workers' only real wage floor is the federal or state minimum wage, from which some agricultural employers are still exempt.

The employers would continue, as under the H-2A program, to be exempt from Social Security and unemployment taxes, depriving foreign workers of social security and creating incentives to use guestworkers rather than U.S. workers.

The above list of serious problems in these lengthy, complicated bills is incomplete. A full examination of the problems in these bills would be too extensive for this article. The concerns stated above, however, should be enough to justify opposition to the legislation.

## *CONCLUSION*

The U.S. Commission on Immigration Reform (Sept. 1997) correctly concluded that a new guestworker program would be a "grievous mistake." Agricultural employers have rejected the recommendations of that Commission and the U.S. Commission on Agricultural Workers (1992) to improve wages and working conditions to attract and retain farmworkers. Instead, agribusiness has responded with a low-wage, high employee turnover strategy on labor practices and with a massive lobbying campaign for new immigration and labor legislation that revolves around guest worker programs. All of it should be rejected.

Farmworkers should be given the economic, legal and immigration status to empower themselves, and employers should be given incentives to modernize their labor practices and improve wages and working conditions.

6

# Comparison of H-1B Bills

LYNN FRENDT SHOTWELL
*American Council on International Personnel*

| 106th Congress | **Hatch/Abraham Bill (as reported out of Judiciary Committee 03/09/00) S. 2045** | **Smith Bill (as ordered reported out of Judiciary Committee 05/17/00) H.R. 4227** | **Dreier/Lofgren Bill H.R. 3983** |
|---|---|---|---|
| **H-1B Numbers** | 195,000 | FY2000: No Cap<br>FY2001-2002: unlimited visas available <u>if</u> median wage condition is met. | 200,000 |
| **Length of Program** | Sunsets FY2002 | Sunsets FY2002 | Sunsets FY2003 |
| **H-1B Cap Conditions** | **Exemptions from the cap:**<br>1. Individuals who are employed/ receive offer of employment from an institution of higher education, affiliated entity, non-profit research organization or governmental research organization.<br>2. Individuals who have a petition filed between 90 days before and 180 days after receiving a masters degree or higher from a U.S. institution of higher education.<br><br>**Recapture of Numbers:** Visa issued fraudulently or by misrepresentation shall be revoked, and the number restored to cap. | **Condition on visas:**<br>In FY01 and 02, unlimited visas available above cap in current law <u>only if</u> employer documents a net increase in median wages paid to U.S. workers in the previous tax year. (Exception: the employer "sold or otherwise legally transferred for consideration, the assets of a division or other severable portion" of the business before the end of the tax year) | **Numbers reserved within the 200,000 cap:**<br>1. 10,000 for persons working for an institution of higher education, or a related or affiliated nonprofit entity, or a nonprofit or governmental research organization.<br>2. 60,000 for persons holding a master's or higher degree, or its equivalent.<br><br>**Additional visas** to clear out the FY99 backlog and overcount so that 115,000 visas are truly available for FY00. |

| | | | |
|---|---|---|---|
| **Improved Immigration Processing** | **Portability:**<br>• H-1B worker may start employment at new employer upon filing of petition. Work authorization will or denied.continue untilpetition is approved<br>• Exception: Individuals who are employed/receive offer of employmentfrom an institution of higher education, affiliated entity, non-profit research organization or governmental research organization who were exempt from the cap may not move to a cap job until petition is approved.<br><br>**Per Country Backlogs:**<br>• Employment-based immigrants will not be subject to per country limits if additional visas are available in other employment-based categories.<br>• H-1B status extended until application for permanent residence is processed<br><br>**Improved Green Card Processing:**<br>• H-1B extended if individual has an approved labor certification (if required) <u>AND</u> who have a pending petition for immigrant status or adjustment of status <u>IF</u> one year has elapsed since they started the green card process. | **Portability:**<br>• H-1B worker may start employment at new employer upon filing of petition. Work authorization will continue until petition is approved or denied.<br>• Exception: Individuals who are employed/receive offer of employment from an institution of higher education, affiliated entity, non-profit research organization or governmental research organization who were exempt from the cap may not move to a cap job until petition is approved.<br>**$200 Processing Fee**<br>• Imposes $200 fee on all H-1B petitions. Money will be split between INS and DOL for improved H-1B and LCA processing. | **Per Country Backlogs:**<br>• Allows rollover of unused visa numbers to oversubscribed countries regardless of the per-country ceilings. Rollover would happen on a quarterly basis beginning October 1, 2000.<br>• Allows H-1B non-immigrants facing lengthy waits for adjustment of status due to per country ceilings to remain in the U.S. on an H-1B visa beyond the six year limitation on stay. Effective October 1, 2000.<br>• Recaptures unused employment-based visa numbers from FY99 and FY00 for use in FY01 and beyond.<br><br>**Improved Green Card Processing:**<br>• Individuals reaching the end of their 6-year H-1B stay who have an approved labor certification (if required) <u>AND</u> who have a pending petition for immigrant status or adjustment of status are eligible to have their H-1B status extended beyond six years <u>IF</u> six months have elapsed since they started the green card process. |

| | | | |
|---|---|---|---|
| | | | **Internet Recruitment:**<br>• Requires DOL to take internet recruitment efforts into account for labor certification and similar activities. Internet advertising as the sole recruitment tool shall not per se be considered unsatisfactory. DOL may require an employer to post on a designated website for up to 30 days.<br><br>**INS Internet Based Technologies:**<br>• INS & DOL must establish a web-based system that will allow employers and other petitioners to check the status of a petition online. This must be established within one year of enactment.<br>• Establishes a "Technology Advisory Committee" made up of industry and government agencies. Requires INS, DOL, and DOC to consult with the TAC and prepare a feasibility study on on-line filing by January 1, 2001. The study must address how 98% of immigrant petitions can be adjudicated within 3 months and 98% of nonimmigrant petitions within one month. |

| | | | |
|---|---|---|---|
| **Filing Fees and Regulations** | **Extension of H-1B Attestation and Fee Requirements:**<br>• Extends provisions due to sunset in FY02, including $500 training fee. | **Extension of H-1B Attestation and Fee Requirements:**<br>• Extends provisions due to sunset in FY02, including $500 training fee.<br><br>**Anti-Fraud Fee:**<br>• A $100 fee will be imposed on each H-1B petition.<br><br>**ACWIA Regulations**<br>• DOL directed to issue final regulations by September 1, 2000. | **Increase in Fee on Initial Petitions:**<br>1. Increases H-1B filing fee to $1000 for an initial petition filed after October 1, 2000.<br>2. Extensions and other petitions will still pay $500.<br>• INS will receive 2% of fees for improved processing instead of 1.5%.<br>3. DOL will receive 4% of fees for improved LCA processing instead of 3%. |
| **Education and Training** | **Low Income Scholarship Program:**<br>• $3,125 per year, up to 4 years National Science Foundation:<br>• NSF grant for K-12 math, science and technology education<br>• 25.8 percent of H-1B funds will go to NSF grant monies<br><br>**After-school Technology Grants to the Boys and Girls Clubs of America:**<br>• Funds of $20,000,000 FY2001-2006 to be derived from the Violent Crime Reduction Trust Fund. | | **Stafford Loan Forgiveness Program:**<br>• 33%, or potentially $66 million annually.<br>• Expands current law by doubling loan forgiveness for those who teach math, science, computer science, or related fields for at least three years from $5000 to $10,000.<br><br>**Upward Bound Math/ Science Program:**<br>• 17%, or potentially $34 million annually. This provision would more than double the Upward Bound budget. |

| | | | |
|---|---|---|---|
| | • Aimed at aiding communities with juvenile crime, violence and drug use<br>• Technology focused activities, such as PowerUp, provide access to technology and supply technological training<br>• Eligibility applications must be submitted with description of what communities are being served | | **National Science Foundation Scholarships:**<br>• 14%, or potentially $30 million annually (under current law, the NSF scholarship program receives $16.2 million in 2000 and less thereafter).<br>• Retains current law to provide up to $2,500 for low-income students studying in math, computer science, engineering and science related fields.<br>• Students agreeing to work in the "public sector" (such as the National Science Foundation or the Department of Defense) for three years would be eligible for scholarships of up to $5,000.<br><br>**Regional Skills Alliances Job Training:**<br>• 25%, or potentially $50 million annually (under current H-1B visa law, job training efforts receive $32 million in 2000 and less thereafter). Federal funding will be matched by local governments and the private sector to allocate grants. |
| **New Requirement on Employers** | | **Minimum Wage Requirement:**<br>• H-1B employee must receive annual salary of $40,000 (includingcash bonuses and similar compensation) | **Filing of W-2 Forms:**<br>• Employers must annually file W-2s with DOL for each H-1B employee. This will apply to H-1B petitions filed on or after October 1, 2000 |

| | | | |
|---|---|---|---|
| | | • Annual Cost of Living Adjustment (COLA)<br>• Exception: Higher Ed, related governmental nonprofit and nonprofit research organization. Hyde amendment exception for public and private elementary and secondary schools.<br><br>**Minimum Education Requirement:**<br>• H-1B alien must have at least a bachelor's degree in some field. Maintains ability to obtain "equivalency" in the specific specialty through a bachelor's degree and related work experience.<br><br>**Minimum Hours Requirement:**<br>• H-1B must work at least 35 hours per week.<br>• Exception: Higher Ed, related nonprofit and nonprofit governmental research organization.<br><br>**Minimum Asset Requirement:**<br>• Employer petitioning for an H-1B visa must maintain a place of business in the United States and must have assets of at least $250,000, or submit documents showing the need for H-1B employees. | and to W-2 forms issued on or after January 1, 2001. The forms may be filed electronically. |

| | | | |
|---|---|---|---|
| | | **Filing of W-2 Forms:**<br>• Employers must annually file W-2s with DOL for each H-1B employee. This will apply to H-1B petitions filed on or after October 1, 2000 and to W-2 forms issued on or after January 1, 2001. The forms may be filed electronically.<br><br>**Internet Posting of Employee Data:**<br>• Employers must post for all H-1B workers: Country of origin, Academic Degrees, Job Title, Date employment commenced, Salary/wage level<br><br>**Change in Visa Issuance:**<br>• Eliminates ability to obtain "B-1 in lieu of H-1B" visa.<br><br>**Minimum Education for Physical Therapists**<br>• Requires physical therapists to have a master's or higher degree or equivalent experience. | |
| **Reports and Studies:** | • National Science Foundation to conduct a study on the "digital divide" with a mandatory report to Congress no later than 18 months after enactment of bill. | • GAO report on minority recruitment and training.<br>• GAO report on INS compliance with efforts to correctly count H-1B visas. | |

| | | | |
|---|---|---|---|
| **Co-sponsors:** | Gramm, Gorton, Hagel, Bennett, DeWine, Edwards, Grams, Helms, Brownback, Smith, Warner, Mack, Specter, Lott, McConnell, Nickles, Graham, Lieberman, Ashcroft, Feinstein, Voinovich | Smith, Goodlatte, Campbell | Ackerman, Armey, Ballenger, Biggert, Boehner, Bonilla, Cramer, Crowley, Cunningham, Davis, Davis, T., Dicks, Doggett, Dooley, Dunn, English, Eshoo, Etheridge, Ford, Gonzalez, Greenwood, Houghton, Hoyer, Inslee, Kennedy, Kind, Knollenberg, Kolbe, Linder, Lofgren, Matsui, McCarthy, McCarthy, K., McDermott, McIntosh, Meeks, Menendez, Millender-McDonald, Moran, Morella, Myrick, Nadler, Northup, Oxley, Pelosi, Peterson, Rangel, Roemer, Salmon, Sandlin, Sessions, Shays, Smith, Sununu, Tauscher, Upton, Weller, Wexler, Wolf |
| **Position/ Comments** | Strongly support. | Oppose | Strongly support |

Prepared by the American Council on International Personnel (ACIP) *www.acip.com*
*Last Updated: May 24, 2000*

# PART III

## INS RESTRUCTURING

7

# An Update from Capitol Hill

LORA L. RIES
*Congress of the United States, Committee on the Judiciary*
*House of Representatives*

There is an overwhelming sense in this country and in Congress that the INS needs to be reorganized and reformed. The INS has two important but conflicting missions: administer immigration benefits and enforce the immigration laws. As is often seen in the news, the INS is unable to perform either function adequately. The backlog of naturalization, adjustment and other applications is unacceptably high. Meanwhile, Americans are frustrated that the INS is not enforcing the immigration laws by deporting illegal aliens, especially aliens who have been ordered deported by an Immigration Judge or the Board of Immigration Appeals. The INS has surpassed the IRS as the agency Americans most want reformed.

Recently, the INS received the worst grade out of 20 federal agencies in a study reviewed by Syracuse University's Government Performance Project. It has become very popular to criticize the INS lately, but what do we do to improve it?

The Commission on Immigration Reform, which was established in the Immigration Act of 1990, began reviewing and evaluating our immigration law and policies and the agencies that handle immigration. The Commission issued its final report in September 1997. On the issue of structural and management reform, the Commission found the current structure for the administration of immigration law problematic. It found that the responsible agencies, particularly the INS, suffer from "mission overload" in that they have so many responsibilities that they are unable to manage all effectively.

To resolve these problems, the Commission recommended the dismantling of the INS and giving its functions to agencies better suited to perform the duties by:

1. Creating a new Bureau of Immigration Enforcement in the Justice Department that would merge the uniformed enforcement officers (Inspectors, Border Patrol and Detention Enforcement Officers) into one officer corps. Other components of this new agency would include: investigators, removal officers, intelligence officers, pre- and post-trial probation officers, INS prosecuting attorneys, and asset forfeiture personnel.
2. Recommending that the Justice Department consider transferring the responsibility for operating detention centers to the Bureau of Prisons or U.S. Marshals' Service.
3. Moving the adjudication responsibility for all domestic and international applications for benefits to the Department of State. There would be four benefit adjudications divisions: the Bureau of Immigration Affairs (for immigrant visas); Refugee and Asylum Affairs; Citizenship and Passport Affairs; and a Quality Assurance division.
4. Moving all employment-based immigration issued to the Labor Department. This would include enforcing the employer sanctions provisions of the INA and adjudicating all applications for employment-based visas.
5. Creating the Agency for Immigration Review to decide all cases and appeals. This would include all the Immigration Judges, an Appellate Board and Administrative Hearing officers to hear employer sanctions appeals.

Following the Commission's Report, Representatives introduced various bills in 1998 to restructure the INS. However, all of this was put on hold by the House Judiciary Committee when the impeachment referral arrived.

In 1999, new attempts were made to restructure the INS in the House.

The House Subcommittee on Immigration and Claims marked-up H.R. 3918, the "Immigration Reorganization and Improvement Act," on March 22. Rep. Rogers introduced the bill along with Rep. Reyes and Chairman Lamar Smith.

The bill establishes two bureaus – a Bureau of Immigration Services and a Bureau of Immigration Enforcement. Each Bureau is headed by a Director, who would be appointed by the President with Senate consent. The Director would report directly to the Attorney General or her delegate.

The Director of the Bureau of Immigration Services (BIS) must have a minimum of 10 years experience in providing services or processing applications for benefits, or both, with at least 5 of those years in management or comparable management experience.

The bill transfers from the Commissioner of the INS to the director of BIS all functions, personnel, infrastructure, and funding provided to the Commissioner in support of the following programs:

1. Adjudications of nonimmigrant and immigrant visa petitions;
2. Adjudications of naturalization petitions;
3. Adjudications of asylum and refugee applications;
4. Adjudications performed at Service centers; and
5. All other adjudications under the INA performed by the INS.

The bill also creates for the BIS a position of Chief Financial Officer.

With respect to the Bureau of Immigration Enforcement (BIE), the Director shall have a minimum of 10 years experience in law enforcement, with at least 5 of those years in management or comparable management experience.

The bill transfers from the Commissioner of the INS to the Director of BIE all functions, personnel, infrastructure, and funding provided to the Commissioner in support of the following programs:

1. The Border Patrol program;
2. The Detention and Deportation program;
3. The Intelligence program;
4. The Investigations program; and
5. The Inspections program.

Like the Bureau of Immigration Services, the bill creates a position of Chief Financial Officer for the Bureau of Immigration Enforcement.

H.R. 3918 has a section on Savings Provisions for legal documents, proceedings, suits, nonabatement of actions, continuance of suits, and administrative procedure and judicial review. So, all orders, rules, regulations, permits, grants, loans, contracts, agreements, licenses that have been issued or made and that are in effect before the effective date of transfer shall continue in effect until they are modified, terminated, superseded, etc. The bill does not affect any proceedings or application for benefits, licenses, permits or financial assistance pending on the effective date or suits commenced before the effective date.

The bill transfers to the two Bureaus the personnel of the Justice Department employed in connection with the functions transferred, the assets, liabilities, contracts, property, records, and unexpended balance of appropriations, authorizations, and allocations. Unexpended funds transferred pursuant to this subsection shall be used only for the purposes for which the funds were originally authorized and appropriated. The bill permits the Attorney General to adjust or realign transfers of funds and personnel for 2 years after the date of Bureau establishment.

The transfer under the Act of full-time and part-time personnel holding permanent positions shall not cause any such employee to be separated or reduced in grade or compensation for 1 year after the date of transfer to the Bureau.

The bill permits the Directors of both Bureaus to delegate any of the transferred functions to officers and employees as may be necessary.

The bill authorizes the Attorney General to provide for an appropriate allocation and/or coordination of resources involved in supporting shared support functions for the two Bureaus. These could include information resources management, human resources and training, security, records and form management, equal opportunity activities, and facilities and procurement administration. Also, the Attorney General, through the Justice Management Division, maintains oversight and control over the shared computer databases and systems and records management.

Within 120 days of the Act's enactment, the Attorney General is to submit to the Appropriations Committees of both the House and Senate a report on the proposed division and transfer of funds between the two Bureaus. Then, 60 days later, each Bureau must submit to both Appropriations Committees an operating plan of resources allocated.

A report on the proposed division of personnel between the two Bureaus must be submitted to the same two Committees by the same deadline, 120 days from the date of enactment.

By the same deadline, the Attorney General must also submit to the Appropriations Committees a plan to carry out this Act. The plan should include details concerning the separation of the Bureaus and address the issues of chain of command, shared services, file and data management and oversight, financial management systems, procedures for interaction between the two Bureaus, fraud detection and investigation, organizational structure, and establishment of a transition team. The plan should also include ways to phase in the costs of separating the administrative support systems of the INS to provide for separate administrative support systems for the Bureaus where best provided for separately.

One hundred eighty days after the date of enactment, the Attorney General is directed to submit to the Appropriations Committees a plan to transfer the detention operations of the Bureau of Immigration Enforcement to the Federal Prison System. The plan should address the detention of criminal aliens, non-criminal aliens, and asylum seekers. Finally, the plan should outline the steps necessary for the transfer to occur no later than 4 years after the plan is submitted.

The transfer of functions shall take effect one year after the date of enactment. By that date, the two Bureaus should be established and the Directors of the Bureaus should be appointed. Details beyond those tasks will be included in the Attorney General's reports.

# PART IV

## INS PROCESSING: ENTRY, APPLICATIONS, CITIZENSHIP

8

# Family Reunification and The Living Law: Processing Delays, Backlogs, and Legal Barriers

DONALD KERWIN
*Catholic Legal Immigration Network (CLINIC)*

The disparity between the law's promise and practice is a defining characteristic of our nation's immigration regime. Nobody suffers more acutely from this disparity than immigrant families. This makes my assigned topic – the impact on immigrants of processing delays by the Immigration and Naturalization Service (INS) – both timely and important. These delays should be considered as immigrant families experience them, in the context of a broader system of laws and practices that threaten their very integrity. Our current system keeps families separated or in a legal limbo for years on end, impedes the educational advancement of children, and prevents potential wage-earners from supporting their families.

This constitutes a problem of national scope because of the historic number of "immigrant" families in the United States, and the reach of our laws. Immigrants and their children comprise 20 percent of our nation's population,[1] a remarkable figure, but one that understates the number of families in the United States with immigrant members. It does not reflect, for example, the families formed by the marriage of an immigrant to a U.S. citizen who already has children. Immigrants typically live in "mixed status" families, narrowly defined as those with at least one non-citizen parent and U.S. citizen children. Nine percent of families with U.S. citizen children have at least one noncitizen parent.[2] Ten percent of all children in the United States live in mixed status families.[3] In immigrant-headed households, the overwhelming majority of children are U.S. citizens.[4] While our nation's vitality increasingly depends on the well-being of its newest members, our immigration laws and practices, many introduced by the 1996 Immigration Act,[5] undermine millions of their families. Consider the following:

- More than 3.5 million family members of U.S. citizens and legal permanent residents, whom INS has approved for family-based immigrant visas, languish in backlogs, either physically separated from their family members (abroad) or in a legal limbo in the United States.[6]

[1]Raumbaut, "Coming of Age in Immigrant America," 1 Research Perspectives on Migration, No. 6 (Carnegie Endowment for International Peace, Jan./Feb. 1998).
[2]Urban Institute, "All Under One Roof: Mixed States Families in an Era of Reform" (June 1999), at 4-5.
[3]*Id.* at 2.
[4]*Id.* at Figures 4 and 6.
[5]The Illegal Immigration Reform and Immigrant Responsibility Act of 1996, Pub. L. No. 104-208, 110 Stat. 3656 (Sept. 30, 1996).
[6]U.S. Department of State, Bureau of Consular Affairs, "Immigrant Visa Waiting List In The Family-Sponsored and Employment-Based Preferences As Of January 1997" (March (1997) (Officials report that these statistics may significantly understate the number of persons in family-based visa backlogs).

- An estimated 41 percent of U.S. households with foreign-born heads do not earn 125 percent of the poverty income guidelines, the threshold for U.S. citizens and legal permanent residents who want to sponsor family members for visas.[7]
- Roughly five million undocumented persons live in the United States.[8] Immigrants "unlawfully present" in the United States for more than 180 days or one year face (respectively) three and ten year bars to "admission."
- In 1999, the INS removed 176,990 persons, and immigration judges ordered an additional 72,000 to depart "voluntarily."[9] Once-removed immigrants who return to the United States face automatic removal and permanent bars to re-entry, notwithstanding their U.S. citizen spouses and children.
- In 1999, the INS removed 62,359 immigrants with criminal convictions.[10] Under current law, long-term legal permanent residents who committed relatively minor crimes years before face removal from the United States and their families here.
- In 1998, the INS detained 153,517 persons.[11] Due to the 1996 Immigration Act's "mandatory" detention provisions, this figure could double in subsequent years. As many as 5,000 immigrants on any given night languish in "indefinite" INS custody because their countries of birth will not accept their return and the INS will not release them.[12] Detention physically divides families, and INS's detention practices make it impossible to sustain even the most attenuated family ties.

This article will outline the family-reunification process through permanent residency and naturalization, as a way to highlight where delays and other problems occur. It will then use two case studies to highlight how delays, backlogs, and common legal problems combine to undermine immigrant families.

[7]Fix and Zimmerman, "Welfare Reform: A New Immigrant Policy for the U.S.," Urban Institute (1997).
[8]*INS Statistical Yearbook for 1997*, at 199 (October 1999).
[9]INS News Release, "INS Sets New Removals Record: Fiscal Year 1999 Removals Reach 176,990" (Nov. 12, 1999).
[10]*Id.*
[11]INS Fact Sheet, "INS Improves Management of Detention Program" (June 8, 1999).
[12]Meeting between Phyllis Coven, Special Assistant to the INS Commissioner for Detention, and non-governmental organizations (Feb. 17, 2000).

## *THE FAMILY REUNIFICATION PROCESS: DELAYS, BACKLOGS AND LEGAL BARRIERS*

Most legal immigrants to the United States come to join U.S. citizen or legal permanent resident family members.[13] Through the visa petition process, these family members ("intending" immigrants) themselves become legal permanent residents, allowing them to live and work indefinitely in the United States. On the other hand, family members eligible for a visa, but subject to delays and backlogs, typically do not enjoy legal status or the right to work in the United States.

Family-based immigration is limited by annual quotas on the number of visas available by "preference" category and by country of nationality. Backlogs occur when the INS approves more persons for visas than the number available. Only "immediate" relatives of U.S. citizens – the spouses, minor children, and the parents of adult U.S. citizens – are exempt from the caps.[14]

Other family members of U.S. citizens and legal permanent residents qualify for visas under "preference" categories. Qualifying relationships include: 1) unmarried, adult children of U.S. citizens; 2) spouses, unmarried adult children, and minor children of legal permanent residents; 3) married adult children of U.S. citizens; 4) brothers and sisters of U.S. citizens.[15]

The visa process begins when a U.S. citizen or legal permanent resident files a petition with INS on behalf of a family member. In approving a petition, the INS certifies that the "intending" immigrant has the proper relationship to the petitioner and the petitioner is a U.S. citizen or legal permanent resident. With the exception of the Vermont Service Center, INS attempts to process petitions for "immediate relatives" of U.S. citizens more quickly than petitions in "preference" category cases. Depending on

[13]Family sponsored immigrants composed 67.1% of all immigrants admitted during 1997. *INS Statistical Yearbook for 1997*, at 19, Table A (October 1999).

[14]INA, § 201(b)(2)(A)(i)(1999).

[15]Under current law, visas are allocated under the preferences as follows: First Preference, unmarried adult children of U.S. citizens, 23,400/year; Second Preference, 2A, spouses and minor children of Lawful Permanent Residents, 87,900/year; Second Preference, 2B, unmarried adult children of Lawful Permanent Residents, 26,300/year; Third Preference, married adult children of U.S. citizens, 23,4000/year; Fourth Preference, brothers and sisters of U.S. citizens, 65,000/year.

[16]American Immigration Lawyers Association, "Immigration Law Today," Vol. 19, No. 3 (March 2000), at 145-146.

the Service Center, processing delays can run from two to eight months for "immediate relatives" and to more than two years in other cases.[16] This initial "processing" delay particularly affects the "immediate relatives" of U.S. citizens (thus, the attempt to expedite their cases) who would otherwise be eligible to apply immediately for permanent residency. It does not affect "intending" immigrants in preference categories who languish concurrently in visa backlogs, their "priority" date (position in the queue) determined by their petition filing date.

Backlogs in visa preference categories constitute the second significant delay in the family immigration process. As stated, their duration depends on the "intending" immigrant's visa category and nationality. For example, a Mexican spouse or minor child of a legal permanent resident would currently face a six year backlog. A Mexican (adult) son or daughter of a legal permanent resident would endure an eight and a half year wait.[17] Similar waits apply to the nationals of other high immigration source countries, like the Philippines and India.

Visa backlogs force many families to remain separated for extended periods, as the "intending" immigrant remains in his native country. In other cases, the family member already lives in the United States, but the duration of the backlog leads him to overstay his temporary visa. In fact, immigrants often run afoul of the law because of delays and backlogs which they cannot control. Undocumented persons eligible for family-based visas cannot work legally or travel abroad. They also accrue time in "unlawful presence" that will bar them from re-entering the United States when their visa becomes available.

The 1996 Immigration Act established a three-year bar for those "unlawfully present" in the United States for more than 180 days,[18] and a ten-year bar for those "unlawfully present" for one year or more.[19] It provides for a discretionary waiver to these bars, if the immigrant's exclusion would result in "extreme hardship" to the U.S. citizen or legal permanent resident spouse or parent.[20] However, the hardship worked on a U.S. citizen or legal permanent resident child by his parents' exclusion from the country cannot be considered.

The three- and ten-year bars apply only to persons seeking admission to the United States. Unfortunately, in 1997, Congress failed to extend a

[17]Department of State, *Bureau of Consular Affairs Visa Bulletin* (February 2000).
[18]INA §212(a)(9)(B)(i)(I).
[19]INA §212(a)(9)(B)(i)(II).
[20]INA §212(a)(9)(B)(v).

provision of the law that allowed undocumented persons to adjust to permanent resident status within the United States.[21] Only undocumented persons with visa petitions filed by January 14, 1998 can still adjust status in the United States. All others must leave the country to obtain permanent residence, thus subjecting themselves to "unlawful presence" and other bars to admission. Undocumented immigrants who qualify for a waiver can still expect to wait outside the country for months, apart from their families.

Children in backlogs often face the problem of "aging out" of their preference categories. For example, if a child reaches age 21 while in the "preference" category backlog for the minor children of legal permanent residents, she would be switched to the "preference" category for adult children which has a longer backlog.[22]

The State Department (DOS) has reported that, as of January 1997, 3,535,430 persons who had been approved for family-based visas, languished in visa backlogs, including 1,052,270 spouses and minor children of legal permanent residents.[23] According to consular affairs officials, these figures almost certainly understated the backlog in 1997, and these numbers would have significantly increased in the interim. The third significant delay in the family reunification process comes at the point that a family member's visa "priority date" becomes current and he applies to become permanent resident. Depending on the applicant, this occurs either through the "adjustment of status" process in the United States or through "consular processing" abroad. In either case, immigrant families face yet another delay at this juncture. Even in relatively simple cases, practitioners report that consular processing can take a year or more, depending on the consulate. In more complicated cases, this delay can be far longer. Overseas adjudication of waivers to bars for "unlawful presence" can alone take a year.

The "adjustment of status" process averages 52 months nationally, with projected delays varying from four months in the INS's Baltimore district office, to 128 months in San Diego.[24] Despite these disparities, applicants pay the same fee throughout the nation. In addition, increased

[21]The Department of Commerce, Justice, State, the Judiciary and Related Agencies Appropriations Act of 1998, Pub. L. 105-119, 111 Stat. 2440 (Nov. 26, 1997), Title I, § 111.
[22]*Id.*
[23]U.S. Department of State, Bureau of Consular Affairs, "Immigrant Visa Waiting List In The Family-Sponsored and Employment-Based Preferences As Of January 1997" (March (1997).
[24]INS Service Center Data, "Projected Processing Time October 1999:I-485s" (Nov. 29, 1999).

delays come in the wake of steep fee increases. In 1998 and 1999, INS raised application filing fees so substantially that most fees nearly doubled.[25] The fee for an application for permanent residence increased from $130 to $220, yet by the end of 1999 pending adjustment cases had skyrocketed to 1,001,550.[26] This represents a stunning development for immigrant families. Only five years before, in 1994, the adjustment backlog numbered 121,000 cases.[27] Furthermore, it continues to grow with no end in sight. At a February 23, 2000 liaison meeting, officials from the INS's Immigration Services Division reported that the agency had received 172,566 adjustment applications in the last quarter of 1999, but completed only 82,498.

The adjustment backlog can be attributed in large part to the INS's significant shift in resources over the last four years to adjudication of naturalization cases. This came in response to intense criticism over naturalization backlogs that exceeded two million persons and average waits of more than two years. Over the same period, Congress enacted legislation to aid Central Americans, former Soviet Bloc nationals, and Haitians, without providing additional resources to INS to handle the resulting work. INS funds its immigration adjudication and naturalization programs through fees paid by applicants.[28] However, the fees collected have failed to cover costs, leaving a $184 million deficit in 1999.[29]

Many legal permanent residents attempt to expedite the family reunification process by trying to become U.S. citizens. As stated, there is no backlog (or numerical limitation) on visas for the spouse, minor child, or parent of an adult U.S. citizen. However, long naturalization backlogs still exist and, in these cases, naturalization can be viewed as the fourth major delay in the family reunification process.

INS officials report that the naturalization backlog had decreased to 1,317,348 by the end of 1999, and remains on a steep downward trajectory. In the last quarter of 1999, the INS received 92,499 naturalization applications, and completed 261,267. Nonetheless, processing times still average one year nationally, running from five to 19 months depending on the

[25]63 Fed. Reg. 43604-10 (August 14, 1998).
[26]INS Service Center Data, "I-485, Application for Adjustment of Status: F.Y. 2000 Year to Date" (Jan. 27, 2000).
[27]Wettstein, "Wasted Days and Wasted Nights: INS Visa Processing Delays and How to Combat Them," 76 Interpreter Releases 1441, 1442 (Sept. 30, 1999).
[28]75 Interpreter Releases 1145 (Aug. 24, 1998).
[29]Viglucci, "Immigrants Complain as Backlogs Slow INS," *Miami Herald* (June 27, 1999).

INS district.[30] Because legal permanent residents cannot become U.S. citizens in a timely manner, their eligible family members cannot become legal permanent residents for years on end.

## *CASE STUDIES: THE INTERPLAY BETWEEN DELAYS, BACKLOGS, AND THE LAW*

INS delays, visa backlogs, and the law often operate as a seamless web to keep immigrant families separated, impoverished, and unsettled. Two cases illustrate the interplay between these factors, and the harsh division between the law in theory and practice.

Mr. M, a 39 year old legal permanent resident from Mexico, applied for citizenship in November 1997. At the time, the naturalization backlog exceeded two years. As a permanent resident, Mr. M had filed a visa petition for his wife and son, which the INS approved. However, their preference category had a four to five year backlog.

In 1998, Mr. M discovered that he had cancer. At that point, citizenship became more important (in practical terms) for him and his family. If Mr. M could naturalize, his wife and child would become "immediate relatives" of a U.S. citizen and, as such, be able to file immediately for permanent residency. If Mr. M died a citizen, his wife could still file a widow's petition which would give her permanent residency. However, if he died a permanent resident, his wife and child's only option would be to request, on humanitarian grounds, that the Attorney General not revoke their visa petition.[31] The long duration of their backlog, however, would mitigate against granting this request.

By December 1999, Mr. M had moved to a hospice. Hospice staff twice wrote the INS district office to request that his naturalization case be expedited, but they received no response. By February 2000, Mr. M had returned home to die. By then, he had been in the naturalization backlog for 27 months. A local Catholic Charities asked the local INS district to expedite the case. The district responded that it still had not received Mr. M's file from the INS Service Center. The Service Center informed the Catholic Legal Immigration Network, Inc. (CLINIC) that the file had not been forwarded because Mr. M's "fingerprints" had expired. For persons in the naturalization backlog, this represents a common problem. After 15

[30] INS Service Center Data, "Projected Processing Time: October 1999" (Nov. 29, 1999).
[31] 8 C.F.R. §205.1 (1999).

months, new prints need to be taken. At this point, the INS became solicitous of Mr. M's needs. They took Mr. M's fingerprints at his home, transferred his file, and in early March, interviewed him and granted him citizenship.

This allowed Mr. M's wife and child to apply for permanent residency. Fortunately, they met the January 14, 1998 cut-off date for in-country adjustment of status. If forced to leave the United States, they would have been subject to the ten-year bar on readmission based on their "unlawful presence." Unfortunately, they still face a 62 month adjustment processing delay.

Mr. M's wife and child will likely receive immigration status in the United States, but only after surmounting delays, backlogs, and various legal barriers. Furthermore, this would have been impossible without extensive advocacy and the INS's ultimate cooperation, neither of which can be assumed in such cases.

Mr. and Mrs. U became legal permanent residents in 1990 through the Special Agricultural Worker ("SAW") program.[32] Shortly after they became residents, their three children – ages 10, 11 and 12 – joined them in the United States, but not in time to qualify for special treatment under the "family unity" program. Today, the family continues to support itself through migrant labor in Georgia, Virginia and Maine. The children regard the United States as their home. All three graduated from high school in a rural Virginia community, and distinguished themselves with their academic and athletic achievements. They hope to attend college.

Mr. and Mrs. U filed visa petitions for their three children in late 1993. Although the INS approved the petitions, as of March 2000 none had become legal permanent residents. When they turned 21, the two oldest moved into a preference category with a backlog of more than eight years.

The priority date of the youngest child, age 20, has become current, and she has filed her application for permanent residence. However, adjustment backlogs mean that she will likely turn 21 prior to a decision on her application. If so, she will revert to the same preference category as her older siblings, and face further delays.

In 1998, Mr. U filed an application for naturalization, which has yet to be adjudicated. In the meantime, the three children do not enjoy legal status in the United States and cannot pursue their education or careers. What is worse, the INS has initiated removal proceedings against them

[32]INA §210 (1999).

after finding them working in a blueberry field during a raid. The children must now present their applications for permanent residency to an immigration judge. The two older children face a particularly difficult situation. If their priority dates have not become current at the time of their final hearing, they will not be eligible to apply for permanent residency. If removed, they will face a 10-year bar to re-entry.[33]

Like millions of immigrant families nationwide, this family met all the legal qualifications for "reunification." However, delays, backlogs, and the law have combined to threaten them with separation. Our nation undermines families like this to its discredit and, given the new face of our country, to its own peril.

[33]INA §212(a)(9)(A)(ii).

# PART V

# HUMAN RIGHTS OF MIGRANTS: REFUGEE PROTECTION, GENDER-BASED VIOLENCE AND TRAFFICKING

9

# Combating Human Smuggling by Enlisting the Victims

ARTHUR C. HELTON[1]
*Council on Foreign Relations, New York*
ELIANA JACOBS[1]
*Council on Foreign Relations, New York*

## *INTRODUCTION*

The scourge of human trafficking is receiving increased attention in the public realm. This is a nasty practice that can produce grave affronts to human rights. But analysis with forward-looking recommendations to curb the practice has been at a premium. This paper offers a law enforcement

[1]The authors wish to acknowledge the financial support of the Open Society Institute and the Ford Foundation in the preparation of this article.

approach which is designed to benefit the interests of the individual victims and is founded on notions of dignity.

A fundamental problem in combating human trafficking is the risk/reward ratio under which traffickers operate. While the rewards are great, the risks have been relatively limited due to a variety of factors. Traffickers rely on the fact that their victims, equally intimidated by the threat of arrest, detention and removal from the United States by government authorities and the threat of violence and reprisals at the hand of their tormentors, will not ordinarily report abuse to the authorities. The removal of trafficking victims as illegal migrants thereby leads to a perversely favorable outcome for traffickers. Indeed, the exile of the victims often removes the only witnesses against traffickers and thus inevitably hampers efforts to prosecute the criminal organizers, thereby helping to perpetuate the phenomenon of human trafficking.

This paper proposes a broad adjustment of immigration status remedy, building upon the S-visa precedent, as an incentive for trafficking victims to come forward and testify against traffickers and the criminal syndicates for whom they work. If status adjustment were more readily available to trafficking victims, then a major factor which currently intimidates victims and prevents them from reporting abuse to the authorities would be eliminated. In the short run, of course, this might actually increase the number of persons receiving status. However, if the policy proved successful in prosecuting traffickers it would have the effect of considerably increasing the risks faced by criminal networks engaged in such operations and U.S. employers collaborating with them. By exposing the U.S. links of such trafficking networks and prosecuting their operatives, this policy would disrupt trafficking networks and provide law enforcement. The long-term effect of such disruptions should be a reduction in the levels of human trafficking and the associated abuses. In addition, as the number of surviving trafficking operations diminishes, this would presumably reduce the available channels for illegal entry into the country and thereby ultimately reduce the number of arriving undocumented migrants.

## *WHAT IS TRAFFICKING*

For our purposes, we define trafficking in human beings as a process involving the recruitment, transport, harboring, sale or receipt of persons, through the use of deceit, fraud, coercion, force, or abduction, for the purpose of placing such persons in situations of slavery-like conditions, including forced prostitution, bonded sweatshop labor, domestic servitude, or other debt bondage. This can occur within national or across international borders. Our paper focuses on a possible remedy under immigration law for cross-border trafficking into the United States.

On the question of definition, there exists some debate as to what are the essential elements of human trafficking. Specifically, there is disagreement about: 1) whether coercion is a necessary element; 2) whether the crossing of an international border is required; and 3) whether the definition should only include trafficking for purposes of sexual exploitation, or should also apply to labor trafficking and marriage marketing.[2] For purposes of this paper, a broad view is taken on the issue of definition. It should also be noted that trafficking has two related but separate dimensions. It consists of the process of recruitment, on the one hand, and the context of work or services, on the other hand.[3] The elements of deceit, coercion and abuse which characterize trafficking operations can occur at either or both ends of the continuum. While involvement of a victim in one of these phases, *e.g.*, recruitment, can be an act of choice, the conditions under which such a person then finds he/she must work may involve the imposition of force, deceit or other forms of violence and abuse. It is not necessary that coercive practices be used at both ends of the process for victimization to occur.

## *THE RISKS AND REWARDS*

Trafficking of men, women, or children for purposes of sexual exploitation, forced labor, debt-bondage, domestic servitude, and other forms of exploitation and abuse, poses relatively few risks for the guilty parties while offering significant financial gain. The United Nations estimates that four million people are trafficked around the world each year, resulting in illicit profits to criminal syndicates of up to 7 billion dollars annually.[4] Over 50,000 women and children are trafficked into the U.S. annually, primarily from Latin America, the former Soviet Union, and South East Asia.

[2]Young, Becki, "Trafficking of Humans Across United States Borders: How the United States Laws can be Used to Punish Traffickers and Protect Victims," *Georgetown Immigration Law Journal*, Vol. 13, No. 1, Fall 1998, p. 75.

[3]Wijers, Marjan and Lin Lap-Chew, *Trafficking in Women, Forced Labour and Slavery-Like Practices in Marriage, Domestic Labour and Prostitution.* Utrecht: Foundation Against Trafficking in Women (STV), April 1997, p. 3.

[4]*Introduction to the Centre for International Crime Prevention.* Web page of the United Nations Office for Drug Control and Crime Prevention. Available at <www.uncjin.org/CICP/cicp.html>, visited June 20, 2000.

Of these 50,000, approximately half fall into the categories of coerced or bonded sweatshop labor and domestic servitude. Men are also trafficked, particularly into forced labor.[5] The illegality of such operations and their attractive economic benefits encourage the involvement of well-established criminal syndicates in trafficking enterprises.[6]

While the rewards reaped by criminal networks involved in the illicit trade in people are considerable, their risks are relatively limited. Because trafficking is addressed primarily as an immigration enforcement issue under the current legal regime, and the government interest in that area is to curtail illegal immigration, victims of trafficking often suffer paradoxically greater punishment than traffickers themselves.

## *THE ENFORCEMENT DILEMMA*

Enacting more restrictive immigration laws and greater enforcement of such laws is unlikely to reduce trafficking significantly. On the contrary, limiting the legal means of entry available to would-be migrants creates a greater reliance on criminal networks offering illegal means of gaining entry and thus enhances the position of traffickers. This is a simple supply and demand equation. Similarly, a policy of summary arrest, detention and deportation of undocumented migrants actually deters victims of trafficking from exposing their victimizers by reporting abuse.[7] From a criminal justice perspective, the primary objective is to prosecute individuals engaged in these systematic and often violent crimes, including exploitative employers, and to significantly disrupt the organized crime networks through which they operate. One might also raise a related moral question, namely, should persons victimized and abused on U.S. soil suffer further punishment in the nature of removal at the hands of government authorities? What then can be done to combat human traf-

[5]Opening Statement of the Hon. Christopher H. Smith, *The Sex Trade: Trafficking of Women and Children in Europe and the United States,* Hearing Before the Commission on Security and Cooperation in Europe, June 28, 1999, CSCE 106-I-9, p. 5. Available at <www.house.gov/csce>, visited March 7, 2000.

[6] Regarding Chinese and Russian criminal networks, respectively, *see,* for example: Kwong, Peter, *Forbidden Workers: Illegal Chinese Immigrants and American Labor,* New York: The New Press, 1997, and Caldwell, Gillian, Steven Glaster and Nadia Steinzor, *Crime and Servitude: An Expose of the Traffic in Women for Prostitution from the Newly Independent States,* Washington, DC: Global Survival Network. 1997, p. 3.

[7]This is particularly true of women trafficked for purposes of sexual exploitation, because prostitution and associated activities are criminalized in most countries, including the United States. *See also,* Caldwell, *et al., supra* note 5.

ficking and prosecute the actual perpetrators of crime, while treating the victims of such crime with dignity?

## *A POSSIBLE REMEDY FOUNDED ON INDIVIDUAL CHOICE*

The immigration consequences of coming forward to report abuse at the hands of traffickers, *i.e.*, removal, generally causes victims of trafficking to endure abuse without reporting the traffickers to the authorities. Most traffickers therefore remain unknown to the authorities; or, if they are known, they remain unpunished for lack of evidence against them. If victims were given immigration incentives to turn against their erstwhile tormentors this equation could change dramatically. The problem is not only that few victims currently report abuse for fear of reprisals. Those who do are often summarily deported as illegal aliens, thus removing the only witnesses who could testify against the traffickers.

There is a provision under U.S. immigration law, which, if expanded, could be used to implement such an incentive-based enforcement program. The "S-visa," colloquially known by the immigration authorities as the "snitch" visa, was created by Congress under the Violent Crime Control and Law Enforcement Act of 1994.[8] It allows the Attorney General to grant a non-immigrant visa to an alien who the Attorney General determines:

I) is in possession of critical reliable information concerning a criminal organization or enterprise;
II) is willing to supply or has supplied such information to Federal or State law enforcement authorities or a Federal or State court; and
III) whose presence in the United States the Attorney General determines is essential to the success of an authorized criminal investigation or the successful prosecution of an individual involved in the criminal organization or enterprise.[9]

The law also provides that under certain circumstances the spouse, and married or unmarried sons and daughters of such an alien, may similarly be granted S-visas.[10]

Currently the law provides for only 200 S-visas to be issued each year.[11] The provision, which expired in 1999, has been extended for an

[8]Act of September 13, 1994, Pub. Law No. 103-322, 108 Stat. 1796.
[9]INA § 101(a)(15)(S)(i)(I-III).
[10]INA § 101(a)(15)(S)(ii)(IV).
[11]INA § 214(k)(2); INA § 214 fn 2a.

additional 2 years and now is scheduled to expire on September 13, 2001.[12] Holders of temporary S-visas can adjust their status to permanent residency if they have provided information which has "substantially contributed to the success of an authorized criminal investigation."[13]

The low numeric ceiling of only 200 visas per annum would have to be expanded significantly in order to make the S-visa program a viable incentive for trafficking victims to come forward and testify against the traffickers. Only if all trafficking victims could potentially receive immigration status in return for incriminating information and testimony would the S-visa provide a real incentive for victims and represent a credible threat of exposure to law enforcement officials of traffickers and the criminal networks for whom they work. Similarly, the requirement that the information provided by an S-visa applicant be "essential" to a criminal prosecution would have to be revisited in this context.[14] Clearly, the number of witnesses "essential" for the prosecution of any one trafficker will be lower than the number of people victimized by such a trafficker and therefore potentially available as witnesses. Only if every victim who cooperates in an investigation or prosecution is a potential S-visa recipient does the trafficker lose the ability to intimidate victims with the prospect of arrest and deportation. The risk to a trafficker of prosecution grows correspondingly, with the likely effect of reducing trafficking operations both through exposure and by deterring those who collaborate with traffickers and engage in the associated abuse and exploitation.

The obstacles to the S-visa as an effective tool to curb trafficking extend to the eventual outcome with respect to status. Unlike the initial allocation of temporary S-visas, the adjustment to permanent resident status is based on the effectiveness of information provided.[15] If S-visas are to motivate trafficking victims to come forward and testify against traffickers, granting temporary status is likely to be insufficient. To make adjustment to permanent status contingent on successful prosecution would significantly undermine any incentive the original offer of temporary status might have on victims of trafficking. Prosecutions can fail for many reasons, including technical factors not bearing on the validity of witness testimony. Also, a witness who is returned to his/her home country after expiration of temporary S-visa status, or his immediate family

[12]INA § 214(k)(2); INA § 214 fn 2a.
[13]INA § 245(i)(1)(A) and (B).
[14]INA § 101(a)(15)(S)(i)(III).
[15]INA § 245(j)(1)(A)and(B).

members, could potentially face reprisals there from traffickers who originally brought them to the U.S.[16] This would give the criminals leverage to prevent victims from coming forward in the first place.

## *CURRENT INITIATIVES*

A UN treaty is currently being negotiated in Vienna which would criminalize trafficking and promote cooperation and information sharing.[17] Significantly, the treaty would also urge countries to grant immigration status to victims of trafficking on humanitarian grounds.[18] The U.S. has been deeply involved in these negotiations, and negotiators hope to finalize a treaty before the end of the year.

Legislation to curb trafficking has also been introduced in the United States House of Representatives as well is in the Senate. The House bill (H.R. 3244), sponsored by Representative Christopher H. Smith (R-NJ), was introduced on November 8, 1999, as the Trafficking Victims Protection Act of 1999. It has undergone some revision and was received by the Senate and placed on its legislative calendar in May 2000 as the Trafficking Victims Protection Act of 2000. The Senate bill (S. 2449), was introduced on April 13, 2000 by Senator Sam Brownback (R-KS) and is known as the International Anti-Trafficking Act of 2000. There are provisions (the so-called "T-visa") in both bills to grant immigration status to victims who cooperate with law enforcement officials.

Both the House and Senate bills note in their respective section on findings that because existing laws and law enforcement procedures often fail to distinguish between victims of trafficking and traffickers who have knowingly and willfully violated laws, and because victims often do not have legal immigration status in the countries into which they are trafficked, the victims are often punished more harshly than the traffickers themselves.[19]

Both the House and Senate bills would amend Section 101(a)(15) of the Immigration and Nationality Act by adding a new subparagraph ('T')

[16]Under INA § 245(j)(1)(B) an alien's spouse, married or unmarried sons and daughters, or parents who were previously admitted under INA § 101(a)(15)(S)(ii)(IV) can also have their status adjusted to permanent residency under the same conditions that apply to the witness.
[17]*Revised draft Protocol to Prevent, Suppress and Punish Trafficking in Persons, Especially Women and Children, supplementing the United Nations Convention against Transnational Organized Crime*, prepared by the Ad Hoc Committee on the Elaboration of a Convention against Transnational Organized Crime. U.N. doc A/AC.254/4/Add.3/Rev.6.
[18]*Ibid*, Art. 5.
[19]H.R. 3244 Sec. 2(b)(17); and S. 2449 Sec. 2(b)(17).

which would allow the Attorney General to grant non-immigrant visas (T-visas) to certain victims of severe forms of trafficking who are in the United States, who have not unreasonably refused to assist in the investigation or prosecution of acts of trafficking, and who would face retribution or other harm if they were removed from the United States.[20] The Senate bill sets a lower burden of proof, requiring only that the victim show a "significant possibility" of retribution or harm, while the revised House bill requires the victim to show a "well-founded fear" of retribution or harm. Both bills also provide for visas for the spouses, children, and parents of trafficking victims under certain circumstances. The Senate bill does not set a numeric limit on the number of T-visas made available for this purpose. The revised House bill limits to 5,000 the total number of aliens who may be provided nonimmigrant status during any fiscal year. This numerical limitation applies only to principal aliens and not to the spouses, sons, daughters, or parents of such aliens.

Furthermore, both bills would amend Section 245 of the Immigration and Nationality Act to allow the Attorney General to adjust to lawful permanent resident status the status of victims (and under certain circumstances their spouses, children and parents) who have been in the United States continuously for three years since admission, who have remained of good moral character, who have not unreasonably refused to assist in trafficking investigations or prosecutions, and who would face a significant possibility (or in the House version, "a well-founded fear") of retribution or other harm if removed from the United States.[21] Once again, the Senate bill does not set a numeric limit on the number of T-visas made available for this purpose. The revised House bill limits to 5,000 the total number of aliens whose status may be adjusted to permanent resident status during any fiscal year. This numerical limitation applies only to principal aliens and not to the spouses, sons, daughters, or parents of such aliens.

Limitations on the number of T-visas available each year and requirements for a higher level of proof regarding a victim's risk of retribution or harm, as have been added to the original House bill, are counterproductive as a method of law enforcement. Additional amendments to the House bill, sponsored during the spring by Representative Lamar Smith (R-TX), would further undermine the visa provision by applying it only to minors under 17 who can demonstrate that they would face persecution

[20]H.R. 3244 Sec. 7(f)(1)(C)(i-iv); and S. 2449 Sec. 7(f)(1)(C)(i-iv).
[21]H.R. 3244 Sec. 7(f)(4); and S. 2449 Sec. 7(f)(4).

upon return home.[22] Lack of protection from deportation for cooperating victims simply gives the traffickers more leverage over them. If the primary objective is to expose and prosecute traffickers then, on the contrary, the remedy should be broadened in order to enlist the victims in bringing as many traffickers as possible to justice.

## *CONCLUSION*

The T-visa provision was designed as a measure of humanitarian relief for those who have been abused. The problem with such an approach is that it is conceived exclusively in humanitarian terms. A more powerful rationale would be to view the granting of immigration status as an incentive to enlist the victims in identifying and prosecuting the traffickers. If immigration status were made widely available to those who have been trafficked and who cooperate with official investigations, then a powerful new tool would be made available to law enforcers in their efforts to curb clandestine trafficking networks. While there might be an initial surge in requests for status, after a period of time migrant trafficking would likely diminish as smugglers reorient their activities to avoid prosecution. With more abuses reported, more trafficking networks would be exposed and investigated. With more victims testifying, more traffickers would be prosecuted and their operations disrupted the knowledge that victims have a valuable incentive to inform on traffickers will inevitably change the perceived risk and act as a deterrent.

We realize that those responsible for immigration law enforcement are likely to view our proposal with alarm. They will worry that fraudulent reports of abuse will be made in order to receive status and that the traffickers themselves will seek to manipulate this new route to status through fraud. For the proposal to be viable it will be necessary to address these concerns.

The primary way to address the potential for fraud will be through a carefully-crafted new statutory provision implemented with scrutiny. For example, the provision could provide for conditional non-immigrant status (like the fiance/fiancee visa)[23] for a period of 90 days, after which time law enforcement authorities are to certify that the report has contributed to a criminal or appropriate administrative investigation, utilizing proce-

[22]"Recent House Immigration Subcommittee Activity," *Immigration Law Today,* (May 2000), 239-240.
[23]*See* INA § 101(a)(15)(K).

dures similar to those now used to address marriage fraud and alien investors.[24] The condition would then be removed and adjustment could follow after some period of time, unless there follows a finding of non-cooperation or fraud, which would lead to a removal proceeding in the immigration court. This mechanism should thus limit the risk of fraud while providing a significant incentive to victims to report abuse and cooperate in the prosecution of offenders. The timelines and procedures should be calibrated, of course, to fit the precise mix of interests at play. It might also be possible to introduce the remedy initially as a pilot program limited in terms of time and place, in order to assess the consequences of the initiative.

This is not a panacea. A whole host of new tools will be needed to address modern forms of international organized crime and terrorism. Traditional notions of border control and immigration policy are not particularly effective in dealing with such issues. While this proposal may not enable law enforcement personnel to weed out all such criminal activities, new tools and options will surely help to break up networks and criminal enterprises.

In sum, our proposal seeks to provide a concrete way to promote humane law enforcement and harmonize immigration, labor, and human rights policy. Initiatives such as this are likely to be required if real progress is to be made in curbing the scourge of human trafficking.

[24]*See* INA § 216 and § 216A.

# 10

# Refugee Protection, Gender-Based Violence and Trafficking in Persons

DEBORAH E. ANKER*
*Harvard Law School*

## *INTRODUCTION*

In an era of restrictionism in the field of immigration law, protection of the rights of some women immigrants stands as a marked, perhaps surprising – although certainly not consistent – exception. On the one hand, Congress has generally cut back on the rights of immigrants. It has restricted judicial review, provided for mandatory detention in many cases, automatic deportation of long-term permanent residents with certain criminal

*The author wishes to thank Nancy Kelly, John Willshire-Carrera, Lauren Gilbert, Ann Jordan and Leslye Orloff for advice and comments, and Allison Tirres for research assistance.

convictions; it has eliminated opportunities for mitigation and discretionary relief, and created new obstacles to legal immigration with profound effects for immigrant families.[1] On the other hand, in two instances, Congress and the administrative authorities have recognized and created opportunities for women immigrants whose human rights have been violated to obtain protection and status in the United States. First, in the spring of 1995, a group of non-governmental organizations, including our Women Refugees Project, convinced the Immigration and Naturalization Service (INS) to issue guidelines instructing adjudicators that women claiming they would face persecution based on their gender could not be excluded from eligibility for asylum and protection from return to their home countries.[2] Following the publication of the *INS Gender Guidelines*, a body of jurisprudence was born specifically acknowledging forms of persecution as gender-based, such as rape and forced female genital mutilation (FGM); and grounds for persecution, including assertions of feminism such as refusal to conform to discriminatory social mores (wearing the veil or chador), fleeing forced marriage, etc., as grounds for refugee protection.[3] Second, in 1994, as part of the Violent Crime Control and Law Enforcement Act,[4] Congress passed the Violence Against Women Act (VAWA) allowing certain women and children immigrants subjected to domestic violence in the United States to obtain status through special cancellation of removal and self-petitioning provisions.[5]

[1]*See generally*, Donald Kerwin, *How Our Immigration Laws Divide, Impoverish and Undermine American Families*, 76 Interpreter Releases 1213 (1999). Following enactment of the Illegal Immigration and Immigrant Responsibility Act of 1996 IIRAIRA), Pub. L. No. 104-208, 110 Stat. 3009, INS reported that legal immigration was at the lowest level in a decade. *See INS Releases Legal Immigration, Removal Numbers*, 76 Interpreter Releases 1234 (1999).

[2]Memorandum from Phyllis Coven, INS Office of International Affairs, to All INS Asylum Officers and HQASM Coordinators, Considerations For Asylum Officers Adjudicating Asylum Claims From Women (May 26, 1995) [hereinafter INS Gender Guidelines], *reproduced in* Deborah Anker, *Women Refugees: Forgotten No Longer?*, 32 San Diego L. Rev. 771, 794-817 (1995).

[3]Deborah E. Anker, Law of Asylum in the United States 252-267, 365-373, 386-394 (1999).

[4]Pub. L. No. 103-322, 108 Stat. 1796.

[5]8 U.S.C.§ 1229b(b)(2) (cancellation of removal); 8 U.S.C. § 1154(a)(1)(A)(iii), (B)(iii)(self-petitioning).Although the title of VAWA uses "women," the immigration provisions generally use gender neutral terminology, *i.e.*, "spouses." In her 1996 report, the Special Rapporteur on Violence Against Women notes that, "Despite the apparent neutrality of the term, domestic violence is nearly always a gender-specific crime, perpetrated by men against women . . . [it is] intended to subordinate women as a group on account of their gender, and deprive them of a range of other rights." *Report of the Special Rapporteur on Violence Against Women, Its Causes and Consequences*, Comm'n Hum. Rts., U.N. GAOR, 52d Sess., Provisional Agenda Item 9(a)¶¶ 23, 53, U.N. Doc. E/CN.4/1996/53 (1996).

It would certainly be interesting to consider why this has occurred, as well as the many contrasting and significant disadvantages women face under the immigration laws.[6] However, this brief discussion instead will focus upon the meaning of these changes and the duality in the conception of women and women's rights that these two important changes in the immigration law represent. One case, gender asylum, recognizes women's rights *qua* rights, grounded in international human rights norms; the other, the VAWA immigrant women provisions, although an extraordinary step forward for women, continues to reflect a view of women as victims subject to statutory and discretionary benefits at the will of Congress – not grounded in rights but in the exceptional plenary power of Congress that, according to many (but not all) commentators, characterizes immigration law.[7] The United States is at an important moment where the rights framework of gender asylum may be lost and swallowed into the political will framework of immigration law generally; there is a significant danger that gender asylum could become or evolve into (at best) a VAWA-like remedy. First this paper will describe the provisions of both bodies of law, their challenges, and then the dilemma.

As noted, the VAWA battered immigrant women and children provisions were part of a larger crime control undertaking and some large part of the motivation for their passage was the idea – shared by many conservative congress people – that protecting women was a critical, indirect means of enabling the prosecution and punishment, of their abusive spouses: if battered immigrant women were not given an opportunity for status and protection, they would not come forward and assist the criminal justice system in the prosecution of their spouses.[8] VAWA has two key provisions. First, immigrant women who otherwise qualify under immigration categories – as the spouse of a U.S. citizen or lawful permanent resident – may "self-petition" for categorization as eligible immigrants.[9]

[6]*See generally*, Joan Fitzpatrick, *The Gender Dimension of U.S. Immigration Policy*, 9 Yale J.L.& Feminism 23, 34-36 (1997).
[7]See, e.g., Stephen H. Legomsky, Immigration Law and the Principle of Plenary Congressional Power, 1984 Sup. Ct. Rev. 255 (1985); Hiroshi Motomura, Immigration Law After a Century of Plenary Power, 100 Yale L. J. 545 (1990). For an article questioning some prevailing views regarding the plenary power doctrine, see Gabriel J. Chin, Is There a Plenary Power Doctrine, 14 Geo. Immigr. L. J. 257 (2000).
[8]See generally, Leslye Orloff, Battered Immigrant Women, in Violence Against Women: Law and Litigation, 21-8 to 21-13 (David Frazee *et al.* editors) (1997).
[9]8 U.S.C. § 1154(a)(1)(A)(iii).

Immigration law generally requires that the lawful permanent resident or U.S. citizen initiate the process for his or her spouse or child to obtain status;[10] for battered spouses and children, VAWA provided an exception. Battered immigrant spouses and children can self-petition, as long as they can establish the relationship and meet other requirements, the most important of which, in addition to proving they were battered or subjected to "extreme cruelty" by the U.S. citizen or lawful permanent resident, is showing that their removal would result in "extreme hardship" to themselves or their children.[11] The second VAWA provision allows women or children in removal proceedings who have been battered or subjected to extreme cruelty by a U.S. citizen or lawful permanent resident (even if the relevant marital relationship has been terminated) and who can show three years residence and extreme hardship resulting from removal, to obtain "cancellation of removal" and ultimately status in the United States, at the discretion of the Attorney General.[12] These represent very significant modifications and lowering of the standards in the general cancellation of removal provisions which, among other differences, for non-battered spouses require ten years residence in the United States, a higher measure of hardship and only to a specified group of U.S. relatives.[13]

The VAWA battered immigrant spouses and children provisions are a very important remedy – hundreds if not thousands of women and children have already benefited – and their enactment is a critical part of the efforts of women's rights groups and others to have the civil rights of women recognized and especially to have domestic violence taken seriously. The critique offered here – if it can even be called that – is that the VAWA provisions are conceptualized and structured as immigration benefits, not as rights. Congress has plenary power in immigration and what it gives it can take away; there is only a whispering of a rights-based independent grounding here. The international human rights community is beginning to understand domestic violence as a human rights issue,[14] but that understanding is not explicit in the structure of VAWA. And VAWA was passed in significant part to aid the prosecution of abusers. This has

[10]*See generally* 8 U.S.C. § 1154(a) (setting forth the family-based immigration petition process).

[11]8 U.S.C. § 1154(a)(1)(A)(iii), (B)(iii).

[12]8 U.S.C. § 1229(b)(2).

[13]8 U.S.C. § 1229b(b)(1).

[14]*See generally* Anker, *supra* note 3, at 258-261.

resulted in real problems for women, especially as, subsequent to VAWA, a domestic violence conviction has been made into an automatic ground of deportation.[15] Our clinic represents several women who, for example, want to bring charges against their abusers but do not want them convicted and removed, which as a practical matter results in the withdrawal of financial support and the opportunity for children to have some contact with their fathers. These women face a terrible dilemma as local district attorneys often refuse to drop charges once brought.

Gender asylum has different roots and a different history than does battered immigrant women and children protection under VAWA. It did not originate as an act of Congress to help women and its purposes do not include prosecution of the criminal law. Rather it is a jurisprudential development, an interpretation of an existing law – the Refugee Act of 1980[16] – a law itself that is not simply an independent act of Congress but domestic implementation of an international human rights treaty, the 1951 UN Refugee Convention.[17] As the *INS Gender Guidelines* state, gender asylum is not new law, but fair application of existing standards to women.[18] Gender asylum recognizes, as the INS has stated, that "women's rights are human rights and women's rights are universal."[19] A brief explanation of the purposes and norms of refugee and asylum protection puts gender asylum in perspective.

The asylum provisions of our law were enacted in 1980 and, as noted, they implement the 1951 UN Refugee Convention, which was part of the post-World War II birth or flowering of international human rights. The refugee treaty is part of the corpus of international human rights instruments which traces its origins to that time, including especially the Universal Declaration of Human Rights[20] and later the International Covenant on Civil and Political Rights [21] and the International Covenant

[15]8 U.S.C. § 1227(a)(2)(E).

[16]Refugee Act of 1980, Pub. L. No. 96-212, 94 Stat. 102 (1980) (codified as amended in scattered sections of 8 U.S.C.).

[17]United Nations Convention relating to the Status of Refugees, opened for signature July 28, 1951, 19 U.S.T. 6259, 189 U.N.T.S. 137; United Nations Protocol relating to the Status of Refugees, opened for signature Jan. 31, 1967, 19 U.S.T. 6223, 606 U.N.T.S. 267.

[18]INS Gender Guidelines, *supra* note 2, at 804.

[19]*Id.* at 795.

[20]Universal Declaration of Human Rights, G.A. Res. 217A, U.N. GAOR, 3d Sess., Supp. No. 16, U.N. Doc. A/810 (1948).

[21]International Covenant on Civil and Political Rights, adopted Dec. 16, 1966, S. Treaty Doc. No. 95-2, 95th Cong., 2d Sess. (1977), 999 U.N.T.S. 171.

on Economic, Social and Cultural Rights.[22] The treaty and statute grant protection from return and status to a person who meets the criteria of "refugee," defined as someone outside his or her country who has a well-founded fear of persecution because of race, religion, nationality, membership of a particular social group or political opinion.[23] Refugee law exists to protect the individual – by providing surrogate state protection – when states have failed in fundamental obligations they have towards their population *and* when that failure of state protection and resulting serious harm or persecution is for a discriminatory reason – race, religion, nationality, political opinion or membership in a particular social group.[24] Gender is not a specific ground stated in the refugee definition, but it has been found by the U.S. Board of Immigration Appeals, the Canadian Supreme Court, the U.K. House of Lords and many commentators to be embraced within the particular social ground.[25] Particular social group is defined either by an "immutable characteristic" or by past or present voluntary association entered into for reasons protected by basic human rights principles that are considered "fundamental to human dignity."[26] Such qualities relate directly to the purposes of refugee law, which are grounded in values similar to those embodied in the non-discrimination principle underlying international and domestic law. Refugee law seeks to protect those persons who are fundamentally marginalized within their societies because of characteristics that are protected as basic rights or over which they have no control.[27] Sex or gender is such a characteristic.[28] As gender asylum law has developed, forms of harm that are specific to or that disproportionately impact upon women – rape, domestic violence, female genital mutilation (FGM), etc. – that previously were dismissed as private acts, have been recognized as serious human rights violations and

[22]International Covenant on Economic, Social, and Cultural Rights, adopted Dec. 16, 1966, 993 U.N.T.S. 3, reprinted in 6 I.L.M. 360.

[23]For discussion of some of the differences between the U.S. definition and that in the treaty, *see generally* Anker, *supra* note 2, at 13-87, 267-415.

[24]*Id.*, at 184-99, 290-92.

[25]The views of the Board of Immigration Appeals, the Canadian Supreme Court and those of commentators are discussed at id., 388-94. Those of the House of Lords are contained in Islam (A.P.) v. Secretary of State for the Home Department, Regina v. Immigration Appeal Tribunal and Another Ex Parte Shah (A.P.), [1999] 2 All ER 545 (House of Lords). The views of the Board were further elaborated in In re R-A-, Interim Dec. 3403 (BIA 1999).

[26]Anker, *supra* at 376-78.

[27]*Id.*

[28]*Id.* at 398-94.

persecution.[29] And in many instances, adjudicators have understood that these harms or other actions against women are gendered. For example, in a case that received a fair amount of publicity a number of years ago, that of Fauziya Kasinga who fled imminent subjugation to female genital mutilation in Togo, to be imposed upon her against her will, the Board of Immigration Appeals adopted a context-sensitive understanding of gender persecution. It looked to the societal context, rather than the private motive of the individual persecutory actor, finding persecution on account of a gender based particular social group because of the cultural purpose of the practice of FGM – to suppress and control the woman on account of her gender.[30] A critically important component in the development of gender asylum is the recognition that the agent of persecution can be a non-state actor because violations of women's human rights are more typically inflicted by non-state actors, including by members of women's families, communities, and traditional cultural authorities.[31] The non-state actor doctrine is long-standing in U.S. law and has been accepted by several other states parties to the 1951 UN Refugee Convention as well as by the United Nations High Commissioner for Refugees; this is because refugee law is concerned with protecting persons where there has been a failure of duty by a state, and states have obligations to protect from non-state harm.[32] Although the non-state actor doctrine had a long history before the development of gender asylum, it has been a challenge to have it applied in women's cases, but there have been many successes.

The current dilemma of gender asylum – the threat of its transformation into an immigration remedy – has arisen in the context of domestic violence. In a recent decision, *In re R-A-*, the Board of Immigration Appeals denied asylum to a Guatemalan woman, who had been subjected to severe abuse by her husband and whom the Board agreed would face similar or worse persecution if returned.[33] The Board failed to recognize – or really to address – the gendered nature of domestic violence, but retreated to a literalist understanding of motives, focusing upon the particular psyche of the perpetrator (and even there, unfortunately, not understanding its gendered nature). The case is more about the issues the Board

[29]*Id.* at 252-66.
[30]*In re Kasinga*, Interim Dec. 3278 (BIA 1996); Anker, *supra* at 388-94.
[31]Anker, supra at 364-66.
[32]*Id.* at 191-98.
[33]Interim Dec. 3403 (BIA 1999).

avoided then what it addressed, but one part of the Board's analysis is particularly interesting and disturbing. The Board commented that if Congress had wanted to protect women facing domestic violence from return it would have addressed it in or simultaneous with the passage of VAWA – after all had not Congress spoken to domestic violence there?[34] But gender asylum is about the application of human rights principles to specific cases; it does not require congressional recognition that women against whom particular forms of abuse have been perpetrated deserve protection. No one has ever suggested that special laws are needed to protect persons who are political prisoners, who protest against particular policies of repressive governments, who face persecution because they belong to a clan or race or religion. These are understood to be embraced by asylum law, with elaboration in the jurisprudence through individual adjudications. Women too have rights; they are rights grounded in international law. Most fundamentally, as the *INS Gender Guidelines* promised, they have the right to equal treatment under the treaty and the U.S. asylum statute.

Since *R-A-*, some congress people initially attempted to address the problem of the result in that case by suggesting amendments to the law through which, for example, women who face domestic violence in their home countries could obtain parole status in the United States – the most discretionary form of relief in the immigration act. Refugee scholars and rights advocates have rejected these offers. Let the issue be whether or not domestic violence constitutes a serious human rights violation and, in individual cases, meets the other criteria of the refugee definition. The *INS Gender Guidelines* state that women's rights are human rights and women's rights are universal. Gender asylum has been an important arena in which that principle has taken concrete form and it has been an exception to the general trend in immigration law where all rights are conceived as creatures of congressional discretion.

This issue – the differing conceptions of women's rights *as* rights or as discretionary immigration benefits – is manifested in other arenas than VAWA and gender asylum. Proposed U.S. legislation to address trafficking in persons, including women, epitomizes these same dilemmas. Proposed bills, among other things, provide for a "T" visa for persons who

[34]*Id.* at 10 (citing VAWA and commenting that, "No changes relative to battered spouses were made in the refugee definition or the asylum statute at the time of enactment of the battered spouse provisions.").

have been subjected to trafficking, which would protect them temporarily or possibly permanently from return. One bill, introduced by Senator Paul Wellstone, for example, speaks in hortatory language of trafficking as a serious human rights violation as well as a critical problem for law enforcement and state sovereignty.[35] On the one hand, what emerges from this legislation – albeit in nascent form – is a norm against return of persons, and most particularly women, who have been subjected to or who face serious human rights violations. On the other hand, a clear emphasis in the trafficking legislation is protection of women and other trafficking victims because such protection facilitates prosecution of the perpetrators. Some proposed bills, for example, require a determination that applicants for "T" visa protection have cooperated in the formal prosecution of their traffickers;[36] others also provide demanding standards of proof on trafficked persons as well as exacting showings of hardship.[37] Watching the development of this legislation over the next several months, it will be critical to see how fulsome and rights-based these protections against return are conceptualized and articulated, and how much the legislation views trafficked persons as holders of rights entitled to protection, rather than as supplicants for discretionary benefits and instruments in facilitating enforcement of the law.

[34]*Id.* at 10 (citing VAWA and commenting that, "No changes relative to battered spouses were made in the refugee definition or the asylum statute at the time of enactment of the battered spouse provisions.").

[35]S. 2414, 106th Congress, 2d Sess. (2000).

[36]*Id.*

[37]Amendment to H.R. 3244, 106th Congress, 2d Sess. (2000) (introduced by Senator Lamar Smith).

# 11

# The Eleventh Circuit, All Elian, and Asylum: How Young is Too Young to Apply?

ELIZABETH HULL
*Rutgers University*

As fiction, the saga of Elian Gonzalez would never sell: too preposterous! As real-life docudrama, however, it attracted worldwide attention for over six months and commanded more airtime by the network evening news than even the deaths of Princess Diana and JFK Jr. (Rich, 2000).

The story began on November 22nd, 1999, when 14 people fled Cuba on a 16-foot motor boat. The crowded vessel capsized the next day, and 11 of those on board perished at sea – including the mother of a boy then five years old. The boy, Elian, survived for two days by clutching an inner tube (that might or might not have been kept afloat by kind-hearted porpoises, as legend soon had it). He was rescued, appropriately, on Thanksgiving Day and handed over to the INS, which placed him in the temporary care of his great-uncle, Lazaro Gonzalez.

The uncle, an expatriate bitterly estranged from his relatives still living in Cuba, resides with his wife and daughter alongside thousands of fellow exiles, in the Little Havana section of Miami. He immediately filed a petition with a Florida state court for his nephew's formal admission to this country. The court awarded him a temporary protective order and ruled that Elian was not to be removed from the United States prior to a March 6th hearing it scheduled. Meanwhile, on November 27th, the child's father, Juan Miguel Gonzalez – unaware until her disappearance that his ex-wife had fled the island with their son – requested that the petition for Elian's admission be withdrawn and that the child be returned to Cuba. At this juncture Attorney General Janet Reno declared that the state court order was without force because only federal authorities have jurisdiction over issues involving admission and asylum (Reno letter, Jan. 13, 2000).

Accordingly, on December 10th, the uncle, Lazaro Gonzalez, applied in federal district court for asylum on Elian's behalf. Three weeks later the Immigration Service interviewed the boy's father in Havana and concluded that he had been a loving, attentive parent. INS Commissioner Doris Meissner consequently ruled that the boy be returned to Cuba by January 14th. In response, the Miami relatives – with the fierce support of most other members of the Cuban-American community (and the many politicians who, whether or not they shared the community's ideological fervor, shared a keen appreciation for its political strength) – vowed never to allow the child's return to a repressive dictatorship that his mother had given her life to escape.

Thus began the riveting soap opera "All Elian, All of the Time." (One veteran INS official reported that the story easily surpassed in terms of public interest any other immigration-related incident he could recall) (Broder & Sciolino, 2000). On January 26th both of Elian's grandmothers made their first airplane trip in order to visit him, and almost everyone with a television set watched as they embraced and then romped with their beloved grandson. As the drama unfolded, viewers continued to watch as a wrenching family drama metamorphosed into a legal, political, and even diplomatic donnybrook (prompting CNN Vice-President Keith McCallister to assert that Elian's story "raises major issues about the foreign policies of two countries") (Rich, 2000).[1]

[1]According to another television executive, however, such a claim is delusional: Elian's "just a very sexy kid" in a sitcom (Rich, 2000).

Meanwhile, on April 6th, Elian's father and five others left Cuba for the United States. Six days later, after Lazaro Gonzalez refused for one reason and then another to hand Elian over to his father, and after a stressful day in which Reno herself negotiated at length with the Miami relatives, she ordered them to surrender Elian by that afternoon. Defiant, the uncle declared that ". . . we will not turn the child over." Federal agents were "training and preparing to attack my house," he charged, and "they would have to come in and get him" (Bragg, April 4, 2000).

All the while a carnival-like atmosphere prevailed outside the Gonzalez home in Little Havana. The sun shone, vendors sold snow-cones, and the crowd, depending on the turn of events, either reveled in the streets or marched angrily down them, chanting and brandishing an occasional clenched fist. In record time they became media savvy, granting interviews and seizing free air time to excoriate both Castro and "fascistic" federal authorities.

## *THE RAID*

The mood changed abruptly on April 22nd. That day, in a predawn raid, eight federal agents, clad in riot gear and bearing automatic weapons, swept through the Gonzalez home, seized Elian, and placed him in the arms of a specially-trained female guard who, in Spanish, whispered in his ear "we are taking you to see your papa" (Orr, 2000). The entire episode, which newscasters, pundits, and editorialists would ponder, dissect, and critique for what, all-tolled, would be hundreds of hours, took exactly three minutes.

The next day the covers of nearly every newspaper in the country featured a picture, snapped by a family friend as the raid was occurring, of a heavily-armed commando aiming a gun at a screaming and clearly terrified child. Many of these papers juxtaposed the picture with another one taken five hours after the raid – this of a beaming Elian, sporting a Batman tee-shirt, walking hand-in-hand with his father at Andrews Air Force Base in Maryland.

The reaction among many Americans, upon learning of the raid, was one of relief. Reaction among most Cuban-Americans, however, was outrage. Within minutes of hearing the news, thousands of protestors swarmed into the streets of Little Havana, some weeping and waving American flags; others, fewer in number, blocking traffic and setting fire to trash bins. Police, numbering in the hundreds and fortified with tear gas, dispersed the crowds and hauled more than 300 rioters off to jail.

Was the raid justifiable? An editorial in *The Washington Post* (May 1, 2000) described it as being "swift, deft and solicitous as regards the boy." *New York Times* columnist Anthony Lewis, rarely one to laud the Immigration Service, said that Reno had been "extraordinarily patient, if not dilatory, in a situation increasingly dangerous to Elian's long-term well-being" (April 29, 2000). He even agreed with Reno's explanation that the armed agents had been necessary – not only because they were entering a hostile atmosphere, but also because the show of force in itself may have prevented violence (Johnston, April 28, 2000).

Yet prominent senators accused the Department of Justice of "running roughshod over the rights of the boy's relatives in Miami" (Mann, 2000; Van Natta, April 23, 2000). Tom Fitton, the president of a conservative organization called Judicial Watch, went so far as to suggest that the raid bordered on treason. Documents the organization had obtained through the Freedom of Information Act, he said, revealed that administration officials, including ones in the INS, had consulted with Cuba on issues that involved Elian. "These smoking gun documents help prove what we've suspected, that the Clinton-Gore Administration was doing the bidding of Fidel Castro when they raided the Gonzalez home using 151 armed federal agents" (Holland, 2000).

Even the generally supportive *New York Times* accused Reno of acting "precipitously" (April 23, 2000)(prompting columnist John Farmer to retort that if she had waited any longer, "her term would have run out") (Farmer, April 24, 2000). Farmer is right. There is one thing the raid was not: precipitous. Government officials, everyone from low-level state department officials to INS Commissioner Doris Meissner and Reno herself, met repeatedly for over five months with Elian's Florida relatives in an effort to facilitate a peaceful solution, culminating in a 44-hour marathon in which some of Miami's most influential leaders served as mediators. More than once a resolution seemed within reach, only to slip away – at least as Reno saw it, because Lazaro Gonzalez and his attorneys "kept raising the stakes" (Davies, 2000). A settlement was *not* imminent, contrary to the claims later made by some of the mediators, and as Reno later disclosed she realized "it wasn't going to get any better" (News Conference, April 23, 2000). Nevertheless, she was still on the phone with the Florida parties when federal agents burst through the front door of the Gonzalez home.

As many critics assailed Janet Reno for being irresolute as for being reckless (Dowd, 2000; Farmer, 2000). Former INS agent Jan Ting, for one, charged the Department of Justice with "an abject act of spinelessness" for engaging in lengthy negotiations with Elian's Miami relatives (Van Natta, April 2, 2000). He said the federal government appeared – in Richard Nixon's unforgettable phrase, like a "pitiful, helpless giant" that time and again "caved in to intimidation and threats of civil disorder." (Ting also blamed President Clinton for failing to send in troops to enforce the law, as Eisenhower did in Little Rock and Kennedy did in Mississippi and Alabama). "Ironically," Ting said, Reno and others in the Clinton Administration ultimately may have encouraged the civil disorder that occurred in Miami, "not because of their action but because of their inaction"(*id.*).

Reno's pre-raid behavior was indeed irresolute – a fact that may be explained, although not justified, by her experiences as both Miami's chief prosecutor, and as the United States Attorney General. As a prosecutor for fifteen years, she was forced to deal with disorderly influxes of immigrants and the civil unrest they incited, and dreaded the prospect of either recurring under her watch. Reno also presided over the Department of Justice during the seven-week standoff in April 1993 between the federal government and members of the Branch Davidian religious sect in Waco, Texas. It was she who eventually gave the order for troops to storm the compound, resulting in the violent deaths of 80 cult members, including many children, and four FBI agents. The specter of South Florida becoming another Waco came close to immobilizing her (Johnston, April 13, 2000; Van Natta, April 2, 2000).

However reluctant Reno's behavior, was it legal? According to some of her antagonists, ordering the great uncle to return Elian to INS custody was the action of a "brazen autocrat." They are wrong, because a long-standing law vests the Immigration Service with custody of any alien who arrives at this country's borders without documents. The law further allows the Attorney General, and by extension the INS, to parole an alien, with this proviso: "When the purposes of such parole shall, in the opinion of the Attorney General, have been served, the alien shall forthwith return or be returned to the custody from which he was paroled" (*Gonzales v. Reno*, 2000 WL381901, 11th Cir.). When Reno notified Lazaro Gonzalez that she had revoked Elian's parole, he was legally mandated to surrender his nephew. By refusing to do so, it was the uncle, *not* the Attorney General, who flouted the law.

## *COURT ACTION*

The drama was playing out not only in the overheated streets of Little Havana, but also in the air-conditioned chambers of the Eleventh Circuit

Court of Appeals in Atlanta. On March 21st, after a federal district court held that Elian was too young to apply on his own for asylum, and should be represented by his father, Lazaro Gonzalez immediately sought a reversal from the higher court. What started out as a simple custody case then became an even bigger *cause celebre* because, on April 19th, a three-judge panel indicated that Elian might indeed be able to represent himself. The immigration law expressly states that "any alien, regardless of age, may seek asylum in the United States (1158(a)(1))," the circuit court said, and according to the record, "plaintiff, although a young child, has expressed a wish that he not be returned to Cuba"(*id.* at 381901 ). In response to the Justice Department's assertion that since the child could not understand the complexities of asylum law, only Elian's father could speak for his son, the court accused the INS of rejecting the boy's asylum application out-of-hand, without even interviewing him. The agency, it said, may not have properly considered "the child's separate and independent interests"(*id.* at 381909).

Although the Eleventh Circuit decided that a definitive ruling would be "premature," since oral arguments and a full hearing were scheduled for May 11th, it prohibited the child from being removed from the United States until his asylum status was resolved. The court's limited injunction, however, did not prevent Reno from ordering the INS to transfer Elian to his father's custody.

On May 1st Gregory Craig, the lawyer appointed by the government to represent Juan Miguel Gonzalez, submitted a brief to the three-judge panel arguing that Elian should be returned to his father. "The child longs for nothing so much as the familiarity of his own bedroom in Cardenas," he said (Marquis, May 2, 2000). "This father seeks to raise his family where he wants and how he wants" – a right that "is no less important to people from Cuba than it is to Americans" (*id.*).

"Distant" relatives pressed Elian to sign a claim for political asylum that he neither wanted nor understood, Craig continued. The fact that he printed his name on the asylum application filed for him by his uncle means nothing. There is absolutely no way Elian could have understood the significance of his actions – especially since the claim was filed in English and the child cannot even read his native Spanish, much less a foreign tongue (*id.*).

Moreover, the father, Juan Miguel Gonzalez, knows his own child, knows he is not afraid to return to Cuba, and knows that even if he were he could not articulate the "well-founded fear of persecution" necessary to win asylum under United States immigration laws (*id.*). (Craig attached the findings of Paulina Kernberg, a physician who concluded after observing and interviewing Elian that his understanding of his environment was "what one would expect from a six-year-old." She noted that Elian asserted himself freely around his father, "refusing to take his vitamin C pill and drink all his milk") (*id.*).

Neither does the father fear persecution if he returns to Cuba, Craig said. He is not being "manipulated" by Castro, and he is at liberty to "openly express his feelings and his opinions" (*id.*). His decision to return to his homeland was "free from Cuban government coercion," "contrary to the claims" made by Elian's great-uncle Gonzalez. "There is nothing stopping Juan Miguel from telling the marshals that he wants to be protected from the Cuban government as much as he wants to be protected from the relatives in Miami," Craig concluded. "He has not done so" (*id.*).

In their "counter" brief, lawyers representing Lazaro Gonzalez accused the INS of "trampling" on the child's rights in its haste to reunite him with his father. "Without ever meeting the child or considering the merits of his claim under established asylum procedures . . . the INS determined that it did not think this boy's claims worthy of traditional adjudication, and then proceeded to ensure that his claims would never see the light of day" (*id.*).

According to one of the uncle's attorneys, Kendall Coffey, Elian might indeed have a legitimate fear of persecution in Cuba, but a child his age is not capable of expressing that fear. If returned, Coffey asserted, Elian would be paraded around Cuba, used as a "trophy," and deprived of a normal life. "There is no parent in Cuba who controls what happens to his or her child, and there is no power in this country that can protect this child if he is removed to Cuba" (Bragg, May 12, 2000).

The May 11th oral arguments included a tense exchange between the Eleventh Circuit panel and attorneys representing both sides. Judge Charles Wilson observed at one point that while he was sure "Elian Gonzalez is a very bright and intelligent six-year-old," "he didn't even have the ability to sign his last name on the asylum petition"(Bragg, May 12, 2000). At the same time, Judge J.L. Edmondson, the senior member of the panel, wondered aloud if returning Elian to "Communist Cuba" would be in the child's best interests, even assuming his father's fitness as a parent (*id.*). He said the case was theoretically comparable to one involving a child who had been rescued from a communist country in the former Soviet Union by a mother who sacrificed her life to deliver him to freedom.

This rhetorical volley did not foreshadow the court's eventual position. On June 1st, three weeks after oral arguments, the Eleventh Circuit panel affirmed the district court's March 21st ruling and, by extension, the position adopted by the Immigration Service: one, that Elian was too young to comprehend a complicated asylum application; and two, that the Immigration Service acted within its legal authority when it determined that only the father – not Elian himself or his relatives in Miami – could speak for the boy (*Gonzales v. Reno*, 212 F.3d 1338).

The ruling, a paean to judicial restraint, was influenced by a 1983 Supreme Court decision holding that the judiciary should accord agencies like the INS wide discretion in interpreting their own regulations as long as their interpretations fit "within the range of reasonable choices" (*Chevron U.S.A. Inc. v. Natural Resources Defense Council, Inc.*, 467 U.S. 837, 1984). Accordingly, said Judge Edmondson, speaking for the panel, "the judicial power is a limited power. It is the duty of the judicial branch not to exercise political will, but only to render judgment under the law" (212 F.3d at 1352). Moreover, he continued, in language that was scarcely an endorsement of the Immigration Service, while he "might disagree with sending the boy back to a communist government with a long, dismal history on human rights, the law gave wide discretion to the INS in such cases" (*id.* at 1349, 1350).

Judge Edmondson made clear that if the Eleventh Circuit had been the appropriate decision-making body, it might have reached a different conclusion; unlike the Immigration Service, he suggested, it would have considered whether Elian merited asylum from what he twice referred to as the "Marxist" government in Cuba, and once as the "Marxist, totalitarian state" (*id.* at 1352). In fact, he as much as said – eleven different times – that the INS might have made the wrong decision, and he also noted that "in some instances" the agency's policy of deferring to parents – especially those residing outside of this country – "might hinder some six-year-olds with non-frivolous asylum claims" (*id.* at 1351). But, he repeated, it was not the job of judges to overturn administrative policy "merely because we personally might have chosen another" (*id.*).

The Miami relatives sought a rehearing by the full twelve-member circuit, primarily on the ground that the three-judge panel had neglected to consider a May 1st Supreme Court ruling holding, essentially, that courts are not obligated to accept agency determinations that conflict with the plain language of the law (Lewis, Neil, 2000).[2] Nine days later, on June 24th, the Eleventh Circuit unanimously – and without even holding a vote – denied a rehearing. (Judge Edmonson, again speaking for his colleagues, declared that the court would not grant any future motions for a stay – writing the "NOT" in large, bold-faced type) (Bragg, June 16, 2000). He also reminded the appellants of something they already knew – *i.e.*, that the injunction prohibiting Elian's removal from the United States would expire at four p.m. the next day. Elian could be on a plane bound for Cuba within 24 hours unless they succeeded with their last trump card: the Supreme Court.

The lawyers for Lazaro Gonzalez, accordingly, asked William Kennedy – the Supreme Court Justice assigned to hear emergency cases from Florida – to issue a stay blocking the boy's return pending a formal appeal. The legal issues in the case, they argued, "boil down to a single straightforward question: Can the INS deprive an alien child of his statutory and constitutional right to apply for asylum without conducting any hearing of any kind – or even without interviewing the child himself?" (Carelli, 2000).

The Supreme Court rarely grants an emergency stay unless a compelling legal issue is raised or the petitioning party has demonstrated a substantial likelihood of success, and predictably it refused to do so in this case. On June 28th, within hours of its refusal, Elian and his entourage flew home.

## *ANALYSIS*

The Eleventh Circuit panel's June 1st ruling is welcome to the extent it granted Juan Miguel Gonzalez sole authority over his son. However, the logic employed by the panel – both in this opinion, and in its preliminary one on April 19th – is both puzzling and worrisome. On the one hand, the court seemed to be making the blanket assertion that the immigration law permits "any alien," regardless of age, to seek asylum in the United States" (1158(a)(1); and, on the other, to be suggesting that the judiciary will not interfere if the INS determines that, notwithstanding this right, children's preferences will never be allowed to supersede that of their parents.

[2]According to the brief submitted by the relatives' attorneys, the decision by the Immigration Service that Elian could not seek asylum independently of his father constituted agency interpretation of existing law, and "[t]his error undeniably affected the outcome of this case."

In its earlier opinion, after stating more than once that the immigration law permits "any alien" to seek asylum, the panel encouraged INS officials to ask six-year-old Elian Gonzalez himself whether he wanted to return to "Marxist Cuba" or remain with his relatives in Miami, regardless of his father's wishes (2000WL at 381905). It explicitly said, as well, that not only might the child apply for asylum, but that "it appears he did so" by signing an application on file with the Immigration Service.

As David A. Martin, a former INS General Counsel, pointed out, by "fixating" on one brief phrase in the immigration statute – the one that reads "any alien . . . irrespective of such alien's status, may apply for asylum," and divorcing this language from the context in which it might be applied, the Court reached the "foolish" conclusion that any child, however young, is legally entitled to apply personally for asylum (Martin, April 21, 2000).

Martin observed that the Eleventh Circuit's ruling prompted fellow immigration lawyers to write him sardonic e-mail messages, like the one recommending that attorneys hang around Disney World, where they're likely to find "foreign kids" to whom they can promise permanent residency if these kids just make a "crayon mark on the signature line of the asylum form"(*id.*). While the message is facetious, it underlines not just the "foolishness," but even the danger of interpreting the immigration statute literally. If the term "any alien" compels the Immigration Service to take seriously any child's resistance – however fleeting – to going home, the agency will be intruding dangerously into family life, maybe even routinely substituting its opinion for that of the parents.

What, then, *did* Congress mean when it wrote "any alien . . . may apply for asylum"? It did not explicitly exclude young children, but, Martin says, neither did it "expressly exclude kids' applications for licenses to operate nuclear power plants" (*id.*). Courts are expected to exercise common sense, and refer for guidance to other laws governing the capacity of minors. By so doing, they easily could reach the "sensible result" that neither judges nor administrators are obliged to accept applications from children "tendered by meddling adults, even if the child made a mark on the page and says that he wants whatever goody is offered" (*id.*).

If six is too young, how old *should* children be before they can file for asylum? In their brief before the Eleventh Circuit, government attorneys cited a 1985 case where a federal appeals court granted asylum to a twelve-year-old Ukrainian boy against his parents' wishes (*Polouchak v. Meese*, 774 F.2d 731, 7th Cir. 1985). Notably, however, the court in that case ruled that twelve years of age was presumably "near the lower end of an age range" entitling children to defy their parents (*id.* at 736-7), and at least until Elian's case judges rarely (if ever) assumed that children under twelve were mature enough to make sound decisions for themselves.

Children, after all, live in the here-and-now, and are often influenced by factors that adults would consider extraneous. "You give a kid a Nintendo and the kid will want to go where the Nintendo's going," said Michael Ratner, an international human rights lawyer who teaches at Yale University (Bynum, 2000). Children also lack an adult's capacity for abstract thinking. How pointless to ask a six-year-old, or probably even a ten-year-old, whether he or she prefers one governmental regime, or one economic system, to another. (How many adults, if asked, could provide a reasoned response?)

Asking children to make critical decisions might even wreak psychological harm, according to Dr. Albert Solnit, Connecticut's former Mental Health Commissioner. He said, in reference to Elian Gonzalez, that while it might be "therapeutic" for him to express his feelings, these feelings should not be accorded equal weight with those of a child of fourteen, say. "He shouldn't be burdened with the responsibility of making decisions that require an adult capacity, cognitively, emotionally, and socially" (Sengupta, 2000). One could not expect a child Elian's age to comprehend what such a decision entails, he said, "how to trust his memory, how to deal with severe trauma" (*id.*).

The June 1st ruling distinguished from the April 19th ruling, is also troubling, but for an opposite reason: The Eleventh Circuit panel seemed to be saying that children will never receive asylum in the United States if their parents object, unless these parents are manifestly unfit. Judge Edmondson, speaking for the court, noted that the boy's father intended to return his son to what he repeatedly called a "Communist dictatorship," and that this same father had waited weeks before coming to the United States to retrieve his child. Nor did the Immigration Service ever grant the boy a single interview. Even so, and with the court's acquiescence, the INS *still* awarded the father sole authority to speak for his son. Yet such concern might prove unwarranted. In 1998 the Immigration Service issued new guidelines governing claims submitted by juveniles, and these guidelines explicitly acknowledge that under some circumstances children would receive asylum even in defiance of their parents' wishes. Indeed, the Justice Department did not foreclose the possibility of Elian's submitting an independent claim until officials had interviewed the child's father in Cuba and determined for themselves that he was a fit parent who had maintained a close relationship with his son.

The INS guidelines are necessarily flexible, and time will tell if immigration officials are able to distinguish between the vast majority of cases, in which children are indeed best served by their parents, and the exceptional cases where they are not. (As a *New York Times* reader asked in a Letter-to-the-Editor, "would anyone like to speculate on how the Clinton Administration or the INS would have handled the Elian Gonzalez case had it involved a six-year-old girl fleeing an Afghanistan ruled by Taliban fundamentalists?") (Salas, 2000).

Finally, the Eleventh Circuit's June 1st opinion was notably deferential to the Immigration Service, vesting it with considerable discretion to decide which claims it will and will not hear.[3] Further, INS officials might interpret the panel's "hands off" position in such a well-publicized case as a signal that the judiciary will rarely interfere. Its ruling, then, could bode ill for other children, frequently unaccompanied minors, whose asylum claims might indeed be compelling.

Again, however, such concern might prove unnecessary. Arguably, the Eleventh Circuit was exhibiting admirable restraint. It is a tenet of responsible jurisprudence, after all, that courts should defer to administrative agencies on factual, as opposed to legal issues, and even more so when a decision reflects their expertise.[4] Since agencies are accountable to elected officials, and their rulings amendable by legislation or executive orders, at least theoretically their action is more democratic than that undertaken by federal judges, who are non-elected and whose pronouncements are less easily modified.

Such judicial solicitude is proper, however, only as long as the action under review is "reasonable," within an agency's delegated power, and does not constitute an abuse of discretion. Certainly the Eleventh Circuit, applying these standards in the Elian Gonzalez case, could easily conclude that the INS action was justifiable. The court will have established a dan-

[3]According to Howard Simon, Executive Director of the American Civil Liberties Union of Florida, such deference is the "logical outgrowth" of the 1996 Immigration Act, which denies most aliens found deportable by the INS the right to seek judicial review (Clymer, 2000).
[4]T. Alexander Aleinikoff, a professor of law at Georgetown University Law School, praised the decision for reaching a proper standard of judicial review of administrative decisions. But, he said, "we seem to always go further in immigration cases where there is an extra dose of deference that is given." He said the Eleventh Circuit probably went further than necessary in this case by emphasizing how immigration policy affected "the president's conduct of our nation's international affairs" (Clymer, *id.*).

gerous precedent only if subsequent tribunals interpret its language to mean that deference is appropriate even when the Immigration Service takes action that is clearly unreasonable or unfair.

## *POLITICS*

Robert Pastor, who directed Latin American relations at the National Security Council during the Carter Administration, observed that "[t]here is no U.S.-Cuban issue that's not politicized"(Broder, 2000). And, he added, "tensions always seemed to rise in election years" (*id.*). As if on schedule, *L'Affaire Elian* emerged shortly before the beginning of the 2000 presidential campaign, and complicated life for one of the candidates for at least the next six months.

The conflict put Vice-President Al Gore, the Democratic nominee, in a bind: he could take a stand supporting Florida's 800,000-strong Cuban-American community, and better his chances to capture the fourth largest state's all-important electoral votes in November. (Texas Governor George W. Bush, his Republican rival, had declared back in January that he favored citizenship for Elian.) Alternately, he could align himself with virtually every other member of the Clinton Administration by declaring that the boy belonged with his father.

In a patently political and perhaps very shrewd move, Gore chose the first option. On March 30th he urged Congress to adopt legislation sponsored by Senators Bob Graham (considered at the time a possible running-mate) and Bob Smith that would grant permanent resident status to Elian and his extended family, thereby allowing the boy to remain in the Untied States while a family court adjudicated his case. "From the very beginning," Gore explained, "I have said that Elian Gonzalez's case is at heart a custody matter . . . that should be decided by courts that have the experience and expertise to resolve custody cases, with due process, and based on Elian's best interests" (*New York Times*, March 31, 2000).

The bill to which Gore referred was only one of several that legislators introduced to impede the boy's repatriation. Ultimately, however, Republicans abandoned their efforts to pass any law after receiving warnings from some of their staunch supporters, including leaders of the conservative Family Research Council, that granting the boy residency would undermine parental authority. (Congressional Republicans also cancelled hearings they had scheduled to investigate the circumstances surrounding the April 22nd raid when public opinion polls revealed that at least sixty percent of the American public supported the government's action (Cohen, 2000).

President Clinton himself was in almost as uncomfortable a position as his vice president. He certainly did not want to hobble Gore's candidacy by alienating Florida's potent Cuban-American voting bloc, but neither did he want to provoke Castro unnecessarily – especially since he had already suffered, however indirectly, from the leader's wrath. In 1980 Castro, in retaliation for what he considered objectionable U.S. policies, launched the so-called "Mariel boatlift," during which he sent to Florida some 125,000 Cubans – including some of the island's most unregenerate criminals. The Carter Administration temporarily resettled 20,000 of these exiles at Fort Chaffee, Arkansas, provoking rioting that injured more than forty Cubans and state police. Clinton, then running for another term as Arkansas's governor, faults Carter for sending the Cubans to his state with inadequate security – a move he believes caused his only gubernatorial defeat (Broder, 2000).

As President, Clinton has been dogged by the fear of another forced migration, and in 1995, in part to foreclose such a crisis, he entered into an accord with Castro obligating the United States to admit a minimum of 20,000 Cubans a year – a move that for the first time in decades regularized immigration patterns between the two countries. Regardless of the accord, however, an aroused Fidel Castro could launch a second boatlift, and in fact Circado Alarcon, head of the Cuban National Assembly, delivered a speech in Havana saying that Castro was prepared to do so if Elian Gonzalez were not sent home (Hentoff, 2000).

Pragmatic as well as partisan considerations influenced members of the Clinton Administration, almost every one of whom – with the notable exception of Gore – agreed with authorities in both immigration and family law that the Elian case, absent its political overtones, would have been resolved from the beginning in favor of the father. As Reno said at an April 8th press conference, "the law is clear. A child who has lost his mother belongs with his sole surviving parent, especially with one who has shared such a close and a continuous relationship with his son" (Johnston, April 8, 2000).

Besides, keeping the boy from his father would establish a dangerous precedent. Every year estranged spouses and other relatives in countries throughout the world hold hundreds of children as virtual hostages, and without the cooperation of foreign governments the parents of American children might never regain custody of their sons and daughters. As a senior INS officer pointed out, if "your child is taken to a foreign country and they think their way of life is better than ours, and make him or her a citizen of that country to prevent his repatriation, that would be in the mind of any parent an absolutely unacceptable position" (Broder and Sciolino, 2000).

## *THE CUBAN-AMERICAN COMMUNITY*

For most Americans, communism is something that effectively ended when the Berlin Wall came down. For Cuban-Americans, however, it remains a personal, almost visceral phenomenon, and Fidel Castro its despised embodiment. Many of the older exiles fled the island when Castro came to power, and as they see it he stripped them of everything – family members, their homes, businesses, the community standing that was theirs by right (Alvarez, April 11, 2000). They follow with passionate interest any political development that could affect the Castro regime. Even young Cuban-Americans, most of whom have never stepped foot in their parents' homeland, can cite the names of individual Cuban heroes, political prisoners, members of the Miami-based exile group, Brothers to the Rescue.

Memories remain fraught. Many in Little Havana can recall the details of a 1994 rampage in which Castro's agents killed twelve unarmed people as they were attempting to flee the island in a tugboat. Some of those demonstrating outside the Gonzalez home carried mimeographed photocopies of the children aboard that vessel (*id.*). Others, unprodded, will tell in exhausting detail about the time Castro's henchmen shot down two planes that were manned by expatriates patrolling the Florida straits in search of refugees fleeing Cuba on rafts.

For four decades United States foreign policy toward Cuba has been guided not by strategic imperatives but by the antipathy the exile community bears for Castro. This community and its supporters have successfully blocked almost every governmental action that might have benefited the island, thereby encouraging the adoption and retention of counter-productive policies that are at odds with those of every other progressive country. These policies have harmed the Cuban people and, perversely, reinforced Castro's grip on power (he has, after all, outlived nine U.S. presidents!) (*See* Friedman, 2000).

Given their successful record, the denizens of Little Havana were understandably confident they could win a showdown over Elian. They did, in fact, succeed in keeping the federal government at bay for five months. In so doing, however, they may at last have overplayed their hand. The entire nation – much of the world, in fact – watched as the uncle, egged-on by the anti-Castro lobby, defied a lawful order issued by the INS that he surrender his nephew. They watched as Miami-Dade County Mayor Alex Penelas – in what was plausibly an invitation to civil disobedience – announced that the police forces under his command would not assist federal authorities if they attempted to seize the boy (La Corte, 2000). As newspaper columnist John Farmer observed, the activists made clear that when Cuba and Castro are concerned, "they have no respect for American law" (Farmer, April 24, 2000).

Further, by exploiting a child to feed its own propaganda campaign, the exile community may have disillusioned the long-sympathetic American public. Indeed, by using every political, legal (and not-so-legal) gambit available to keep Juan Miguel Gonzalez from his son it managed not only to generate sympathy for the father, but also, and more significantly, to alert the citizenry to the anachronistic and self-defeating policies pursued by its elected officials. In fact, Farmer said, the expatriates may have scored what English soccer fans call an "own goal" – a term, he explains, that means a "blunder" benefiting the opposing team – like kicking the ball into the wrong net (*id.*).

That the Cuban-American community may indeed have scored an "own goal" was suggested the day before Elian flew home: House Republican leaders, in a move that would have been unthinkable even a few months earlier, agreed to terminate the sanctions that for forty years had prohibited U.S. farmers from selling food to Cuba.[5]

[5]Although the United States has not yet renounced its 38-year-old embargo against Cuba, in 1999 the Clinton Administration announced that it would permit additional charter flights to the island, and would approve substantially more visas for those wishing to engage in noncommercial travel (Friedman, 2000).

On June 7, 2000, in an equally significant move, the Immigration Service forcibly repatriated Andy Morales, a baseball star on Cuba's national team, who was apprehended as he attempted to enter the United States by sea. The Coast Guard returned the third baseman after he was unable to convince immigration authorities that he qualified for political asylum. One official explained that "[h]e said he came here to play baseball. That does not constitute a "well-founded fear of persecution" (Marquis, June 8, 2000). Perhaps not, but another government official said that he could recall no other instance in which this country had repatriated a well-known Cuba athlete who had attempted to defect. *Id.*

This country, in fact, has opened its arms to dozens of such defectors, including Orlando Hernandez, a pitcher for the New York Yankees, and his brother, Livan, who joined the Florida Marlins and, in 1997, pitched the game that won his team the World Series. *(Continued)*

## *CONCLUSION*

What lessons should the United States have learned from the Elian imbroglio? That its relationship with Cuba needs a major reassessment, and its asylum policies some fine-tuning; that political pandering *a la* Gore, or the rhetoric of lawlessness, *a la* Mayor Penelas, may yield short-term reward but rarely long-term respect; and that despite Janet Reno's exasperating forbearance, and the posturing and bellicosity of some members of the Cuban-American community in South Florida, the country's legal system plodded forward in a more or less reasonable fashion, providing all parties their day in court, and eventually producing what most Americans consider a just result.

## *REFERENCES*

Alvarez, L.
2000 "Hatred of Castro Feeds Outrage Among Exiles," *The New York Times,* April 11, A22.

———
2000 "Raid in Miami Opens New Front in Struggle Over the Cuban Boy," *The New York Times,* April 24, A1.

Bragg, R.
2000 "Boy's Cuba-based Family to be Issued U.S. Visas," *The New York Times,* April 24, A1.

———
2000 "Miami Family Told to Turn Over Boy After Talks Fail," *The New York Times,* April 13, A1, A29.

———
2000 "Judges Ask Tough Questions About Cuban Boy's Custody," *The New York Times,* May 12, A16.

———
2000 "Appeals Court Rejects Bid by Cuban Boy's Relatives," *The New York Times,* June 24, A6.

Broder, J. M. and E. Sciolino
2000 "A Legal Process Snarled by Politics," *The New York Times,* March 31, A20.

Bumiller, E.
2000 "Seizure of Cuban Child Is Grist for Senate Race," *The New York Times,* April 25, B4.

[5](Morales, incidentally, is not one to give up easily. He tried again to enter the United States, and on July 20th reached the Marquesas, a group of islands near Key West that are U.S. territories. This time he was allowed to stay, by virtue of this country's bizarre "wet foot, dry foot" policy. Under federal rules, Cuban refugees who actually reach United States soil are ordinarily allowed to remain, and they become eligible for permanent residence within one year. Those interdicted at sea, however, are returned unless they are able to demonstrate a well-founded fear of persecution, in which case the United States will attempt to find a haven for them in a third country (Nobles, 2000).

Bynum, R.
2000 "Appeals Court Like Will Mark Last Stand for Elian's Relatives," *The Newark Star-Ledger,* May 11, p. 5.

Carelli, R.
2000 "Elian's Kin Take Appeal to the Supreme Court," *The Newark Star-Ledger,* June 27, p. 7.

Clymer, A.
2000 "Debate on Miami Raid Rides on Whether Deal was Near," *The New York Times,* April 25, A1.

Cohen, R.
2000 "Lott Says Inquiry Will Probe Elian Tactics," *The Newark Star-Ledger,* April 26, p. 10.

Davies, F.
2000 "Reno 'Pained' Over Decision to Seize Boy," *The Miami Herald,* April 23, A19.

DeYong, K.
2000 "Elian's Kin Rebuffed as Court Backs Dad," *The Newark Star-Ledger,* April 28, p. 20.

Dowd, M.
2000 "Never on Sunday, Monday or . . .,"*The New York Times,* April 19, A23.

Editorial
2000 "Elian Goes Home," *The New York Times,* June 29, A30.

———
2000 "The Elian Operation," *The Washington Post National Weekly Edition,* May 1, p. 24.

———
2000 "A Precipitous Raid," *The New York Times,* April 23, A10.

Farmer, J.
2000 "Miami Cubans are the Ultimate Loser," *The Newark Star-Ledger,* April 24, p. 5.

Friedman, T. L.
2000 "Reno for President." *The New York Times,* April 25, A23.

Glaberson, W.
2000 "Tepid Endorsement of Government's Actions," *The New York Times,* June 2, A16.

"Gore Supports Permanent Residency Status for 6-Year-Old in Volatile Custody Case
2000 "*The New York Times,* March 31, A1, A20.

Hentoff, N.
2000 "'Doing the Right Thing'...for Castro and Clinton," *The Newark Star-Ledger,* May 2, p. 15.

Holland, J. J.
2000 "Senate Seeks Justice Data on Elian Raid," *The Newark Star-Ledger,* June 9, p. 7.

Johnston, D. A.
2000 "Raid Leaders Explain the Use of Automatic Weapons," *The New York Times,* April 28, A20.

———
2000 "For Reno, A Custody Case Is Now a Personal Crusade," *The New York Times,* April 13, A29.

———
2000 "U.S. Set to Order a Speedy Return of Boy to Father," *The New York Times*, April 8, A1.

LaCorte, R.
2000 "Miami Mayor Ousts City Manager who Balked at Order," *The Newark Star-Ledger*, April 28, p. 21.

Lewis, A.
2000 "Elian and the Law," *The New York Times*, April 29, A13.

Lewis, N. A.
2000 "Miami Relatives Seek Review of Decision That Would Let Boy Return to Cuba," *The New York Times*, June 16, A12.

Mann, W. C.
2000 "GOP Leaders Fault Clinton for Castro-like Tactics," *The Newark Star-Ledger*, April 23, p. 13.

Marquis, C. A.
2000 "United States Sends Cuban Athlete Home," *The New York Times*, June 8, A14.

———
2000 "Relatives Pressured Boy to Seek Asylum, Father's Lawyer Says," *The New York Times*, May 2, .

Martin, D. A.
2000 "In Elian's Interest?," *The New York Times*, April 21, A25.

Nobles, C.
2000 "Cuban Slugger Makes It to U.S. on Second Try," *The New York Times*, July 20, A23.

Orr, J. S.
2000 "Raid, then Reunion," *The Newark Star-Ledger*, April 23, A25.

Rich, F.
2000 "America Finds Another JonBenet," *The New York Times*, April 22, A13.

Reno, J.
2000 "Excerpts from Press Conference," Reprinted in *The New York Times*, April 7, A9.

———
2000 "Excerpts from Reno's Letter on Cuban Boy," Reprinted in *The New York Times*, January 13, A30.

Salas, A.
2000 Letter-to-the-Editor, *The New York Times*, June 3, A12.

Sengupta, S.
2000 "In Custody Battles, Children Get Unequal Time," *The New York Times*, April 23, A3.

Van Natta, Jr., D. A.
2000 "When Policy and Personal History Mix," *The New York Times*, April 2, A3.

———
2000 "Bush Criticizes Administration for Removing Boy 'At Gunpoint'," *The New York Times*, April 23, p. 18.

———
2000 "When Policy and Personal History Mix," *The New York Times*. P. A-3. April 2.

12

# The Escalation of Migrant Trafficking

JAMES PULEO
*U.S. Department of State*

The end of the Cold War, the globalization of the world economy, intensive regional populations pressures, and the diffusion of sovereign state power have created fertile conditions for the growth of a multitude of international security problems that currently plague a number of Western nations – terrorism, narco-trafficking, migrant smuggling and trafficking, and transnational crime. Although many believe migrant smuggling is a relative newcomer to this group, it is not but it is a threat that is growing and interacts closely with the above mentioned security issues. The United Nations estimates that nearly four million human beings are smuggled and trafficked across national boundaries every year, and roughly $7 billion is paid to criminal organizations involved in the smuggling.

Viewed from a global perspective, smuggling of illegal migrants is an enormous criminal industry. Enormous levels of official corruption make this growing trade in human cargo possible. In many countries, alien smuggling is not a crime or only draws minimal penalties, thereby allowing smugglers to operate with near impunity, often with the tacit cooperation of indigenous government officials.

If I may turn a commonly used phrase on its ear, "Strong fences do not necessarily make good neighbors but strong neighbors make good fences." No one nation alone can stop the flow of illegal migration. Networks of government, similarly linked in an open architecture that enables them to come together as quickly and efficiently as the criminals, must join together to combat criminal networks. That means an unprecedented degree of international bilateral cooperation, extending multilaterally from government to government, in a series of inter-operating links. The United States cannot protect its citizens and its territory without simultaneously changing the environments in the transit and sending countries.

Alien smuggling as a growth industry is escalating from the domain of the small businessman and travel agent and increasingly involves organized and international criminal elements. In the past five years the number and sophistication of the international smuggling rings have increased in response to the soaring demand and profits that can be generated by this trade. These smugglers are also increasingly involved in drug trafficking, as well as trafficking in women and children for illicit purposes. Today these smuggling networks are moving hundreds of thousands of migrants around the globe. Sophisticated smuggling rings can offer full-service to their clients: providing airline tickets, obtaining valid or fraudulent passports, visas and entry permits, staffing safe-houses, circumventing airport exit controls, and recruiting local guides to move their clients to their final destinations.

Major smuggling rings have escalated their efforts to threaten government authority by their corrupting influence. To be successful, a smuggler must have the cooperation of some government official to facilitate the movement of his clients in cities used as a transit point. No country is immune to the effects of corruption.

The dramatic rise in alien smuggling, especially by criminal syndicates, unfortunately has also seen a rise in smugglers abusing the migrants they are transporting. Smugglers are not afraid to engage in kidnappings and murder to enforce collection for their services, or to resort to physical abuse during the transport of the migrants.

Many countries believe illegal migration has little or no effect on their country, as the migrants are simply passing through. Unfortunately, this is far from true. Besides the negative effect which official corruption has on the country's social infrastructure, many illegal migrants engage in criminal activities to support themselves or to pay the smugglers. It is the law-abiding citizens who must pay the price.

What can we do together to combat illegal smuggling? First, every country should have strong anti-smuggling laws in place. These laws should, at a minimum, penalize the smugglers and those who aid and abet them by moving any person from and through our countries. They should also include penalties for the manufacture of counterfeit documents used by smugglers to move their human cargo across international borders.

Corrupt government officials must be removed and punished for aiding in a criminal act. Removing such officials will severely hamper smugglers' ability to freely move illegal migrants. The smuggler must spend time and resources to cultivate a replacement along the smuggling pipeline.

It is important that we raise the consciousness of our international partners regarding this issue. Foreign governments and law enforcement authorities are sometimes reluctant to dedicate resources to migrant smuggling cases because they see this as a victimless crime. The reality is that migrants are often subjected to inhumane or dangerous treatment and in some cases to violence. Migrants die from suffocation, abandonment, accidents or brutality by smugglers. They are transported by sea in unsafe and unsanitary vessels that were not designed to carry passengers.

We have integrated migrant smuggling into our regular bilateral dialogue with other governments. We have systematic and deep exchanges with key multilateral partners in our effort to develop a global approach to this international problem. In addition to our diplomatic exchanges, the United States has been instrumental in leading the discussions of two international instruments currently under debate within the UN Crime Commission. One, which we introduced, deals with the trafficking of persons, especially women and children. The other, first introduced by Austria and Italy, and rewritten by the United States, deals with the smuggling of migrants, including smuggling by sea. These protocols, as addenda to the Organized Crime Convention, will be the first international instruments that deal with migrant smuggling. There are instruments that deal with smuggling for slavery and prostitution, but neither covers the smuggling/trafficking of persons.

Briefly, these law enforcement protocols call upon member states to criminalize smuggling and trafficking of persons, for aiding and abetting in the smuggling, and for producing fraudulent documents. Both require states to improve training and share information on the smugglers/traffickers. The trafficking protocol also directs states party to the Convention to take the necessary steps to prevent the trafficking of persons by establishing programs to inform potential victims of the dangers that may befall them once they are trafficked. Even those individuals who may know they are being trafficked as prostitutes or to work in sweatshops cannot imagine what may happen.

The trafficking in persons protocol calls upon states parties to enact laws which permit victims of trafficking to remain in their territory, temporarily or permanently, in appropriate cases. This affords the victims the proper protection as material witnesses during the prosecution of the trafficker.

As you can see, the State Department is concerned about the increase in the smuggling and trafficking of migrants. We are engaged on many fronts including within the United Nations. It is only through cooperation among concerned states that we can address this ever-growing problem.

# PART VI

# INTEGRATION OF IMMIGRANTS AND THEIR DESCENDANTS

13

# Assessing Assimilation: Cultural and Political Integration of Immigrants and Their Descendants

MICHAEL LEMAY
*California State University – San Bernardino*

## *INTRODUCTION*

Nathan Glazer's *Beyond the Melting Pot*, first published in 1963, is a classic statement about race and ethnicity as well as an articulate presentation of the argument that the assimilation model, understood in the sociological literature of the time as a paradigm, simply did not happen as the model posited.[1] He posited an alternative view, that of cultural pluralism. An extensive body of literature since than has questioned many of the assumptions of the assimilation model. Since the 1970s many studies have offered insights into just how complex is the acculturation/assimilation process, and why it is important to modify the classic assimilation model in various ways to allow for a richer understanding of the variety of approaches with which racial and ethnic groups respond to a migration process that places them in minority status. They demonstrate that while racial and ethnic groups resulting from the European immigration or from internal migrations (from the South, from Puerto Rico or other U. S. territories) did not always amalgamate into unhyphenated Americans, they did not maintain over time the traits, norms, customs, and language of the first generation migrants from which they arose.

Table 1 offers another schema employing an elaboration of Edgar Litt's (1970) analysis of American ethnic politics. Some racial and ethnic minority groups, especially those developing through the process of voluntary migration, do desire assimilation and employ a strategy of accommodation. Other such groups reject assimilation and attempt to maintain separatism. Still other groups pursue a strategy of radicalism, attempting to modify the majority society's value-system to be more compatible to their own. Table 1 distinguishes two basic tactical approaches for each of these three overarching strategies. It suggests various racial and ethnic groups that serve as examples of each strategy/tactical approach (LeMay:45-60).

Most racial and ethnic minority groups do pursue some variation of the accommodation strategy and exhibit varying degrees of assimilation. Trying to account for the varying rates and routes of the acculturation to assimilation of immigrants to the United States has long been a focus of social science scholars of immigration, as well as of persons serving the immigrant communities, and of policy makers revising immigration pol-

[1]See the excellent series of articles (by Alba, Portes, Kasinitz, Foner, Anderson, and Glazer) which "re-visit" BMP in the Spring volume of the *International Migration Review*, 34(1):243-279. Besides Glazer, many scholars reject the view that assimilation is inevitable or even likely. Barth and Noel, for example, maintain that besides assimilation four other stable outcomes of intergroup contact are possible: exclusion (including both expulsion and annihilation), symbiosis, stratification, and pluralism. *See* "Conceptual Framework for the Analysis of Race Relations: An Evaluation," *Social Forces*, 50 (1972): 333-347. For a more recent such critical view of the assimilation model, *see* Conrad Kottak and Kathryn Kazaitis, *On Being Different*. Boston: McGraw-Hill, 1999. Pp. 48-51.

**TABLE 1**
**Strategies and Tactics of Racial and Ethinics Minority Groups' Responses to Discrimination and Placement in Minority Status**

| Strategy | Tactics and Groups Employing Them | |
|---|---|---|
| Accommodation | The Economic Approach<br>Occupational queuing and use of special niches.<br>Groups using:<br>Scots, Welsh, Germans, Scandinavians, Dutch, Japanese, Chinese,<br>Koreans, blacks (Booker T. Washington followers). | The Political Approach<br>Machine politics and coalitions, electoral-generated gains.<br>Groups using:<br>Irish, Italians, Greeks, Jews, Slavs, Women (e.g., NOW). |
| Separatism | Physical Separatism<br>Moving to isolated areas.<br>Groups using:<br>Chinese, Amish, Mennonites, Mormons, Native Americans, blacks (Marcus Garvey followers). | Psychological Separatism<br>Building shell around members.<br>Groups using:<br>Black Muslims, Hasidic Jews, millennial religious groups. |
| Radicalism | Old-Style Radicalism<br>Ideological "isms."<br>Groups using:<br>Socialism—Jews, Poles, Germans, Slavs, Russians<br>Communism—same as Socialism<br>Fascism/Nazism—Germans, Italians, White Russians, radical agrarianism, Utopian movements. | New-Style Radicalism<br>Nonviolent to violent protest actions.<br>Groups using:<br>SCLC, SNCC, CORE, Black Panthers, SEA, AIM, UFW of Cesar Chavez. |

Source: Michael LeMay, *The Perennial Struggle*, Upper Saddle River, N. J.: Prentice-Hall, 2000: 60.

icy. A classic paradigm of the process is provided by Milton Gordon (1964).

Table 2 shows the acculturation/assimilation process as a continuum along which is arrayed Gordon's schema. It illustrates the process both for a group and for an individual immigrant member of a group. It demonstrates that assimilation, the gradual cultural and legal integration of an individual into a new culture/society, is a complex process of absorption which can be viewed analytically as progressing through seven stages as the person or the whole group acculturates and moves toward what Gordon refers to as civic assimilation. Once total assimilation takes place the individual member of a former immigrant subculture group becomes so integrated that neither its former members nor the majority society can

**TABLE 2**

**A Continuum of Acculturation/Assimilation**

*Subcultural Group* — *The Group as a Whole* — *Majority Culture* →

| | | | | | | |
|---|---|---|---|---|---|---|
| Begins to shed some cultural norms (e.g., food, clothing style) typical of the subculture and acquire those of the majority. | Begins to enter job market structure, voluntary associations, etc., of working-class and lower-middle-class levels. | Outgroup marriage becomes common (greater than 50%). | Most group members begin to think of themselves as "hyphenated" Americans, or Americans of "*n*-descent." | Majority no longer shows prejudice against the group. | Absence of discrimination against the group. | Group participates fully in the civic life of the majority culture; no value and power conflict. |

***Gordon's Continuum***

| *Cultural* | *Structural* | *Marital* | *Identificational* | *Attidude Receptional* | *Behavioral Receptional* | *Civic* |
|---|---|---|---|---|---|---|
| Name change (anglicized); acquires some norms typical of the new culture (food, clothing style, some language) and begins to shed those of the subculture. | Gets job on working-class or higher level; begins to join voluntary associations of that level (unions, Lions Club, etc.). | Marries out of own group into the majority group. | Think of himself/herself as belonging to majority but still recognizes the subcultural heritage. | Feels no prejudice on the basis of subcultural background. | Individual no longer experiences discrimination. | Individual participates fully in the civic life of the majority. |

Source: Michael LeMay, *The Perennial Struggle*, Upper Saddle River, N. J.: Prentice-Hall, 2000: 32.

realistically distinguish him or her as living in a separate subculture. Civic assimilation is seen as the end stage of the process.[2] An increasing body of studies have shown just how richly complex and varied is that process.The systems model provides a useful view of this gradual process by focusing attention on the *inherently reciprocal* nature of the process of

[2]Other early scholars of race-relations suggest similar "stages." *See, e.g.,* E. S. Bogardus who posits the following stages: curiosity, economic welcome, industrial and social antagonism, fair play tendencies, quiescence, and second-generation difficulties. *See also* "Race Relations Cycle," *American Journal of Sociology,* 35:613; W. O. Brown, who describes a "natural history" of initial contact, emergence of conflict, temporary accommodation, struggle for status,

assimilation, that is, simultaneously involving the actions of both members of the majority society and members of the immigrant subculture group within it. The systems model reflects the interactions – the feedback effect – among the various factors that influence the process. Figure 1 graphically portrays the model of assimilation incorporating Gordon's paradigm or stages (LeMay:38). The graphic model posits that the rate of assimilation varies according to the level of acculturation that any particular immigrant group has achieved at any given point in time. The level is determined by two major variables: 1) *tolerance*, the majority's willingness to accept the acculturation of members of the immigrant subculture; and 2) *adaptability*, the minority members' ability to acculturate. The model portrays each of these variables, in turn, as being determined by three functions.

Tolerance is shaped by the *majority's fear function*, reflecting the degree to which a majority society perceives the immigrant group as a threat. Such threat may be economic, value-based, cultural, and so on. The greater the degree of fear felt by the majority, the less willing it is to accept acculturation by the immigrant group. Closely linked is the influence of the *size of minority function*. This must be understood as relative; the size of the immigrant group in relation to the majority is key to how that size function influences the majority's willingness or not to allow the minority to assimilate. The majority's *perception* of the minority's size is critically important. The visibility of the minority to the majority (for example, racially different immigrant groups with more highly visible physical features, or whether the immigrant group settles in geographically concentrated patterns versus dispersed settlement, and so on) impacts their perception of size. A sense of threat is implicit in the size function if the majority feels that the immigrant group is large enough to pose a threat to job availability, influence wage scales and working conditions, access to housing, or similar social or economic benefits. Finally, the model portrays that the majority's willingness to accept immigrant groups is also a function of the *time of entry* of the immigrant subculture into the majority society. This function likewise interacts with the majority's perception of the minority. An immigrant group arriving during a period of economic recession or

mobilization, and solution in his "Cultural Contacts and Race Conflicts," in *Race and Cultural Contacts*. Ed. E. B. Reuter. New York: McGraw-Hill, 1934. Pp. 34-37. E. C. Glick suggests "phases" he labels precontact, contact and predomination, domination, and accommodation, in his "Social Roles and Types in Race Relations," in *Race Relations in World Perspective*. Ed. A. W. Lind. Honolulu: University of Hawaii Press, 1955. Pp. 239-241.

depression, or in a time of social upheaval and instability, for example, will be less accepted by the majority than one coming during an economic boom period.

The second major variable determining the level of acculturation of the immigrant group is an *adaptability variable* – that is, its ability to acculturate. The adaptability rate results from three functions that cause it to vary over time. The first is the *minority's ability to organize function*. Groups cannot cope with prejudice and discrimination or develop new values, norms, and customs among their members unless they are well organized. The more organized the immigrant group is to acculturate, the faster is its rate of so doing. The less organized a group, the slower is its rate of acculturation. The second function of adaptability is its *marginal membership* function. The greater the number of a group's marginal members, the faster its rate of acculturation. More rapid exogamy rates among Japanese Americans than among Chinese Americans, for instance, illustrates this function.[3] Finally, the minority's adaptability rate is influenced by a *similarities of culture function*. The closer in basic norms, customs, and values two cultures are, the easier it is for the minority culture (an immigrant group in this case) to acquire the majority culture and the more likely it is that dominant culture will adopt some aspect of the incoming culture. A foreign language linguistically closer to English enables members of the group to learn the language more readily. This function also concerns such cultural aspects as urban living patterns, clothing styles, child-rearing practices, religious beliefs/practices, and so on.

The model specifies the process as being *simultaneously influenced* by these two major variables. It incorporates a feedback process indicating that as a group acculturates it becomes easier and more desirable for its members so to do. Likewise, members of the dominant culture become more willing to accept as an aspect of their own culture some of the norms and values of the immigrant group. Acculturation is a sharing process, a two-way flow. Therefore, even without changing, the immigrant group members may become more like the dominant members and thus be seen

[3]*See Asian Americans.* Ed. Pyong Gap Min. Newbury Park, CA.: Sage, 1995. Rates of intergroup marriage have long been shown to be important in numerous studies. *See, e.g.*, B. R. Bugelski, "Assimilation Through Intermarriage," *Social Forces*, 40:148-153; J. P. Fitzpatrick, "Intermarriage of Puerto Ricans in New York City," *American Journal of Sociology*, 71:395-406; C. Peach, "Which Triple Melting Pot? A Re-Examination of Ethnic Intermarriage in New Haven, 1900-1950," *Ethnic and Racial Studies*, 3:1-16; and B. B. Wessel, *An Ethnic Survey of Woonsocket, Rhode Island*. Chicago: University of Chicago Press, 1931.

as more acceptable to it. Italian, Chinese, and Mexican foods, for example, become "Americanized." A dominant culture may drastically alter its perceptions of some aspect of the immigrant culture. Norms and customs may suddenly become more acceptable without changing. Since World War II many Chinese norms and customs have come to be viewed as charming, quaint, or desirably exotic rather than as strange, clannish, or inscrutable. This feedback influence increases the willingness of the majority to accept members of the immigrant group. It reinforces their desire to acculturate, thereby speeding up their rate of assimilation. The systems model stresses the dynamic nature of the interrelationship between the variables and functions of the process. The explanatory or even predictive usefulness of the model, however, is contingent upon collecting and analyzing empirical data to serve as operational measures or indicators of the functions, rates, and levels described in the model.

FIGURE 1 A SYSTEMS MODEL OF ASSIMILATION

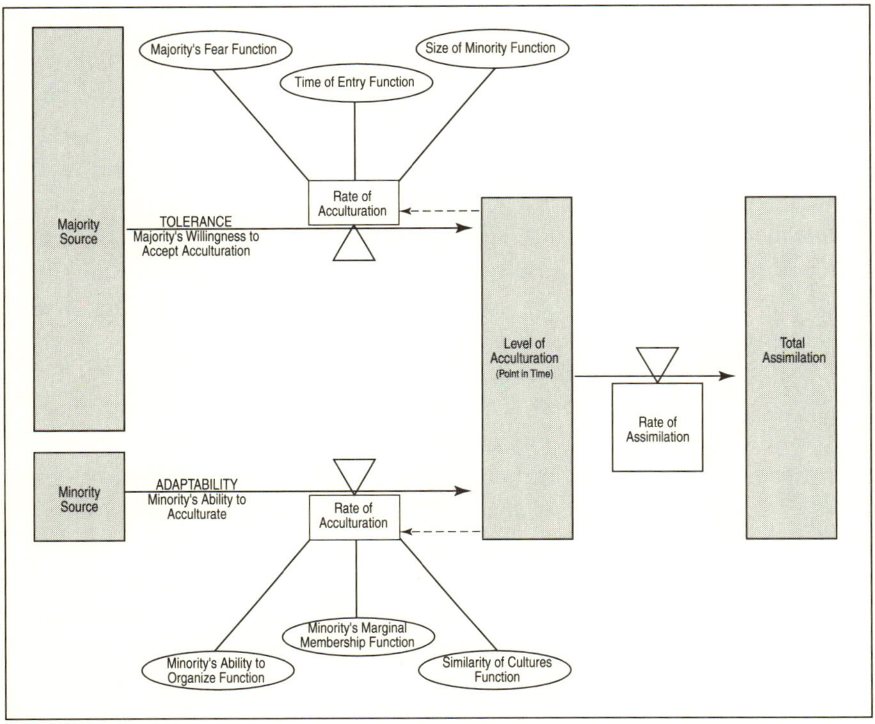


Source: Michael LeMay, *The Perennial Struggle*, Upper Saddle River, N. J.: Prentice-Hall, 2000: 38.

## *RECENT TRENDS IN STUDYING INCORPORATION*

The essays which follow here exemplify and add importantly to a trend among studies of immigration – a focus on the cultural and legal incorporation of immigrants and their descendants. Alejandro Portes and Ruben Rumbaut report on their study of the children of immigrants, data on the second generation. Gillian Stevens presents an interesting essay on language acquisition and language politics in the United States, and Lorraine Minnite discusses a study of the political incorporation of new immigrants in New York. These essays add significantly to a growing body of contributions that establish empirical data that increasingly enable measurement of the processes of cultural, economic, and political incorporation of immigrants and their descendants.

The essay by Alejandro Portes and Ruben Rumbaut reports on and continues their analysis of data drawn from the Children of Immigrants Longitudinal Study (CILS), the largest (at over 5000 teenagers) study of its kind to date in the U. S., including 77 nationalities in two major metropolitan areas: Southern California (San Diego) and South Florida (Miami/ Fort Lauderdale). It covers the period 1992-1996. Their analysis documents the rapid language shift among these children of immigrants, their declining bilingualism, and their increasing fluency in English. They link the language acquisition form of assimilation, moreover, to ethnic self-identity. Their findings show that their respondents turn conventional expectations on their head, a result that they note has potentially significant long-term political consequences. Ethnic identity among San Diego youth of Mexican and Filipino origin increased, apparently in response to the anti-immigrant climate of the period of their study. They note further the "pan-ethnic" group identity gains among Hispanics and Blacks in South Florida. Despite these teenagers' growing awareness of prejudice, they evidence a change over time that has not been toward assimilative mainstream identities, but rather toward a reaffirmation of the immigrant identity for some groups, and a pan-ethnic identity for others. Despite experiences of discrimination, these teen-age respondents had an increasingly positive view of U.S. society. Portes and Rumbaut measure explicitly the progress of their respondents in educational and occupational goals and distinguish factors that enhance or impede that progress. National origin exerted an important influence, with a wide range of differences between ethnic groups in achievement and ambition, portending a significant ethnic segmentation of socioeconomic trajectories as these youth enter the adult labor force. Portes and Rumbaut note that both the family structure and the strength of parent-child bonds are key predictors of successful outcomes. They find that the worst outcomes of achievement and ambition are associated with negative peer pressure groups.

This essay contributes importantly to a growing body of studies that seek to more accurately measure ethnic identity and its change over time as immigrant groups and their children evidence cultural incorporation (Alvarez and Butterfield, 2000; Bedola, 2000; DeSipio, 1996; Newton, 2000; Porter and Washington, 1993; Rumbaut and Cornelius, 1995; and Welch and Sigelman, 2000). This essay and the others cited here add considerably to the insights about language, ethnic identity, and cultural incorporation drawn from the current body of literature. They link in important ways to the studies, previously more often examined, of the economic incorporation of immigrants into the U.S. labor force (Borjas, 1995; Davila and Mora, 2000; Logan *et al.*, 2000; McCarthy and Vernez, 1997).

Gillian Stevens' essay on language acquisition uses interesting cohort demographic measures of English language acquisition and proficiency. It examines a diversity of groups and employs a variety of socio-cultural variables. She demonstrates that the extent to which immigrants become proficient in English is one of the best predictors of their eventual social and economic adaptation to the larger American society. She demonstrates that the nature of the newest (post 1965) immigrants leads scholars to question the applicability of the classic assimilation model. She empirically measures the linkages between language acquisition and the social and economic adaptation of immigrants. Her essay adds to a number of interesting and insightful studies on the effects of language acquisition that similarly employ multivariate analysis techniques of extensive survey databases (Carliner, 2000; Chiswick and Miller, 1995; Davila and Mora, 2000; Espenshade and Fu, 1997; Lazear, 1999; Mora and Davila, 1998).

Lorraine Minnite's essay reports on an innovative study of the political incorporation of new immigrants in New York state. Using data from an extensive state-wide survey, it examines evidence of political incorporation among a wider variety of immigrant groups and delving into a rich array of variables by using the logistic regression analysis for a multivariate analysis of their data. Her study notes some of the somewhat unique aspects of New York's richly diverse immigrant pool, in contrast to studies concentrating on California or Florida, for example, and on Asian and Latino immigrant groups or their children. This study probes politically relevant behavior beyond voting, and distinguishes some effects of group organization or association variables on their political behavior. It notes important differences that can be discerned using their type of telephone survey data instead of using only national survey data such as the Latino National Political Survey or the Current Population Survey. It points out the limitations as well as the value of employing state-wide telephone survey data.

This essay and the study it reports on adds an important contribution to an impressive array of studies of the political incorporation of immigrants or the second generation published during the 1990s. This veritable outburst of studies have to date concentrated mostly on Asian and Latino groups and have used mostly national survey data or site-specific surveys of thousands of respondents to examine political incorporation mostly within the six major immigrant receiving states or within the top ten metropolitan areas in terms of their percent of foreign-born populations (*see, e.g.*, de la Garza and DeSipio, 1996; DeSipio, 1997; 2000; Edmonston and Passel, 1994; Espenshade, 1997; Graves and Lee, 2000; Hritzak and Park, 2000; Iyer, 2000; Michelson, 2000; Money, 2000; Sigelman and Welch, 1993; Welch and Sigelman, 1993; Wong, 2000; Yanez-Chavez, 1996; and Yang, 1994 for a representative although hardly an exhaustive list of such recent studies).

## *CONCLUSION*

These essays, and the growing body of literature to which they add significant contributions, share some common characteristics. They all tend to employ logistic regression models to enable multivariate analysis of the linkages between language acquisition and ethnic identity to job and occupational integration and to gradual political incorporation. They tend, as noted, to concentrate on Latino groups (Mexican, Cuban, Puerto Rican) and Asian groups (Chinese, Japanese, Korean). Most employ either national survey data (*e.g.*, Current Population Survey, American National Election Studies, Latino National Political Survey, PUMS) or large-scale state-wide or metropolitan area databases with thousands of respondents. To date, the best-studied areas are Los Angeles, San Diego, San Francisco, New York state and New York City, Chicago, Miami, and metro-areas in New Jersey.

These studies demonstrate the value of and the need for more carefully constructed, empirically-based analyses of the incorporation processes. Groups that are clearly under-studied from among the newest immigrant groups are the Hmong, Arab-Americans, and Russians. The Minnite essay and the study it reports on demonstrate the value of "combination" studies that blend insights gained from national survey databases with those developed through an original survey of a particular state or region. The Portes/Rumbaut essay shows the value of more comparative studies that examine the process across a greater variety of groups, regions, and over periods of time.

Additional multivariate analysis, such as those discussed here, may help to account for differing rates among geographic regions of the U. S. – contrasting LA and California, for example, with Texas and Florida in how such wedge issues as Proposition 187 and 209 impact the political incorporation among Latino groups. To date the emphasis on studies of metropolitan areas have concentrated, understandably, on those areas that are the greatest receiving areas of immigration. They beg, however, for contrasting studies among states and metropolitan areas with significant but smaller concentrations of immigrants. We need additional studies of metropolitan areas such as New York City and Chicago, with their far richer array and diversity of immigrant groups, with areas such as LA and Miami, where one or at best a few immigrant groups predominate. These essays point out the value of examining the connections between the characteristics of immigrant groups and their children and the specific array of government policy that either enhances or impedes their political incorporation. There are numerous indications in these essays and related studies, for instance, that support the view that the more open and receptive the political system, the more and the faster immigrant groups incorporate. Finally, these studies demonstrate the value of replicating them with data that will be available after the 2000 Census to compare and contrast the effects of the variables they have examined over even more time.

## *REFERENCES*

Alvarez, R. M. and T. L. Butterfield
2000 "The Resurgence of Nativism in California? The Case of Proposition 187 and Illegal Immigration," *Social Science Quarterly*, 81(1):167-179.

Bedolla, L. G.
2000 "They and We: Identity, Gender, and Politics Among Latino Youth in Los Angeles," *Social Science Quarterly*, 81(1):106-122.

Borjas, G. J.
1995 "Assimilation and Change in Cohort Quality Revisited: What Happened to Immigrant Earnings in the 1980s?" *Journal of Labor Economics*, 13(2):201-245.

Carliner, G.
2000 "The Language Ability of U. S. Immigrants: Assimilation and Cohort Effects," *International Migration Review,* 34(1):158-182.

Chiswick, B. and P. Miller
1995 "The Endogeneity Between Language and Earnings: International Analysis," *Journal of Labor Economics,* 13(2):246-288.

Davila, A. and M. T. Mora
2000 "English Skills, Earnings, and the Occupational Sorting of Mexican Americans Along the U.S.-Mexico Border," *International Migration Review,* 34(1):133-157.

———
2000a "The English Skill Acquisition of Hispanic Americans During the 1980s," *Social Science Quarterly,* 81(1):261-275.

de la Garza, R. O. and L. DeSipio, eds.
1996 *Ethnic Ironies: Latino Politics in the 1992 Elections.* Boulder, CO: Westview Press.

DeSipio, L.
2000 "The New Urban Citizen: Electoral Participation Among the Naturalized." In *In Defense of the Alien XXII.* Ed. L.F. Tomasi. New York: Center for Migration Studies.

———
1997 "Migrants and Settlers: Political Opportunities and Political Behaviors Among New Jersey Immigrants." In *Keys to Successful Immigration.* Ed. T. J. Espenshade. Washington, DC: The Urban Institute Press.

———
1996 "Are We Incorporating the Next Generation? Citizenship and Naturalization Among U.S. Immigrants," *Harvard Journal of Hispanic Policy,* 9:7-24.

Edmonston, B. and J. Passel, eds.
1994 *Immigration and Ethnicity: The Integration of America's Newest Arrivals.* Washington, DC: The Urban Institute Press.

Espenshade, T. J. and H. Fu
1997 "An Analysis of English-Language Proficiency Among U. S. Immigrants," *American Sociological Review,* 62:288-305.

Espenshade, T. J., ed.
1997a *Keys to Successful Immigration: Implications of the New Jersey Experience.* Washington, DC: The Urban Institute Press.

Gordon, M.
1964 *Assimilation in American Life.* New York: Oxford University Press.

Graves, S. and J. Lee
2000 "Ethnic Underpinnings of Voting Preferences: Latinos in the 1996 U. S. Senate Election in Texas," *Social Science Quarterly,* 81(1):226-236.

Hritzuk, N. and D. K. Park
2000 "The Question of Latino Participation: From an SES to a Social Structural Explanation," *Social Science Quarterly,* 81(1):151-166.

Iyer, D.
2000 "The Growing Electorate: Asian Pacific American Political Participation in the 1990s and Beyond." In *In Defense of the Alien XXII*. Ed. L.F. Tomasi. New York: Center for Migration Studies.

Lazear, E. P.
1999 "Culture and Language," *Journal of Political Economy*, 107(6):S95-S126.

LeMay, M.
2000 *The Perennial Struggle*. Upper Saddle River, NJ: Prentice-Hall.

Logan, J. *et al.*
2000 "Ethnic Segmentation in the American Metropolis: Increasing Divergence in Economic Incorporation, 1980-1990," *International Migration Review*, 34(1):98-132.

McCarthy, K. and G. Vernez
1997 *Immigration in a Changing Economy: California's Experience*. Santa Monica, CA: The Rand Corporation.

Michelson, M. R.
2000 "Political Efficacy and Electoral Participation of Chicago Latinos." *Social Science Quarterly*, 81(1):136-150.

Money, J.
2000 "New Citizens: Immigrant Electoral Participation and the Host Polity." In *In Defense of the Alien XXII*. Ed. L. F. Tomasi. New York: Center for Migration Studies.

Mora, M. T. and A. Davila
1998 "Gender, Earnings, and the English Skill Acquisition of Hispanic Workers in the United States," *Economic Inquiry*, 36(4):631-644.

Newton, L. Y.
2000 "Why Some Latinos Supported Proposition 187: Testing Economic Threat and Cultural Identity Hypotheses," *Social Science Quarterly*, 81(1):180-193.

Porter, J. R. and R. E. Washington
1993 "Minority Identity and Self-Esteem," *Annual Review of Sociology*, 19:139-161.

Rumbaut, R. and W. E. Cornelius
1995 *California's Immigrant Children*. San Diego, CA. University of California- San Diego: San Diego Center for U.S. – Mexican Studies.

Sigelman, L. and S. Welch
1993 "The Contact Hypothesis Revisited: Interracial Contact and Positive Racial Attitudes," *Social Forces*, 71:781-795.

Welch, S. and L. Sigelman
2000 "Getting to Know You? Latino-Anglo Social Contact," *Social Science Quarterly*, 81(1):67-83.

———
1993 "The Politics of Hispanic Americans: Insights from National Surveys, 1980-1988," *Social Science Quarterly*, 74:76-94.

Wong, J. S.
2000 "The Effects of Length of Residence and Community Context on Political Attitude Formation and Participation Among Asian and Latino Immigrants." In *In Defense of the Alien XXII.* Ed. L. F. Tomasi. New York: Center for Migration Studies.

Yanez-Chavez, A., ed.
1996 *Latino Politics in California.* San Diego, CA. University of California-San Diego: Center for U.S. – Mexican Studies.

Yang, P. Q.
1994 "Explaining Immigration Naturalization," *International Migration Review,* 28(3):449-477.

14

# U.S. Immigration Policy and the Language Characteristics of Immigrants

GILLIAN STEVENS
*University of Illinois at Urbana-Champaign*

Although the United States is firmly dominated by the English language, there are large non-English language populations in the United States. In 1990, over 30 million Americans – almost 1 in 7 – reported speaking a language other than English at home, and almost 14 million were not fully proficient in English (U.S. Bureau of the Census, 1993a). Some speak indigenous languages, others speak languages introduced by immigrants and maintained by their descendants, and still others speak languages established in the country by virtue of the redrawing of boundaries or the incorporation of territories and other sovereign entities.

The use of non-English languages and, in particular, lack of proficiency in English, is, however, much more common among the foreign-born generation than among the native-born generations. While only about 10 percent of the native-born population spoke a minority language in 1990, almost 80 percent of the foreign-born population spoke a minority language and almost half did not speak English fluently (U.S. Bureau of the Census 1993a, 1993b). The ability to speak a non-English language, and the inability to speak English well, is thus heavily identified with the foreign-born population.

In many ways, the enduring stance of the United States towards the language characteristics of its population – in particular, of its foreign-born members – has been one of apparent oversight. Unlike other major immigrant-receiving countries, language characteristics have never been part of federal legislation regulating the flow of immigration.[1] Moreover, the country has never had an overarching official language policy at the federal level that attaches special significance to the English language (or a set of languages) vis-à-vis other languages within the country. The early and continuing silence about the official status of the English language does not mean, however, that the United States considers itself to be multilingual. Many Americans, native-born and foreign-born alike, believe the English language binds the nation together.

At the turn of the 21st century, the United States can therefore be described as having several major attributes. Although firmly dominated by the English language, it contains sizeable non-English language populations, which are largely, although not entirely, a product of recent immigration. It does not have an official policy concerning the English language or non-English languages at the federal level. In this chapter, I discuss how the combination of these attributes have had several consequences.

First, the lack of official policy at the federal level means that the language characteristics of immigrants are largely a by-product of the nature of immigration streams to the United States. Second, the more negative responses toward the language characteristics of immigrants (and of minority language populations in general) become most apparent when immigration levels are high and the proportions of immigrants lacking fluency in English are also high. Third, the lack of an over-arching policy

[1]One exception is the 1986 Immigration Reform and Control Act, which provided an opportunity for undocumented aliens to gain legal status if they met certain conditions. One of the conditions was a demonstration of English literacy. *See* Terdy and Spener (1990) for a description of the conditions.

about language skills of potential immigrants means that public and political responses to the language skills (or lack of them) of immigrants occur at local or state levels and are highly variable.

## *IMMIGRATION AND LANGUAGE, 1600s-1800s*

The first few waves of immigrants to the United States, during the 1600s, were English immigrants. The first major wave consisted of Puritans, the second wave of a few Royalists and many indentured servants, the third wave of English Quakers, and the fourth wave of persons of English, Scottish, and Scots-Irish ancestry. Although these waves of immigrants each had a distinctive culture, they shared a commitment to the English language (Fischer, 1989). Later immigrant streams, however, began to draw from non-English language countries.

Scholars have debated the reasons underlying the early absence of a language policy in the face of the immigration of non-English language speakers. Some argue that the predominance of English in the general American population meant there was no need to formalize the position of English through an official policy. Some point out the awkwardness of formally declaring English as an official language while formally separating from England. Others argue that the language in which the Declaration of Independence was written is *prima facie* evidence that the writers intended English to be the official language of the country (*e.g.*, Hernández-Chávez, 1995; Leibowitz, 1984).

Heath (1992) argues that political leaders recognized immigrants' reliance on languages other than English as a social problem, but also viewed fluency in languages other than English as pragmatic tools of access to codes of law, institutions, and written sources of learning. It was in this pragmatic vein that Benjamin Rush, a signer of the Declaration of Independence, urged that German and French be taught in America's "English schools" (Heath, 1992). In a similar vein, Thomas Jefferson presciently advised his nephew and young correspondents to learn Spanish because of the increasing importance of diplomatic relations with Spain and Spanish America (1787-1853). The general attitude towards languages other than English – and towards continued immigration – was one of tolerance and even encouragement.

## *IMMIGRATION AND LANGUAGE, 1800s – PRESENT*

In the early part of the 1800s, U.S. government agencies began tallying and publishing data on immigration. By the 1820s, these data, although incomplete (immigration from Mexico, for example, is not included), show that the numbers of immigrants from non-English language countries had become sizeable. Figure 1 graphs the numbers of immigrants legally admitted to the United States by the language characteristics of their country of origin. The overall shape of the graph is familiar. It shows the large numbers of immigrants admitted to the country in the late 1800s with peaks in the 1880s and 1900s, the rapid decline in immigration beginning in the 1910s, the virtual cessation of immigration during the 1930s and 1940s, and the rapid increases in immigration occurring after the 1960s.

FIGURE 1 LEGALLY ADMITTED IMMIGRANTS BY DECADE AND LANGUAGE CHARACTERISTICS OF COUNTRY OF ORIGIN

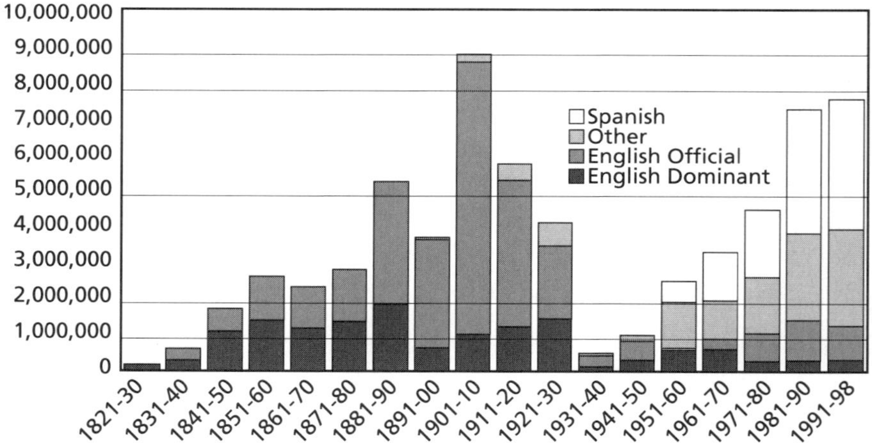


Source: Immigration and Naturalization Service, 2000. Statistical Yearbook of the Immigration and Naturalization Service, 1998, D.C.: U.S. Government Printing.

What may be unfamiliar is the categorization of the immigrant streams. The categories refer to the language characteristics of the immigrants' countries of origin. A more accurate description of immigrants' language characteristics – their "mother tongue" or their level of proficiency in English – would require information on individuals rather than on the characteristics of their countries of origin. Not all immigrants from a specified country speak the same language or share a level of proficiency in English. Unfortunately, the historic data on immigrants' language characteristics are limited. The Immigration and Naturalization Service does not gather information on the language skills of legally admitted immigrants (perhaps because immigration policy is silent about language). The U.S. Bureau of the Census has gathered and published information on the English skills of the foreign-born population only episodically after 1880 (Stevens, 1999a). I therefore use contemporary data to assess the correspondence between immigrants' levels of proficiency in English upon arrival in the U.S. and the language characteristics of their country of origin.

## *LANGUAGE CHARACTERISTICS OF COUNTRIES OF ORIGIN*

The categories used in Figure 1 are (i) "English dominant," (ii) "English official," (iii) "Spanish," and (iv) "Other." "English dominant" refers to countries such as the UK, Canada, Australia and New Zealand in which English is a dominant language spoken by the general population. "English official" refers to countries such as India, and some African or Caribbean countries such as South Africa in which English is an official language although it is not predominantly spoken by the country's residents. "Spanish" refers to countries such as Mexico, Spain, and most of the Latin American countries, in which English is neither a dominant nor an official language and Spanish is the dominant language. This category is separate from the last category, "Other," which refers to countries in which English is neither a dominant nor an official language, and Spanish is not a dominant language.

Table 1 provides the rationale for linking the language characteristics of immigrants' countries of origin with individual immigrants' levels of proficiency in English shortly after their arrival in the United States. The data are from the 1989 Current Population Survey and refer to immigrants who had arrived in the country in 1987-1989 and who therefore had not had much time to learn English in the United States.

Overall, only about half of the recently arrived immigrants speak English "well" or "very well," although the percentages vary widely by the official or dominant language of their country of birth. Almost all of the immigrants from countries dominated by the English language speak English "very well"[2] while most immigrants from countries in which English is an official language speak English "well" or "very well." In contrast,

[2]Immigrants who reported speaking only English at home were not asked to evaluate their level of proficiency in English but are presumed to be fluent speakers of English.

**TABLE 1**
**THE PERCENTAGES OF RECENT IMMIGRANTS REPORTING EACH LEVEL OF PROFICIENCY IN ENGLISH BY OFFICIAL OR DOMINANT LANGUAGE OF THEIR COUNTRY OF BIRTH**

| | Official or Dominant Language of Immigrant's Country of Birth[1] | | | | |
|---|---|---|---|---|---|
| Speaks English | Total | English Dominant | English Official | Spanish Dominant | Other |
| Not well at all | 21.7 | .0 | .0 | 41.6 | 14.4 |
| Not well | 30.1 | .0 | 9.0 | 40.0 | 32.9 |
| Well | 18.5 | 3.3 | 19.8 | 13.0 | 25.9 |
| Very well[2] | 29.7 | 96.7 | 71.2 | 5.4 | 26.8 |
| Total | 100.0 | 100.0 | 100.0 | 100.0 | 100.0 |

Source: Jasso *et al.*, 2000, Demography.
1 See text for description of categories.
2 Includes immigrants who stated that they spoke only English at home and therefore did not answer the question on English proficiency.

most immigrants from countries in which English is neither a dominant nor official language report low levels of proficiency in English. Levels of English proficiency are particularly low among newly arrived immigrants from Spanish-language countries even when compared with immigrants from countries dominated by some other non-English language. Presuming that the relationship between immigrants' skills in English and the language characteristics of their country of origin has remained fairly stable with the passage of time, the table provides a basis for describing the changing linguistic skills of immigrants over the last century and a half. Returning to Figure 1, it is easy to see the continuing migration from English-language dominated countries (particularly from Ireland) to the U.S. during the first part of the 1800s. Until the mid-1800s, non-English languages were tolerated and sometimes encouraged. There were, for example, numerous non-English language schools, as well as non-English language school boards, in Ohio, Pennsylvania, and Wisconsin. Many states, such as Colorado, Illinois, Indiana, Iowa, Kentucky, Ohio, Missouri, Texas, and Wisconsin, routinely published state documents in languages other than English.

The latter half of the 1800s, however, saw a shift in the relative numbers of immigrants from English dominant countries to immigrants from countries dominated by other languages. The numbers of immigrants from non-English language countries, such as Poland and Italy, grew rapidly. As immigration streams continued to shift away from countries dominated by English, the tolerance of non-English languages began to wane. Inspired in part by antipathy towards Catholic immigrants, the states of Wisconsin and Illinois passed English-only instruction laws for both public and parochial schools. States enacted language restrictions in response to pressures from native laborers who resented the competition of foreigners. In 1897, for example, Pennsylvania imposed an English-speaking requirement for coal miners – a measure that especially targeted Italians and Hungarians. Concurrently, immigration policy began to incorporate provisions designed to discourage or halt immigrants from specified countries or areas – all of which happened to be non-English speaking. In 1906, the federal government instituted proficiency in English as a requirement for the naturalization of foreign-born residents.

The dramatic increase in the absolute numbers of immigrants just before and after the turn of the century, and the shift in the national origins of the immigrants, was followed by the "Americanization" movement, which reached its zenith in the 1910s. The leaders of the Americanization movement hoped to mold foreigners into good Americans by teaching them civics, English, and the values of American society (Dixon, 1916). It was a movement of "structured experiences" (Knobel, 1996). Settlement houses, schools, and the YMCA, all offered numerous evening programs aimed at Americanizing foreigners. In practice, however, the main focus of these programs was the teaching of English, considered to be the "first step" in the assimilation of "aliens" (Drachsler, 1920; Hartmann, 1985:24). Near the beginning of the Americanization movement, the rhetoric underlying the teaching of English to immigrants emphasized the utility of English for national unity.

"To be great a nation need not be of one blood, it must be of one mind . . . . If we think together, we can act together, and the organ of common thought and action is common language" (Commons, 1907).

Embracing the philosophy of Americanization, the Federal Bureau of Labor produced publications and patriotic events aimed at immigrant workers. The value of teaching English to "alien-born" workers and so increasing their social opportunities – as well as their work productivity – was trumpeted (Leiserson, 1971). The job-related benefits of learning English were advertised widely. In the city of Syracuse, for example, forty thousand handbills, printed in five languages (English, Polish, Italian, Yiddish, and German) read:

> Can you speak well? Do you want to be an American citizen? It is hard to get a job in America without English. Go to night school and learn it! (Dixon, 1916:23)

By the end of WWI, the movement had became coercive. Theodore Roosevelt, one of the most strident voices in the Americanization movement, argued for the deportation of any immigrant who had not learned English.

> I would have the Government provide that every immigrant be required to learn English, with instruction furnished free. If after five years he has not learned it, let him be returned to the country from which he came. (Roosevelt cited in Drachsler (1920))

There were several attempts to institute a literacy test *in English* for prospective immigrants, although all were vetoed. But by 1930, levels of immigration had subsided because of the implementation of the 1921 and 1924 National Quota Acts. The new immigration policy explicitly referred to national origins, rather than to language per se, but the correspondence between national origins and language is close, and was recognized at the time (Garis, 1927).

During the 1930s and 1940s immigration ground to a virtual halt first because of the Great Depression and then because of the political and social turmoil produced by World War II. Levels of immigration remained low until the mid-1960s. The low levels of immigration during the mid 20th century, and the fact that a significant proportion of the arrivals were English speakers from countries such as Canada, shrank the numbers of immigrants living in the United States who spoke a non-English language. Non-English language populations, and the tie between immigration and non-English languages, thus disappeared from view.

A general shift in federal policy towards civil rights in the 1960s resulted in the passage of important legislation affecting minority populations and minority language populations in particular. The Bilingual Education Act in the late 1960s provided, for example, federal support to local educational agencies for the instruction of minority language students. The 1975 amendment to the Voting Rights Act of 1965 mandated the use of non-English language ballots when the votes of selected language groups[3] constituted more than 5% of the electorate in a voting district. The Hart-Cellar Act, which emphasized family reunification rather than national origins, and thus implicitly de-emphasized language skills, was passed in 1965 and fully implemented in 1968.

High levels of immigration returned after the passage and implementation of the Hart-Cellar Act. During the 1970s, almost 4 million immigrants

[3]A language minority group member was defined as a person of American Indian, Asian American, Alaskan Native, or of Spanish heritage.

entered the country. An additional 7 million entered during the 1980s and at least 8 million more entered during the early and mid 1990s (Immigration and Naturalization Service, 2000). This increase in the volume of immigration was accompanied by an explicit shift in the national origins of immigrants and thus an underlying shift in the distribution of English language skills among new immigrants.

As the proportions of immigrants from Spanish-language countries, and from countries dominated by some other non-English language increased, the overall proportion of immigrants fluent in English declined. The general increases since the 1960s in the absolute numbers and proportions of legally admitted immigrants from Spanish-language and other non-English language countries can be seen in Figure 1. The increases in the numbers and proportions of new arrivals from Spanish-language countries (which send migrants with particularly low levels of proficiency in English) are under-stated because the figure refers only to legally admitted immigrants and so it omits the large numbers of undocumented aliens entering the country during the time period. Using 1980 and 1990 census data, which include the entire foreign-born population, Carliner (2000) estimates that the percentage of foreign-born persons entering the country who were fluent in English declined by an average of .3 percentage points each year between 1950 and 1990.

The immigration streams around the beginning and near the end of the 20th century share a number of features. In each case, the volume of immigration was substantially greater than the decades before. In each case, the shift in the national origins of immigrants was unanticipated, and in each case there were large increases in the numbers and proportions of immigrants who – judging from their countries of origin – were apt to lack fluency in English.

The general growth in immigration and the shift in the national origins of immigrants after implementation of the 1965 immigration act is a product of numerous factors, not just changes in formal immigration policy. However, the provisions of the act appear to have played at least a minor role in helping shift the distribution of English skills among legally admitted immigrants.

Table 2 shows the influence of the details of the formal immigration policy on the language skills of immigrants by visa category. Among immigrants entering through "employment" provisions, over 40 percent speak English "very well." However, much lower proportions of immigrants entering as spouses, or as close relatives (*e.g.*, siblings), and particularly

**TABLE 2**
**English Language Deficiency and Category of Entry into the U.S.: Immigrants Who Entered the U.S. in 1996**

| Visa Category | % Not Speaking English "Very Well" |
|---|---|
| Spouse of US citizen | 66.5 |
| Sibling: Principal & spouse | 100.00 |
| Employment: Principal & spouse | 58.3 |
| Refugee/Asylee: Principal & spouse | 98.0 |
| Diversity Principal & spouse | 73.5 |
| Other | 78.9 |
| All immigrants aged 18-39 | 73.6 |

Source: Jasso et al., 2000, *Demography*.

immigrants entering as refugees or asylees speak English "very well."

Early in the 20th century, the increasing levels of immigration from "new" (and non-English language) countries of origin were followed by the "Americanization" movement, which focused on encouraging and then coercing immigrants to learn English. The high levels of immigration in the 1970s through the 1990s have been accompanied by a backlash against the stream of legislation in the 1960s and 1970s supporting minority languages in various American institutions. Before 1980, for example, only three states had official language statutes. By 1998, twenty five states[4] had adopted official-English legislation (U.S. English Inc., 1998). Meanwhile, in 1996, the U.S. Congress voted on (and the House approved) a bill declaring English the sole language of official government business (Crawford, 1998). In 1999, the House approved a bill that constrains states' abilities to use Title VII funds for bilingual educational programs (Zehr, 1999). In 1994, the U.S. Commission on Immigration Reform reaffirmed the benefits of "Americanization" and the importance of immigrants becoming proficient in English:

> Immigration carries with it obligations to embrace the common core of the American civic culture, to become able to communicate – to the extent possible – in English with other citizens and residents . . . . (U.S. Commission on Immigration Reform (1994:115))

## *CONCLUSIONS*

In this chapter, I started with several general statements. Although the

[4]Alabama (1990), Alaska (1998), Arkansas (1987), California (1986), Colorado (1988), Florida (1988), Georgia (1986 and 1996), Hawaii (1978), Illinois (1969), Indiana (1984), Kentucky (1984), Louisiana (1811), Massachusetts (1975), Mississippi (1987), Missouri (1998), Montana (1995), Nebraska (1920), New Hampshire (1995), North Carolina (1987), North Dakota (1987), South Carolina (1987), South Dakota (1995), Tennessee (1984), Virginia (1981 and 1996), Wyoming (1996).

United States is considered to be an English-speaking country, it contains sizeable non-English language populations, which are largely, although not entirely, a product of recent immigration. The country does not, however, have an official stance towards non-English languages and does not grant a special status to English. In particular, potential immigrants are not evaluated on the basis of their language skills.

The combination of these general characteristics has several consequences. First, the lack of attention paid to the language skills of potential immigrants means the language characteristics of new immigrants are often a by-product of changes in immigration policy. The largely unanticipated shifts in the national origins of immigrants after the implementation of the 1965 Immigration Act, for example, resulted in higher proportions of immigrants from countries in which English was neither a dominant or an official language. Post-1965 immigrants are therefore less likely than immigrants entering during the middle part of the century to have entered the U.S. with high levels of proficiency in English.

General attitudes towards immigrants are the end product of a wide and complex array of factors. One persistent, and according to Higham (1999), under-appreciated factor, is demographic: the aggregate features of the foreign-born population, *e.g.*, size and concentration. Historically, decades of low levels of immigration have been marked by a general tolerance – and sometimes appreciation – of immigrants and their distinctive cultural attributes, while decades of increasing levels of immigration have often been marked by evidence of nativism. The influx of non-English speaking immigrants around the turn of the 20th century was followed by increasing levels of nativism and increasingly restrictive legislation affecting minority language populations. The mid-century lull in immigration in turn was followed by a quieting of concerns about immigrants and non-English languages. The more recent upturn in levels of immigration has re-awakened questions surrounding the role of English in United States and the treatment of minority language populations, especially immigrant minority language populations. It is unlikely that the recent upturn in immigration will be followed by a lull anytime soon.

Although nativism is a complex phenomenon that varies over time, one common feature is the use of cultural and racial criteria to identify the foreigners as different and un-American. An increase in numbers of new immigrants from non-English speaking countries means an increase in the number of foreign-born persons who have not yet had the time and opportunities to learn English and therefore an increase in the proportion of non-English speakers among the foreign-born population. The inability to speak the nation's "common" language becomes a convenient way to demarcate the boundary between Americans and "foreigners." In 1913, for example, the U.S. Bureau of the Census (1913:1267-68) expressed concern about the growing number of immigrants who lacked proficiency in English and pointed to the "new" immigrant streams from Southern and Eastern Europe as the source of the problem. More recently, the increases in the numbers of new immigrants from non-English language countries have re-awakened the lament that immigrants are not learning English. Research based on historic and contemporary data show that immigrants and their children quickly become more proficient in English the longer they live in the United States (*e.g.*, Espenshade and Fu, 1997; Labov, 1999; Stevens 1999b). Yet recent immigrants in general have been vilified as not setting the learning of English as a high priority, and Hispanic immigrants have been singled out as particularly unwilling to learn English (*e.g.*, Lam and Imhoff, 1985: 99-124).

Expressions of concern about the language attributes of immigrants often invoke the need for a shared language for national cohesion. Yet the lack of an official national policy allows the acquisition of skills in English to be perceived as the personal responsibility of the immigrants rather than the responsibility of the nation as a whole. Neither the United States as the receiving country, nor major immigrant-receiving areas within the country, take on the formal responsibility in helping immigrants become fluent in English. Instead, concerns are raised about the "huge" costs of providing special services such as bilingual education, government documents in languages other than English, multilingual ballots, and translators (*e.g.*, Unz and Tuchman, 1998; Gribbon, 2000). Many analysts argue that the cost quotations are inflated and that the focus on language characteristics belies a racist focus on non-English speakers' national origins (Chen, 1995).

Because the public and political responses to immigrants' language skills are not governed by an overarching national policy governing immigration or the reception of immigrants, the responses are largely *ad hoc*, pertain to particular contexts, and are highly variable. One result of the *ad hoc* and often highly politicized reactions to immigrants' language skills is a high degree of variance across time and across local or state areas in policy. While twenty-five states have "Official English" legislation, for example, twenty-five states do not. The passage of Proposition 227 in California in 1998 undermined the provision of bilingual educational programs.

I began by saying that the longstanding attitude of the United States towards the language characteristics of the potential immigrants has been one of apparent oversight. Strictly speaking, at least at the federal level, this statement has some truth. In reality, however, because the language skills of immigrants are so important to the immigrants themselves and to the wider society, they cannot be, and are not, overlooked. Immigration policy, or lack of it, affects the distribution of language skills among newly entering immigrants. In times of high levels of immigration, the common equating of low English skills with "foreignness" allows immigrants to be criticized for what is often a temporary inability to communicate in the nation's dominant language. The patchwork of public and political responses to immigrants' language skills is a direct reflection of the difficulties – and benefits – of welcoming America's newest members in a country that prides itself on being an immigrant nation while maintaining its position, although not recognized in federal policy, as an English-speaking nation.

## *REFERENCES*

Carliner, G.
2000 "The Language Ability of U.S. Immigrants: Assimilation and Cohort Effects," *International Migration Review,* 34(1):158-182.

Chen, E. M.
1995 "Implications of 'Official English' Legislation Before the United States House of Representatives Committee on Economic and Educational Opportunities Subcommittee on Early Childhood, Youth and Families." American Civil Liberties Union. Available online at: www.aclu.org/congress/chen.html

Commons, J. R.
1907 *Races and Immigrants in America.* New York: Macmillan Publishing Company.

Crawford, J.
1998 "Anatomy of the English-Only Movement: Social and Ideological Sources of Language Restrictionism in the United States." In *Language Legislation and Linguistic Rights.* Ed. D. A. Kibbee. Amsterdam: John Benjamins.

Dixon, R.
1916 *Americanization.* New York: Macmillan Publishing Company.

Drachsler, J.
1920 *Democracy and Assimilation. The Blending of Immigrant Heritages in America.* New York: Macmillan Publishing Company.

Fischer, D. H.
1989 *Albion's Seed: Four British Folkways in America.* New York: Oxford University Press.

Garis, R. L.
1927 *Immigration Restriction.* New York: Macmillian Publishing Company.

Gribbin, A.
2000 "Learning English not a Priority for Immigrants." *The Washington Times*, May 30.

Hartmann, E. G.
1967
(1948) *The Movement to Americanize the Immigrant.* New York: AMS Press.

Heath, S. B.
1992 "Why No Official Tongue?" In *Language Loyalties.* Ed. J. Crawford. Chicago: University Of Chicago Press. Pp. 20-30.

Hernández-Chávez, E.
1995 "Language Policy in the United States: A History of Cultural Genocide." In *Linguistic Human Rights: Overcoming Linguistic Discrimination.* Ed. R. Phillipson, T. Skutnabb-Kangas, and M. Rannut. New York: Mouton de Gruyter.

Higham, J.
1999 "Instead of a Sequel, or, How I Lost My Subject." In *The Handbook of International Migration.* Ed. C. Hirschman, P. Kasinitz, and J. DeWind. New York: Russell Sage Foundation.

Immigration and Naturalization Service
2000 *Statistical Yearbook of the Immigration and Naturalization Service, 1998.* Washington, DC: U.S. Government Printing Office.

Jasso, G., D. S. Massey, M. R. Rosenzweig, and J. P. Smith
2000 "The New Immigrant Pilot Survey (NIS-P): Overview and New Findings about U.S. Legal Immigrants at Admission," *Demography*, 37:127-138.

Jefferson, T.
1878
(1853-54) *The Writings of Thomas Jefferson.* Vol. II. Washington, DC: United States Congress.

Knobel, D. M.
1996 "America for the Americans: the Nativist Movement in the United States." In *Social Movements Past and Present.* Ed. R. D. Benford. New York:

Labov, T.
1998 "English Acquisition by Immigrants to the United States at the Beginning of the Twentieth Century," *American Speech*, 73:368-398.

Lamm, R. D. and G. Imhoff
1985 *The Immigration Time Bomb.* New York: Truman Talley Books.

Leibowitz, A. H.
1984 "The Official Character of Language in the United States: Literacy Requirements for Immigration, Citizenship, and Entrance into American Life," *Aztlan*, 15:25-70.

Leiserson, W. M.
1971 "Adjusting Immigrant and Industry." In *The Acculturation of Immigrant Groups into American Society.* Ed. W. S. Bernard. Montclair, NJ: Patterson Smith.

Portes, A. and R. G. Rumbaut
1996 *Immigrant America. A Portrait.* Berkeley: University of California Press.

Roosevelt, T.
1992
(1917) "One Flag, One Language." In *Language Loyalty.* Ed. J. Crawford. Chicago: University of Chicago Press. Pp. 84-85.

Stevens, G.
1999a "A Century of U.S. Censuses and the Language Characteristics of Immigrants," *Demography,* 36:387-397.

———
1999b "Age at Immigration and Second Language Proficiency Among Foreign-born Adults," *Language in Society,* 28:555-578.

Terdy, D. and D. Spener
1990 "English Language Literacy and Other Requirements of the Amnesty Program. ERIC Q & A." Washington, DC: Office of Educational Research and Improvement.

U.S. Bureau of the Census
1993a 1990 Census of Population and Housing. Summary Social, Economic, and Housing Characteristics. 1990 CP-2-1. Washington, DC: Bureau of the Census.

———
1993b 1990 Census of Population. The Foreign-Born Population in the United States. 1990 CP-3-1. Washington, DC: Bureau of the Census.

———
1913 Thirteenth Census of the United States Taken in the Year 1910. Vol. 1. Population 1910. General Report and Analysis. Washington, DC: Government Printing Office.

U.S. Commission on Immigration Reform
1994 *U.S. Immigration Policy: Restoring Credibility.* Washington, DC: U.S. Government Printing Office. Also available online.

U.S. English, Inc.
1998 U.S. English Home Page. http://www.us-english.org/index.html

Unz, R. and G. M. Tuchman
1998 "The Unz Initiative." Available online at: http://www.catesol.org/unztext.html

Zehr, M. A.
1999 "Bilingual Ed. Advocates Decry Changes to Title VII." Education Week 11/3/99. Available online at: www.edweek.org/ew/ewstory.cfm?sug=101ing.h19

15

# The Political Participation of Immigrants in New York[1]

LORRAINE C. MINNITE
*Barnard College, Columbia University*

JENNIFER HOLDAWAY
RONALD HAYDUK
*City University of New York*

[1]The authors would like to thank Robert Y. Shapiro, Michael LeMay, and John Mollenkopf for their many helpful comments on an earlier draft of this paper prepared for presentation at the 1999 Annual Meeting of the American Political Science Association. Any errors are the sole responsibility of the authors. The survey analyzed in this paper was conducted at the 1199 Communications Center, Inc. (33 West 42nd Street, New York, New York 10036) through generous research support provided by Local 1199, National Health and Human Services Employees Union, SEIU/AFL-CIO.

## *INTRODUCTION*

Since 1965 the U.S. has experienced the greatest wave of immigration since the turn of the last century. Over the last thirty years, the number of immigrants living in the U.S. has nearly tripled to a historically unprecedented 26.3 million people (Camarota, 1999).[2] Almost as important as the numerical increase is the change in the country of origin of the post-1965 immigrants who come mostly from Latin America, Asia and the Caribbean. More than a third are from Mexico, Central America, Cuba, and the Dominican Republic, and nearly 20 percent from Asia — particularly China and the Philippines. (Fix and Passel, 1994).

The demographic changes spurred by this new immigration have far-reaching political implications, reviving questions of pluralism and the openness of the American political system to new constituencies. As new immigrants naturalize and the second generation children of earlier cohorts reach adulthood, the pool of immigrant voters is increasing. There are at least 10 million legal aliens living in the U.S. who are potential citizens and voters (Raskin, 1993; Fix and Passel, 1994; Passel and Clark, 1998).[3]

Geographically, most immigrants entering the U.S. since 1965 have gone to just six states: California, New York, Florida, Texas, Illinois, and New Jersey, with more than half of all new arrivals over the last two decades settling in the metropolitan areas of several big cities: Los Angeles, New York, Miami, Anaheim, Chicago, Washington D.C., Houston, and San Francisco (Fix and Passel, 1994; Portes and Rumbaut, 1996). These immigrant receiving states and cities play a large role in determining political representation both in Congress and in the electoral college for the presidency, and population growth caused by immigration will also affect the apportionment of seats in the House (Poston *et al.*, 1998).[4] At the state and local level, where they make up a larger proportion of the potential electorate,

[2]This number is derived from the March 1998 Current Population Survey, which is believed to underestimate the size of the foreign born population by five to ten percent (see Camarota, 1999, 11, n. 1).

[3]According to the November 1996 Current Population Survey, 15.5 percent of non-voters (an estimated 13.7 million people) said that they did not vote because they were not citizens (U.S. Department of Commerce, 1997).

[4]Thirteen of the 31 seats that changed hands in 1990 or will change in 2000 will do so because of recent immigration. Low immigrant states lose seats and high immigration states either gain them or lose fewer seats than they otherwise would to population loss. This figure may be an underestimate because it does not include the effect children born to recent immigrants have on congressional apportionment.

immigrants can have an even greater impact, reshaping group relations and creating new political fault lines in urban politics.

Yet despite their growing potential significance for electoral outcomes and policymaking, we know little about how contemporary immigrants are being absorbed into the U.S. political system. Although the number of empirical and ethnographic studies of new immigrants has increased over the last decade, the available data remain thin. This paper contributes to our understanding of the political incorporation of new immigrants in the U.S. through a study of immigrant political participation in New York State.

## *IMMIGRANTS IN NEW YORK*

New York State has an estimated foreign born population of 3.8 million people or 21 percent of the state's population, second only to California (U.S. Department of Commerce, 1998). The profile of immigrants in New York is distinctive in several important ways. The state has a large third generation population, mostly of European descent, and sizable African American and Puerto Rican populations. The second generation includes a high proportion of the "old" second generation, children of immigrants who arrived in the early years of the twentieth century.

Since 1965, a very heterogeneous flow of "new" immigrants has come to New York State. No one group dominates and, in addition to migrants from East and South Asia, the Caribbean, and Central and South America, the foreign born population includes many Europeans, primarily from Eastern Europe and the countries of the former Soviet Union.[5] Latinos are a large and important ethnic group in the state and in New York City, but New York's foreign born population is considerably less Latino than that of California, Texas and Florida because, until recently, the majority of Latinos in New York were Puerto Rican.[6] New York City's Mexican population is relatively small, but growing rapidly; the largest *foreign born* Latino group in New York, however, is Dominican (Hernandez and Rivera-Batiz, 1997).

[5]According to Dr. Joseph P. Salvo, Director of the Population Division of the New York City Department of City Planning, in the 1995-96 period, the latest period for which there is data, people from the countries of the former Soviet Union constituted the single largest group of new immigrants entering New York City annually, with 85 percent of them entering as refugees.

[6]In 1960, Puerto Ricans were 80.9 percent of all Latinos in New York City. As immigration from the Dominican Republic and Central America increased over the last three decades, the Puerto Rican share of the Latino population shrank to 67.5 percent in 1970, 61.2 percent in 1980, to approximately 44 percent today (New York City Department of City Planning, 1994; Haslip-Viera, 1996; Miranda and Muzzio, 1997).

## *IMMIGRANT POLITICAL PARTICIPATION: ONE PATH OR MANY?*

Debates about the political behavior of immigrants center on three questions: 1) To what extent are immigrants being incorporated or assimilated into the political system? 2) What are the factors that impede or promote their participation? and 3) What are the implications of immigrant participation for electoral outcomes and public policy?

The political incorporation of immigrants has often been discussed as one piece of a larger process of assimilation in which immigrants eventually make a break from their country of origin and become "American" (Gordon, 1964; Hirschman, 1983). As ethnic groups work their way into the economic mainstream and achieve income parity with the native born, their separate ethnic identity and attachments weaken, and they adopt the characteristics and tastes of the dominant culture. The traditional assimilation model assumes that ethnic groups become politically incorporated in similar ways, gaining citizenship, participating in the political process and, over generations, becoming indistinguishable in their attitudes and behavior from the native born (Dahl, 1961). In support of the gradual or generational assimilation model, political scientists point to the fact that new immigrants – whether turn-of-the-century or recent immigrants – tend to vote less than native born citizens (Burnham, 1965; Burner, 1975).[7] They also argue that "ethnic voting" – ethnic patterns of partisanship and policy preferences – is strongest for the first generation and declines progressively as the group assimilates (Dahl, 1961; Campbell *et al.*, 1960).

The assimilationist model has been criticized on several grounds. Some have questioned its historical accuracy, challenging the claim that earlier immigrants voted at lower rates than native born citizens, at least in urban areas (Gamm, 1986; Tuckel and Maisel, 1994). Moreover, some have argued that different ethnic immigrant groups apparently voted at different rates (Erie, 1988; Shefter, 1994), making broad generalizations difficult. Others have argued that ethnic allegiances persisted among earlier immigrants and carried over into the second and third generations (Wolfinger, 1965). McNickle claims that in New York City an ethnic analy-

[7]Explanations for low voting rates include apathy (Campbell *et al.*, 1960), the absence of popular democratic traditions (Ladd, 1970), the introduction of electoral reforms such as voter registration (Converse, 1972; Rusk, 1974) or the effective disenfranchisement of eligible voters (Piven and Cloward, 1988). *See* DeSipio (1998) for the contemporary period.

sis of the number and direction of votes cast by a group still "explains electoral results with more power and consistency than any other form of analysis" (McNickle, 1993:2).

Many who do not question the validity of the assimilation thesis for earlier European immigrants nonetheless argue that post-1965 immigrants cannot be expected to follow the same trajectory but will rather experience "segmented" assimilation (Portes and Zhou, 1993). Because the new arrivals come mostly from non-European countries, they may experience prejudice and discrimination in the U.S. beyond the first generation.[8] Furthermore, economic restructuring and the loss of unionized manufacturing jobs may limit the employment opportunities available to them, channeling some into the marginal sectors of the economy (Gans, 1992; Waters and Eschbach, 1995; Portes and Rumbaut, 1996). There is considerable debate over the role that race and ethnicity, human and social capital, and the changing opportunity structures of the receiving society play in shaping the economic and social incorporation of the new immigrants, but many scholars concur that the process of "assimilation" may work differently for different racial and ethnic groups (Alba and Nee, 1997; Bonilla-Silva, 1997; DeWind and Kasinitz, 1997; Perlmann and Waldinger, 1997).

Similarly, the new immigrants may experience differential political incorporation both in terms of their level of participation and the form it takes. Those who achieve upward mobility may become politically indistinguishable from native born white citizens, while those who are marginalized may become more like traditionally excluded U.S. born minorities. Through a process that has been described as "reactive ethnicity," group identity may be intensified (and sometimes created) by the experience of discrimination and thwarted mobility in the U.S. (Portes and Zhou, 1993). This may result in alienation and depressed participation; it may also lead to the formation of ethnic-based political organizations that operate outside the mainstream political institutions (Yancey, Eriksen and Juliani, 1976; Portes and Bach, 1985).[9] The emergence of transnational communities, supported by the constant flow of new arrivals and

[8]Many nineteenth and early twentieth century immigrants were not regarded as "white" at the time of their arrival, but became so as a result of violent social conflict and historical processes forging different patterns of ethnic group identity (Saxton, 1990; Roediger, 1991; Ignatiev, 1995).

[9]Portes and Rumbaut (1996) point out how many Mexican American political organizations, from radical groups to the more moderate Mexican American Legal Defense and Education Fund, modeled themselves on African American equivalents. A similar pattern is evident among some sectors of the Asian American community.

improved transportation and communication, may also enable immigrants to maintain stronger ties to their home countries, perhaps delaying incorporation or fostering a generation of immigrants with dual political allegiances (Glick-Schiller, Basch and Szanton Blanc, 1992). In terms of political behavior, then, segmented assimilation may result in a range of outcomes that differ across groups.

The current wave of renewed immigration is still too recent to assess fully the process of political incorporation or assimilation, but existing work reveals complex trends. Several researchers have found that most newly naturalized immigrant adults register and vote at slightly lower rates than natives (DeSipio, 1998; Lien, 1998; Mollenkopf, Ross and Olson, 1999) but there appear to be substantial differences in voting patterns across ethnic groups. Latino immigrants naturalize later than Asian Americans, for example, but have significantly higher rates of voter registration and turnout than Asian Americans (Brackman and Erie, 1994). Nor do the native born always participate at higher rates than immigrants. In their study of immigrant voting patterns in the 1996 presidential election, Mollenkopf *et al.* (1999) found that foreign born black and Latino citizens voted at higher rates than their native stock counterparts, while foreign born whites and Asians voted at lower rates. In the second generation, whites were considerably more likely and Asians a little more likely to vote than the native stock of these groups, but Latinos were less likely to vote, and second generation blacks considerably less likely to vote. The same study shows considerable variation in immigrant voting behavior in New York and Los Angeles, demonstrating the importance of local political contexts in shaping immigrant participation.

## *WHY IMMIGRANTS DON'T VOTE*

First generation immigrants face unique obstacles to political participation. They must learn English and become citizens, a demanding process that often entails the loss of legal and political rights in the home country (Jones-Correa, 1998). Their attitude toward naturalization will be influenced by the circumstances of their migration and their relationship to the home country, whether they are voluntary migrants, sojourners who intend to return, or refugees (Portes and Rumbaut, 1996). Finally, previous experience with democratic politics will most likely play a role in orienting the immigrant toward political participation.

In other respects, with differences of degree, immigrants face the same barriers to participation as native born Americans. Political scientists have offered several competing explanations for electoral non-participation. The first emphasizes the individual characteristics of non-voters, including education and income, ethnicity, age, and their attendant lack of motivation, party identification, or sense of political efficacy.[10] Those who expect a linear process of political incorporation for immigrants assume that, on arrival, they are over-represented in the non-voting categories, but that these effects diminish over time. In recent years, scholars have also noted the importance of civic skills (Verba, Schlozman and Brady, 1995) and "social capital" (Putnam, 1995a, 1995b) in determining electoral and other forms of political participation. More recently, Fuchs *et al.* (1999) have argued that membership in specifically political organizations is key, far outweighing general association membership, and emerging as the single most important factor when socioeconomic status is controlled.

Electoral institutions and legal requirements can facilitate or retard political participation. The decline of party competition (Schattschneider, 1960; Burnham, 1965), the decay of local political party organizations (Ware, 1988; Shefter, 1994), and the imposition of restrictive legal and procedural requirements, such as voter registration procedures, residency requirements, and literacy tests (Piven and Cloward, 1988) have affected the voting behavior of both immigrant and native born citizens.[11] Other factors, such as the gradual elimination of non-citizen voting rights, which existed in twenty-two states and federal territories until 1924 (Raskin, 1993), had a direct impact on immigrants.

Mobilization is another key factor in political participation (Rosenstone and Hansen, 1993) and the behavior of political parties affects immigrant mobilization. Although Erie has argued that the role of the political machines in mobilizing voters has been exaggerated, parties were certainly more active in mobilizing earlier waves of immigrants to naturalize and vote than they are today. Jones-Correa (1998) has shown how the current Democratic Party organization in Queens, New York has *discouraged* Latino immigrants from participation and responded only to immigrant communities that have already successfully mobilized themselves. He

[10]This "social-psychological school" is represented in the works of Campbell *et al.* (1960); Verba and Nie (1972); Brody (1978); Shaffer (1981); Conway (1985); Wolfinger and Rosenstone (1980); and Teixera (1987, 1992).

[11]The "political-behavioral" school is represented by the work of Burnham (1965, 1970, 1982); Schattschneider (1960); Kleppner and Baker (1980) and Kleppner (1982). Regarding the decline of parties and the rise of new campaign technologies, *see* Ware (1988); and Wattenberg (1990).

argues that this lack of mobilization is the second major factor responsible for the low participation of voters observed among even middle-class Latinos.[12] This perspective is significant because it shifts the responsibility for non-voting from "apathetic" immigrants to political parties that are reluctant to mobilize unpredictable "high risk" voters and share their limited resources with newcomers.

## *RESEARCH QUESTIONS*

In addition to presenting new data on New York State, this paper addresses some issues that have been neglected in the literature on immigrant political participation discussed above. Notably, few studies consider non-electoral participation, and few try to distinguish the effects of individual level characteristics from mobilization or other factors. Specifically, we address the following questions.

1) Do the foreign born in New York State participate less than the U.S. born in electoral and non-electoral politics? Is there a gradual increase in participation over generations as the assimilation model would suggest?

2) What factors most effectively explain differences in participation? Do socioeconomic factors or mobilization-related variables account for more of the difference in participation rates?

## *DATA AND MEASURES*

To explore these questions, we analyze data from a telephone survey of 1,662 adult residents of New York State conducted in December 1997.[13] The survey includes a sample of 218 foreign born residents. We compare the foreign born and U.S. born groups in terms of their levels of political participation, including measures of electoral and non-electoral political participation, and attitudes and behaviors that research suggests are related to political participation, such as political efficacy, organizational membership, and socioeconomic status. We divide the U.S. born into the second generation and all others, and the foreign born into citizens and non-citizens to test the hypothesis of generational stages of incorporation and to control for the most important barrier to participation and voting for the foreign born: citizenship status. Unfortunately, our data set is not

[12] Jones-Correa found that the most important factor for first generation migrants is the cost of naturalization in terms of loss of legal and political rights in the home country.

[13] A detailed description of the variables and complete question wording is available from the authors upon request.

large enough to allow for comparisons across different foreign born groups by national origin or among co-ethnics. Second, we explore multivariate models to determine the influence of nativity and citizenship on electoral and non-electoral forms of political participation, and to compare models of participation for the different sub-groups, with a focus on naturalized citizens. We use logistic regression techniques to model the probability of voting in 1994 and 1996.

As a check on the representativeness of our survey sample we compared our data to data drawn from the U.S. Census Bureau's March 1998 Current Population Survey (CPS) (U.S. Bureau of the Census, 1998). Table 1 indicates that our data are reasonably representative of the adult resident population of New York State.[14] Table 2 provides a more detailed demographic profile of the sample by nativity and citizenship status.

## *MEASURING POLITICAL PARTICIPATION*

We define political participation broadly to include a range of activities aimed at influencing government action (Verba, Schlozman and Brady, 1996). Following Verba and Nie (1972), our general measure of political participation is an eleven point scale that combines factors measuring respondents' voting behavior over the previous three years,[15] and whether respondents participated in any of the following political acts over the previous twelve months: volunteered for a political party or candidate; contributed money to a party or candidate; attended a rally for a candidate; attended a political meeting; made calls for a party or candidate; contacted an elected official; wrote a letter to a public official; signed a petition about a problem of concern; or cooperated with others to solve a problem of concern.[16] Table 3 reports the distributions by nativity and

[14]There are two notable exceptions. First, those educated beyond high school are overrepresented in the New York State survey, a not uncommon public opinion survey problem. The proportion of people in the New York State survey lacking a high school education is just over a third that reported in the CPS, whereas the proportion of people with a college degree is more than twice as large. The sample of the foreign born also over-represents the young. This may be because we conducted the New York State survey only in English and the older, less educated among the foreign born are less likely to speak English than younger, educated people.

[15]Municipal elections were held in New York State in 1997. Voter turnout is typically lower in municipal elections in New York State, which by law are held in off-federal and off-state election years.

[16]In a principal components factor analysis, nearly all the variables of the general participation scale loaded on one dimension at .5 or better. The Cronbach's alpha for the reliability of this scale was .79.

**TABLE 1**
**NEW YORK STATE SURVEY**
**SELECTED SOCIOECONOMIC CHARACTERSTICS BY CITIZENSHIP STATUS COMPARED TO MARCH 1998**
**CURRENT POPULATION SURVEY VOTING AGE POPULATION**

| | March 1998 CPS | | | | 1997 New York State Survey | | | |
|---|---|---|---|---|---|---|---|---|
| | Total | Native Born Citizen | Naturalized Citizen | Not A Citizen | Total | Native Born Citizen | Naturalized Citizen | Not A Citizen |
| TOTAL | 100.0 | 75.3 | 10.6 | 14.1 | 100.0 | 85.9 | 8.3 | 5.8 |
| | (13458) | (10134) | (1419) | (1904) | (1662) | (1327) | (129) | (89) |
| EDUCATIONAL ATTAINMENT[a] | | | | | | | | |
| Less Than High School | 18.5 | 15.0 | 22.5 | 34.5 | 6.8 | 6.2 | 7.9 | 10.9 |
| High School or Some College | 54.7 | 57.5 | 49.2 | 43.8 | 53.1 | 54.0 | 42.7 | 36.4 |
| College Degree | 16.4 | 16.6 | 18.8 | 13.5 | 34.9 | 35.2 | 40.4 | 40.0 |
| Graduate/Professional Degree | 10.3 | 10.9 | 9.5 | 8.1 | 5.2 | 4.2 | 9.0 | 12.7 |
| | (11775) | (8851) | (1353) | (1571) | (1144) | (914) | (89) | (55) |
| FAMILY INCOME | | | | | | | | |
| "$20,000 or Less" | 26.1 | 23.5 | 26.7 | 39.6 | 21.2 | 20.6 | 12.4 | 30.8 |
| "$50,000 or More" | 41.4 | 43.9 | 42.9 | 26.7 | 32.4 | 32.9 | 38.1 | 26.9 |
| | (13069) | (9852) | (1399) | (1818) | (1496) | (1202) | (113) | (78) |
| RACE | | | | | | | | |
| White | 66.8 | 78.4 | 41.1 | 24.3 | 70.7 | 77.4 | 32.8 | 21.3 |
| Black | 13.1 | 11.5 | 19.3 | 17.5 | 14.1 | 11.1 | 26.6 | 37.1 |
| Latino | 15.2 | 9.2 | 22.6 | 41.7 | 9.1 | 7.9 | 19.5 | 16.9 |
| Other | 4.8 | 1.0 | 16.9 | 16.6 | 6.2 | 3.6 | 21.1 | 24.7 |
| | (13458) | (10134) | (1420) | (1904) | (1651) | (1321) | (128) | (89) |
| AGE | | | | | | | | |
| 18 – 24 | 12.5 | 12.7 | 4.7 | 17.5 | 12.8 | 12.0 | 13.6 | 24.1 |
| 25 – 29 | 9.0 | 8.4 | 7.0 | 13.2 | 10.9 | 10.7 | 7.6 | 19.0 |
| 30 – 34 | 10.8 | 10.4 | 9.4 | 14.2 | 11.7 | 11.2 | 11.9 | 17.7 |
| 35 – 44 | 21.3 | 21.1 | 20.9 | 22.8 | 24.5 | 24.3 | 28.8 | 20.3 |
| 45 – 64 | 28.5 | 28.8 | 32.7 | 23.4 | 27.7 | 28.4 | 29.7 | 13.9 |
| 65 and Over | 17.9 | 18.6 | 25.4 | 9.0 | 12.4 | 13.4 | 8.5 | 5.1 |
| | (13458) | (10134) | (1420) | (1904) | (1486) | (1186) | (118) | (79) |
| GENDER | | | | | | | | |
| Male | 47.0 | 47.1 | 43.2 | 49.4 | 44.4 | 44.2 | 42.6 | 48.3 |
| Female | 53.0 | 52.9 | 56.8 | 50.6 | 55.6 | 55.8 | 57.4 | 51.7 |
| | (13458) | (10134) | (1420) | (1904) | (1661) | (1326) | (129) | (89) |

[a]Educational attainment reported for all those 25 years of age and older.

**TABLE 2**
**New York State Survey**
**Socioeconomic Characteristics by Nativity and Citizenship**

| | N.Y. S. | U.S. BORN | 3rd Generation or More | 2nd Generation | FOREIGN BORN | Foreign Born Citizen | Foreign Born Noncitizen |
|---|---|---|---|---|---|---|---|
| SAMPLE | 100.0 | 85.9 | 65.0 | 20.9 | 14.1 | 8.3 | 5.8 |
| | (1662) | (1327) | (1004) | (323) | (218) | (129) | (89) |
| EDUCATIONAL ATTAINMENT | | | | | | | |
| Less Than High School | 7.2 | 6.6 | 6.8 | 6.2 | 8.1 | 6.1 | 9.6 |
| High School | 27.3 | 27.4 | 27.6 | 26.7 | 21.7 | 17.4 | 27.7 |
| Jr. College or Some College | 28.8 | 29.2 | 28.9 | 30.1 | 27.3 | 28.7 | 25.3 |
| College Degree | 30.8 | 31.3 | 30.9 | 32.5 | 34.3 | 39.1 | 27.7 |
| Some Graduate School or Degree | 5.9 | 5.5 | 5.9 | 4.5 | 8.6 | 8.7 | 8.4 |
| | (1487) | (1180) | (888) | (292) | (198) | (115) | (83) |
| MEAN Years of Education | 14.0 | 14.0 | 14.0 | 14.0 | 14.2 | 14.6 | 13.6 |
| | (1487) | (1180) | (888) | (292) | (198) | (115) | (83) |
| INCOME | | | | | | | |
| $12,000 or Less | 10.3 | 9.8 | 8.4 | 14.4 | 8.9 | 4.4 | 15.4 |
| $12,001 — 20,000 | 10.9 | 10.8 | 10.6 | 11.5 | 11.0 | 8.0 | 15.4 |
| $20,001 — 30,000 | 20.0 | 19.8 | 19.6 | 20.5 | 20.9 | 21.2 | 20.5 |
| $30,001 — 40,000 | 15.7 | 15.6 | 16.1 | 14.0 | 14.7 | 15.9 | 12.8 |
| $40,001 — 50,000 | 10.8 | 11.1 | 11.4 | 10.1 | 11.0 | 12.4 | 9.0 |
| $50,001 — 60,000 | 9.4 | 9.4 | 9.5 | 9.0 | 11.0 | 11.5 | 10.3 |
| $60,001 — 80,000 | 10.2 | 10.1 | 10.7 | 7.9 | 12.6 | 15.9 | 7.7 |
| $80,001 — 100,000 | 6.1 | 6.7 | 7.6 | 4.0 | 3.7 | 4.4 | 2.6 |
| $100,001 — 150,000 | 3.8 | 3.7 | 3.7 | 3.6 | 4.2 | 3.5 | 5.1 |
| Over $150,000 | 2.8 | 3.0 | 2.4 | 5.0 | 2.1 | 2.7 | 1.3 |
| | (1496) | (1202) | (924) | (323) | (191) | (129) | (89) |
| RACE | | | | | | | |
| White | 70.7 | 77.4 | 79.7 | 70.2 | 28.1 | 32.8 | 21.3 |
| Black | 14.1 | 11.1 | 12.0 | 8.1 | 30.9 | 26.6 | 37.1 |
| Latino | 9.1 | 7.9 | 5.7 | 14.9 | 18.4 | 19.5 | 16.9 |
| Other | 6.2 | 3.6 | 22.6 | 6.8 | 22.6 | 21.1 | 24.7 |
| | (1651) | (1321) | (999) | (322) | (217) | (128) | (89) |

**TABLE 2 (CONTINUED)**
**NEW YORK STATE SURVEY**
**SOCIOECONOMIC CHARACTERISTICS BY NATIVITY AND CITIZENSHIP**

| | N.Y. S | U.S. BORN | 3rd Generation or More | 2nd Generation | FOREIGN BORN | Foreign Born Citizen | Foreign Born Noncitizen |
|---|---|---|---|---|---|---|---|
| AGE | | | | | | | |
| 18 — 24 | 12.8 | 12.0 | 11.4 | 13.9 | 17.8 | 13.6 | 24.1 |
| 25 — 34 | 22.6 | 21.9 | 23.2 | 17.8 | 26.4 | 19.5 | 36.7 |
| 35 — 44 | 24.5 | 24.3 | 25.4 | 20.6 | 25.4 | 28.8 | 20.3 |
| 45 — 54 | 17.1 | 17.0 | 18.0 | 13.9 | 16.8 | 20.3 | 11.4 |
| 55 — 64 | 10.6 | 11.4 | 10.8 | 13.2 | 6.6 | 9.3 | 2.5 |
| 65 — 74 | 8.5 | 9.4 | 8.2 | 13.2 | 4.1 | 4.2 | 3.8 |
| Over 75 | 4.0 | 4.0 | 3.0 | 7.5 | 3.0 | 4.2 | 1.3 |
| | (1486) | (1186) | (905) | (281) | (197) | (118) | (79) |
| MEAN Age | 42.5 | 43.2* | 42.4 | 45.8 | 38.9* | 42.0 | 34.2 |
| | (1486) | (1186) | (905) | (281) | (197) | (118) | (79) |
| GENDER | | | | | | | |
| Male | 44.4 | 44.2 | 43.2 | 47.4 | 45.0 | 42.6 | 48.3 |
| Female | 55.6 | 55.8 | 56.8 | 52.6 | 55.0 | 57.4 | 51.7 |
| | (1661) | (1326) | (1003) | (323) | (218) | (129) | (89) |
| FOREIGN BORN ONLY | | | | | | | |
| MEAN Years Living in U.S. | | | | | 19 | 25 | 11 |
| | | | | | (211) | (123) | (88) |
| MEAN Years Naturalized | | | | | | 16 | |
| | | | | | | (109) | |

*p<.01

citizenship for all of the measures making up the scale.

*EXPLAINING POLITICAL PARTICIPATION*

In this paper we are less concerned with arguing for any one model of participation than we are with comparing the political behavior and attitudes of the foreign born with those of the U.S. born. We have therefore adopted a fairly inclusive measure of political participation that goes beyond the well-established socioeconomic model to incorporate levels of organizational association and embeddedness in participatory networks, a few very rough measures of what might be referred to as 'a capacity to be mobilized' for political participation, and measures of attitudes toward politics known to influence participation. The multivariate analysis considers 1) a basic socioeconomic model; 2) a socioeconomic model that includes measures of organizational association and networks; 3) the same model with attitudinal measures included as independent variables.[17]

## *Socioeconomic Measures*

The socioeconomic model of political participation predicts that individuals with high levels of education and income will be more active in politics. Our multivariate analysis includes measures of educational attainment and income as well as other personal characteristics frequently associated with political participation in America, such as age, race, and gender.[18] To assess the impact of nativity on participation, we include a dichotomized variable for being born in the U.S.[19] and when we analyze the foreign born separately we also include a variable for the mean years living in the U.S. Because our survey was conducted only in English, the sample does not include non-English speaking foreign born residents of New York State. Differences in the behavior and attitudes of the foreign born can thus be

[17]We are interested in direct effects of these variables and, therefore, make assumptions about the exogeneity of the institutional and psychological measures which may in fact not be true. For example, we assume that organizational affiliations and inclusion in participatory networks produce certain attitudes toward politics and not the other way around. We leave the consideration of interaction effects and non-linear functional forms for further research.

[18]Whites and blacks exclude Latinos, who can be of any race. Asians were too small a group in our survey for statistical analysis and are included in the 'Other (non-white) Race' category, along with those reporting their background as mixed race and other race.

[19]Rather than use categorical variables for education and income, we created dichotomized variables for each category of educational attainment and income (matched to the CPS categories). This allowed us to control for missing cases and ensure the largest possible number of cases in the final models.

**TABLE 3**
**NEW YORK STATE SURVEY**
**POLITICAL PARTICIPATION BY NATIVITY AND CITIZENSHIP**

| | N.Y. S. | U.S. BORN | 3rd Generation or More | 2nd Generation | FOREIGN BORN | Foreign Born Citizen | Foreign Born Noncitizen |
|---|---|---|---|---|---|---|---|
| VOTING | | | | | | | |
| Registered to Vote[a] | 80.9 | 85.2 | 84.9 | 86.0 | 54.7 | 79.4 | 19.3 |
| | (1652) | (1323) | (1001) | (322) | (214) | (126) | (88) |
| Voted in 1994 | 65.6 | 71.7 | 70.9 | 74.0 | 33.0 | 48.8 | 10.1 |
| Gubernatorial Election | (1662) | (1327) | (1004) | (323) | (218) | (129) | (89) |
| Voted in 1996 | 73.3 | 78.4 | 78.4 | 78.3 | 43.6 | 65.9 | 11.2 |
| Presidential Election | (1662) | (1327) | (1004) | (323) | (218) | (129) | (89) |
| NON-ELECTORAL PARTICIPATION | | | | | | | |
| In Last Year: | | | | | | | |
| Volunteered for Party/Candidate | 10.1 | 10.5 | 10.2 | 11.5 | 8.7 | 8.5 | 9.0 |
| | (1662) | (1327) | (1004) | (323) | (218) | (129) | (89) |
| Contributed Money to Party/ | 19.9 | 21.3 | 20.4 | 23.8 | 14.2 | 19.4 | 6.7 |
| Candidate | (1662) | (1327) | (1004) | (323) | (218) | (129) | (89) |
| Attended Rally for Candidate | 14.0 | 14.8 | 14.2 | 16.7 | 10.6 | 13.2 | 6.7 |
| | (1662) | (1327) | (1004) | (323) | (218) | (129) | (89) |
| Attended Political Meeting | 20.2 | 20.8 | 21.2 | 19.5 | 17.4 | 18.6 | 15.7 |
| | (1662) | (1327) | (1004) | (323) | (218) | (129) | (89) |
| Made Calls for Party/Candidate | 7.2 | 7.6 | 7.8 | 7.1 | 5.5 | 4.7 | 6.7 |
| | (1662) | (1327) | (1004) | (323) | (218) | (129) | (89) |
| Contacted Elected Official | 34.4 | 36.8 | 36.5 | 37.8 | 22.0 | 27.1 | 14.6 |
| | (1662) | (1327) | (1004) | (323) | (218) | (129) | (89) |
| Wrote Letter to Public Official | 29.8 | 31.7 | 31.4 | 32.5 | 21.6 | 31.8 | 6.7 |
| | (1662) | (1327) | (1004) | (323) | (218) | (129) | (89) |
| Signed Petition About | 45.8 | 48.5 | 48.5 | 48.3 | 32.1 | 41.9 | 18.0 |
| Problem of Concern | (1662) | (1327) | (1004) | (323) | (218) | (129) | (89) |
| Cooperated with Others | 42.0 | 42.8 | 42.8 | 42.7 | 39.9 | 43.4 | 34.8 |
| to Solve Problem | (1662) | (1327) | (1004) | (323) | (218) | (129) | (89) |
| MEAN Score on Political | 3.6 | 3.9** | 3.8 | 3.9 | 2.5** | 3.2 | 1.4 |
| Participation Scale *(0-11)* | (1662) | (1327) | (1004) | (323) | (218) | (129) | (89) |
| MEAN Score on Non-electoral | 2.2 | 2.4** | 2.3 | 2.4 | 1.7** | 2.1 | 1.2 |
| Participation Scale *(0-9)* | (1662) | (1327) | (1004) | (323) | (218) | (129) | (89) |

[a]Not included in Political Participation Scale.

**p<.01.

attributed to factors other than a lack of English language proficiency.

### *Mobilization Capacity Measures*

The first measure of mobilization capacity is citizenship status. This is the minimal threshold for voting in most national and state elections, but non-citizens are not barred from participating in the other (non-voting) measures of political activity making up our overall scale of political participation.

Membership in voluntary organizations can create a capacity to be mobilized for politics. To analyze the importance of organizational affiliation for predicting participation, we developed two measures of organizational membership similar to those used by Fuchs *et al.* (1999) in their examination of the social capital thesis and political participation in New York.[20] The first measure represents the number of formal social organizations to which the respondent belongs. The second measure, which is mutually exclusive of the first, represents the number of organizations the respondent belongs to and also perceives to be engaged in political activity.[21]

Other important organizational or institutional affiliations linked to political participation are variables for union membership and frequency of church attendance. Union membership is particularly important in New York because New York has one of the highest levels of union density of any state in the country and a tradition of politically engaged unionism (Master, 1998). Religion and participation in religious life are of special concern to social capital theorists because of the sustained role of

[20]This paper analyzes the same New York State dataset used by Fuchs *et al.* (1999).

[21]Respondents were asked whether they were members of the following types of organizations: neighborhood or community organization, charitable or service club (*i.e.*, Lions, Elks, Masons), professional association (*i.e.*, American Medical Association, Bar Association), religious association other than a church (Knights of Columbus, campus-based religious group, Christian Coalition), Parent/Teacher Association, veteran's association, civic association (*i.e.*, League of Women Voters, Junior League), or ethnic or racial group association (i.e., NAACP, other group organized by people of the same nationality). Respondents were also were asked if they were a member of a group active on one particular political issue (*i.e.*, anti-abortion, National Rifle Association, environmental, consumer group). All questions were coded 1=Yes, 2=No. All respondents who answered that they were members of any of these organizations were then asked the follow up question, "Does this organization engage in political activity?" Two dummy variables were created for each organizational membership question, one for organizational membership in a non-politically engaged organization, and the other for organizational membership in a politically engaged organization. Two scales, organizational memberships – social, and organizational memberships – political were then created by tallying for each respondent all organizational memberships for organizations that 1) *did not* engage in political activity, and 2) *did* engage in political activity, respectively.

activist churches in a range of political and community development activities, particularly in communities lacking the material conditions (*i.e.*, high socioeconomic status) associated with higher levels of political participation. We therefore include a variable measuring the frequency of attendance at church or religious services.

We also include several approximate measures of respondents' connections to political networks, and measures of residential stability, variables sometimes linked to higher participation. The network measures include 1) a scale for the frequency with which the respondent discusses politics with other family members, friends, and co-workers, and 2) a scale indicating whether family, friends, or co-workers vote. A dichotomized variable indicating whether respondents had been contacted recently to participate in some kind of political activity indicates whether the respondent is in a position to be reached for mobilization efforts (Rosenstone and Hansen, 1993). Residential stability and commitments to place, which are also associated with higher participation, are operationalized with a dichotomized variable indicating whether the respondent owns his or her home, and with an ordinal variable for the length of time (in years) the respondent has spent at his or her present address. Lastly, we created a measure of issue mobilization from an open-ended survey question that asked the respondent to name the most important issue facing his or her neighborhood.[22] Here, we reasoned that the awareness of neighborhood problems might indicate a higher level of engagement in the political process, and expected this variable to be associated with greater political participation. Table 4 reports the distributions by nativity and citizenship for the mobilization capacity measures used in the multivariate analysis.

## *Attitudinal Measures*

The most important attitudinal variable is partisan strength. We expected it to have a positive, significant effect on political participation in New York State, where the experience of non-partisan elections at the state or local level is negligible. To assess the degree of partisan attachment, we constructed a dichotomized variable that took on a value of 1 (and 0 otherwise) if the respondent was both registered to vote in a political party

[22]Respondents were coded 1 if they named any issue at all, and 0 if they said there were no important issues facing their neighborhood. This question was part of a series of four questions about the most important issue or problem facing 1) the state; 2) the respondent's town or city; 3) the neighborhood; and 4) the family

**TABLE 4**
**NEW YORK STATE SURVEY**
**MOBILIZATION MEASURES BY NATIVITY AND CITIZENSHIP**

| | N.Y. S. | U.S. BORN | 3rd Generation or More | 2nd Generation | FOREIGN BORN | Foreign Born Citizen | Foreign Born Noncitizen |
|---|---|---|---|---|---|---|---|
| Citizenship | 94.6 | 100.0 | 100.0 | 100.0 | 59.2 | 100.0 | 0.0 |
| | (1564) | (1327) | (1004) | (323) | (218) | (129) | (89) |
| *Voluntary Associations:* | | | | | | | |
| Belong to At Least One | 45.7 | 46.2 | 46.7 | 44.4 | 47.5 | 47.3 | 47.7 |
| Social Organization | (1659) | (1326) | (1004) | (322) | (217) | (129) | (88) |
| MEAN Social Organizational | .74 | .74 | .75 | .71 | .81 | .84 | .77 |
| Memberships *(0-8)* | (1654) | (1323) | (1002) | (321) | (217) | (129) | (88) |
| Belong to At Least One | 31.2 | 32.9 | 32.5 | 34.1 | 24.3 | 26.4 | 21.3 |
| Political Organization | (1658) | (1326) | (1003) | (323) | (218) | (129) | (89) |
| MEAN Political Organizational | .58 | .62** | .58 | .74 | .39** | .43 | .33 |
| Memberships *(0-9)* | (1654) | (1323) | (1002) | (321) | (217) | (129) | (88) |
| *Union Membership:* | | | | | | | |
| Among All | 20.0 | 20.4 | 21.3 | 17.6 | 18.9 | 25.6 | 9.1 |
| | (1656) | (1325) | (1002) | (323) | (217) | (129) | (88) |
| Among Currently Working | 25.2 | 25.4 | 26.7 | 20.9 | 25.0 | 32.6 | 12.5 |
| | (1056) | (841) | (659) | (182) | (148) | (92) | (56) |
| *Church Attendance:* | | | | | | | |
| Never | 24.0 | 23.4 | 24.1 | 21.1 | 26.4 | 23.6 | 30.3 |
| A Few Times A Year | 27.6 | 28.1 | 28.2 | 28.0 | 21.8 | 22.8 | 20.2 |
| Once or Twice A Month | 12.6 | 13.0 | 12.6 | 14.2 | 12.5 | 12.6 | 12.4 |
| Every/Almost Every Week | 29.6 | 29.1 | 28.7 | 30.5 | 34.3 | 37.0 | 30.3 |
| Several Times A Week | 6.2 | 6.4 | 6.4 | 6.3 | 5.1 | 3.9 | 6.7 |
| | (1641) | (1316) | (998) | (318) | (216) | (127) | (89) |

**TABLE 4** (Continued)
NEW YORK STATE SURVEY
MOBILIZATION MEASURES BY NATIVITY AND CITIZENSHIP

| | N.Y. S. | U.S. BORN | 3rd Generation or More | 2nd Generation | FOREIGN BORN | Foreign Born Citizen | Foreign Born Noncitizen |
|---|---|---|---|---|---|---|---|
| *Political Network Measures:* | | | | | | | |
| MEAN Discuss Politics Scale | 8.9 | 9.0 | 9.0 | 8.8 | 9.3 | 9.1 | 9.6 |
| *(3-15)* | (1592) | (1270) | (965) | (305) | (212) | (125) | (87) |
| MEAN Family, Friends, | 2.0 | 2.1 | 2.1 | 2.0 | 1.8 | 1.8 | 1.8 |
| Co-Workers Vote Scale *(0-3)* | (1662) | (1327) | (1004) | (323) | (218) | (129) | (89) |
| Asked By Others to Get | 23.7 | 24.7 | 24.3 | 26.2 | 19.9 | 25.8 | 11.4 |
| Involved in Political Activity | (1654) | (1322) | (1001) | (321) | (216) | (128) | (88) |
| *Residential Stability:* | | | | | | | |
| Home Owner | 57.1 | 60.8 | 60.7 | 60.9 | 38.7 | 50.0 | 22.5 |
| | (1651) | (1320) | (998) | (322) | (217) | (128) | (89) |
| *Length of Time at Present Address:* | | | | | | | |
| Less Than 6 Months | 7.4 | 7.1 | 7.6 | 5.6 | 8.3 | 6.3 | 11.2 |
| 6 Months – 1 Year | 5.5 | 4.8 | 4.8 | 4.6 | 10.1 | 7.8 | 13.5 |
| 1 – 2 Years | 13.8 | 13.3 | 13.0 | 14.2 | 13.4 | 9.4 | 19.1 |
| 3 – 4 Years | 12.0 | 11.8 | 11.8 | 12.1 | 15.2 | 12.5 | 19.1 |
| 5 – 10 Years | 22.2 | 22.5 | 24.2 | 17.3 | 22.6 | 21.1 | 24.7 |
| 11 – 20 Years | 19.0 | 18.8 | 19.2 | 17.6 | 20.3 | 28.9 | 7.9 |
| 21 – 30 Years | 9.9 | 10.1 | 9.0 | 13.6 | 6.5 | 9.4 | 2.2 |
| More Than 30 Years | 10.1 | 11.6 | 10.6 | 14.9 | 3.7 | 4.7 | 2.2 |
| | (1658) | (1325) | (1002) | (323) | (217) | (128) | (89) |
| *Issue Mobilization:* | | | | | | | |
| Cite Serious Issue Facing | 67.8 | 67.4 | 67.1 | 68.3 | 71.1 | 72.7 | 68.8 |
| Neighborhood | (1521) | (1214) | (911) | (303) | (201) | (121) | (80) |

**p<.01

**TABLE 5**
**New York State Survey**
**Atitudes Toward Politics by Nativity and Citizenship**

| | N.Y. S. | U.S. BORN | 3rd Generation or More | 2nd Generation | FOREIGN BORN | Foreign Born Citizen | Foreign Born Noncitizen |
|---|---|---|---|---|---|---|---|
| Partisan Strength | 22.6 | 24.6 | 23.6 | 27.8 | 14.7 | 22.5 | 4.7 |
| | (1405) | (1116) | (853) | (263) | (197) | (111) | (86) |
| *Interest in Politics:* | | | | | | | |
| Not Interested at All | 7.8 | 6.3 | 6.6 | 5.6 | 12.8 | 9.3 | 18.0 |
| Not Much Interested | 16.4 | 15.5 | 16.4 | 12.7 | 19.7 | 16.3 | 24.7 |
| Somewhat Interested | 50.8 | 52.2 | 53.0 | 49.8 | 44.5 | 50.4 | 36.0 |
| Very Much Interested | 25.0 | 25.9 | 24.0 | 31.9 | 22.9 | 24.0 | 21.3 |
| | (1661) | (1327) | (1004) | (323) | (218) | (129) | (89) |
| MEAN Efficacy Scale | 4.0 | 4.1** | 4.1 | 4.0 | 3.7** | 3.7 | 3.8 |
| *(0-6)* | (1589) | (1269) | (960) | (309) | (207) | (123) | (84) |

**p<.01

and reported that he or she strongly identified with the Democratic or Republican parties.[23] Other attitudinal measures include a dichotomized variable for interest in politics, and a scale measuring political efficacy adapted from the NORC General Social Survey. We expected an interest in politics and higher levels of political efficacy to be correlated with higher levels of political participation. Table 5 reports the distribution for all attitudinal measures by nativity and citizenship status.

## *RESULTS*

*Comparative Rates of Political Participation Naturalized and U.S. Born Citizens.* Naturalized citizens are somewhat less likely to be registered to vote (79.4%) than are the U.S. born (85.2%). Less than half of naturalized citizens in New York (48.8%), however, said they voted in the 1994 gubernatorial election compared to nearly three-quarters (71.7%) of the U.S. born citizens. Interestingly, voting rates for the two groups in the 1996 presidential election were much closer (65.9% for naturalized citizens versus 78.4% for the U.S. born).[24]

With respect to non-electoral political participation, foreign born rates of participation are uniformly lower than those of the U.S. born (*see* Table 3). And while in many cases being a citizen seems to influence whether the foreign born engage in non-electoral political participation (naturalized citizens are more likely than non-citizens to contribute money to parties or candidates, attend political rallies and meetings, contact elected officials, sign petitions, and work with others to solve problems they care about), being a citizen does not fully erase the difference between the for-

[23]Empirically, the partisan strength variable is a mixed measure of behavior (registering to vote in a party) and attitudinal qualities (feelings of attachment to one of the two major parties). However, we consider partisan strength an attitudinal rather than an institutional variable because expressed feelings of attachment to one of the two parties drives it. Moreover, because the two major political parties are not really membership organizations we think this variable reflects more of the affective rather than behavioral qualities it implies.

[24]We have no immediate explanation for the disproportionate drop off in voting between the 1996 presidential election and the 1994 gubernatorial election among naturalized citizens and the U.S. born. The data do not support the argument that the drop off is due to higher rates of mobility or late naturalization among naturalized citizens. Naturalized citizens and the U.S. born share the same mobility rates, with just over a third of both groups (36% of naturalized citizens and 37% of the U.S. born) reporting that they had lived at their present address for four years or less. The sample's naturalized citizens on average came to the U.S. at the age of 17, have been in the U.S. for 25 years, and have been naturalized for 16 years. This suggests they naturalized within a reasonable amount of time upon arrival in the U.S. and are subject to the same forces of internal physical mobility as other New Yorkers.

eign born and the U.S. born when it comes to this form of civic engagement. The foreign born score on average one and one half political acts lower on the cumulative 11 point participation scale than do the U.S. born (with mean scores of 2.5 and 3.9, respectively). When voting is excluded from the scale, the size of the difference between the foreign and U.S. born shrinks but the difference remains (with mean scores of 1.7 and 2.4, respectively). When non-citizens are excluded from the sample, the size of the difference shrinks again, from a mean score of 3.2 for the foreign born and 3.9 for the U.S. born, but it still does not entirely disappear.

The foreign born do not appear to be less connected to voluntary organizations and networks fostering participation than the U.S. born. The mean membership rate of the foreign born for social organizations is .81 out of a possible score of 8. The mean for the U.S. born is .74, but the difference is not statistically significant.[25] The reported unionization rate among naturalized citizens is higher than that of the U.S. born (25.6% compared to 21.3%) and grows wider if taken as a proportion of only those currently working (32.6% and 26.7%, respectively). The frequency of church attendance and the degree to which respondents reported talking to family members, friends, and co-workers about politics were similar for the foreign and native born citizen.

On our measures of mobilization capacity, there are differences between the two groups, but these differences are not consistently in the same direction. U.S. born New York State residents (24.7%) are more likely than foreign born residents (19.9%) to have been asked to participate in some kind of political activity in the last year, although this difference appears to be driven by the small number of non-citizens in our sample; the native born (60.8%) are more likely to own their own home (compared to 38.7% of the foreign born), and twice as likely to have lived at their present address for more than 20 years (21.7% versus 10.2% for the foreign born). On the other hand, the foreign born are just as likely as the native born to have lived at their present address for five to 20 years (42.9% versus 41.3% for the native), and marginally more likely to have said there was a major problem facing their neighborhood (71.1% versus 67.4%).

The major difference between the foreign born and U.S. born with respect to institutional affiliations and participatory networks is the degree to which the foreign born belong to voluntary associations they

[25]The foreign born were just slightly more likely to belong to at least one social organization (47.5%) than the U.S. born (46.2%), but this difference is not statistically significant.

perceive to be engaged in *political activity.* Whereas the foreign born reported membership in non-politically engaged organizations at a similar if not slightly higher rate than the U.S. born, they claimed membership in politically engaged organizations at only a third the rate of the U.S. born (with a mean membership rate of only .39 compared to a statistically significant higher mean of .62 for the U.S. born, out of a possible score of 9). This finding has important implications and may partly account for the lower political participation rates we observe among the foreign born.

Interestingly, there is little difference between naturalized citizens, or the foreign born more generally, and the U.S. born when it comes to our measures of attitudes toward politics. The foreign born show an interest in politics and feel efficacious about politics at about the same rate as the U.S. born. Likewise, roughly the same proportion (between a fifth and a quarter) of naturalized citizens as U.S. born exhibit strong attachments to the two major political parties.

*The Second Generation.* With few exceptions, the differences between the second generation and other native born New Yorkers in the sample are negligible. They share a similar socioeconomic profile, though the second generation is more Latino and less white. There are no pronounced differences in patterns of political participation, attitudes toward politics or the policy preferences of the second generation and all other natives. These adult children of immigrants, like the foreign born themselves, are more likely to be registered as Democrats than the native born, though they are nevertheless similar to natives when it comes to candidate choice in the 1994 and 1996 elections. Their similarity to other native born Americans suggests the successful incorporation of this group within two generations. However, due to New York's long history of mass immigration, a high proportion of our second generation respondents are "old" second generation. We should therefore be wary of generalizing from their experience to that of the children of the post-1965 immigrants.

*Non-citizens.* The non-citizen sample is too small to analyze with any confidence that the findings are valid. Moreover, this sample is most likely very unrepresentative of the non-citizen population in New York. Whereas the CPS reports non-citizens are 11.3 percent of the state's population, and 63.8 percent of the foreign born the population, the non-citizens in our sample are only 5.8 percent of the total sample, segment of and 40.8 percent of the foreign born represented in the sample. As the survey used only simple random sampling techniques, no special effort was made to reach non-citizens. Rather, the non-citizens who participated in the survey had telephones and spoke English well enough to complete the survey, two conditions much less likely to prevail in the non-citizen population than in the general population of the state, or even among naturalized citizens. To provide a full picture of the data, we report distributions for the non-citizen population but do not analyze them separately.[26]

## *MULTIVARIATE MODELS OF POLITICAL PARTICIPATION*

### *All Citizens*

To understand the influence of nativity and citizenship on political participation we used multivariate analysis techniques to model participation, first for the entire sample, and then for naturalized citizens. The models for naturalized citizens must be interpreted with caution, given the small sample size. Tables 6A, 6B, and 6C report the OLS results for our three basic models of participation (as described above) for the New York State sample, excluding the small number of non-citizens. Non-citizens were excluded from the multivariate analyses because they are ineligible to participate in voting. Their inclusion would artificially depress scores for the foreign born on the participation scale used in this study.

The basic socioeconomic model confirms what we know about the importance of higher socioeconomic status and material resources for political participation. Participation increases substantially as education and income increase. Age and gender also matter, with increasing age and male gender demonstrating positive influences on participation.[27] The coefficients for non-white racial categories are negative but they are not statistically significant, suggesting that racial differences in political participation are small in New York State when age and socioeconomic status are taken into account. When we control for these basic socioeconomic characteristics, we find that nativity has a statistically significant effect on participation, increasing the number of political acts engaged in by three quarters of an act

[26]Ten percent of non-citizens in the survey reported voting in the 1994 gubernatorial election and 11 percent said they voted in the 1996 presidential election. We believe it is more likely respondents falsified their answers to the voting questions at the beginning of the survey than they did at the end of the survey when they were asked about their citizenship status. These findings are consistent with studies of the general electorate that find a marginal misreporting of actual voting behavior.

[27]Contrary to our expectations, female gender depressed participation in all three models, though it was statistically significant only when socioeconomic variables alone were controlled.

for the U.S. born over the foreign born.[28] These findings, however, are only suggestive of possible relationships because the fit of the model to the data is poor, explaining just 17 percent of the variance in political participation.

Mobilization capacity measures mediate the influence of nativity on political participation. When we add these measures to the basic socioeconomic model the proportion of the variance in the dependent variable explained increases to 46 percent. Moreover, the strength of the effect of being U.S. born on participation diminishes by half, suggesting the important role organizations and networks play in promoting and increasing civic and political participation among citizens. On the other hand, controlling for institutional affiliation and nativity produces different effects for race.

**TABLE 6A**
**NEW YORK STATE SURVEY**
**INFLUENCES ON POLITICAL PARTICIPATION[A]**

| | *Citizens Only* Unstandardized Coefficients | Standardized Coefficients | t-Values |
|---|---|---|---|
| *Socioeconomic Measures*[b] | | | |
| EDUCATION[c] | | | |
| High School Graduate | .610* | .100** | 2.224 |
| Some College or Trade School | 1.342** | .225** | 4.887 |
| College Graduate | 1.718** | .298** | 6.187 |
| Graduate or Professional Degree | 1.975** | .147** | 4.879 |
| *INCOME*[d] | | | |
| Annual Income $20,001 to $50,000 | .609** | .115** | 3.508 |
| Annual Income Over $50,000 | .978** | .171** | 5.015 |
| *AGE*[e] | | | |
| 25 – 29 Years of Age | .111 | .012 | |
| 30 – 34 Years of Age | .447 | .052 | 1.672 |
| 35 – 44 Years of Age | 1.106** | .176** | 4.821 |
| 45 – 64 Years of Age | 1.706** | .285** | 7.622 |
| Over 65 Years of Age | 1.817** | .222** | 6.921 |
| *RACE*[f] | | | |
| Black | -.116 | -.015 | -.610 |
| Latino | -.137 | -.015 | -.608 |
| Other (Non-white) Race | .175 | .015 | .608 |
| Female | -.265* | -.050* | -2.142 |
| U.S. Born | .756** | .104** | 3.258 |
| **Constant** | .333 | | .819 |

*t-value significant at the .05 level
R2=.180
**t-value significant at the .01 level
Adj. R2=.169
N=1,563
[a]OLS Regression, Dependent Variable: Political Participation Scale (0-11)
[b]Dichotomized variables for missing cases for the education, income, and age categories are not reported.
[c]Base category="Less Than High School"
[d]Base category=Annual Income Less Than $20,000
[e]Base category=18 – 24 Years of Age
[f]Base category=White

[28]The mean number of participatory acts is 3.6.

**TABLE 6B**
**NEW YORK STATE SURVEY**
**INFLUENCES ON POLITICAL PARTICIPATION[a]**

| | *Citizens Only* Unstandardized Coefficients | Standardized Coefficients | t-Values |
|---|---|---|---|
| *Socioeconomic Measures[b]* | | | |
| *EDUCATION* | | | |
| High School Graduate | .200 | .033 | .894 |
| Some College or Trade School | .572* | .096* | 2.545 |
| College Graduate | .697** | .121** | 3.049 |
| Graduate or Professional Degree | .232 | .017 | .691 |
| *INCOME* | | | |
| Annual Income $20,001 to $50,000 | .244 | .046 | 1.694 |
| Annual Income Over $50,000 | .101 | .018 | .602 |
| *AGE* | | | |
| 25 – 29 Years of Age | .185 | .021 | .825 |
| 30 – 34 Years of Age | .395 | .046 | 1.816 |
| 35 – 44 Years of Age | .757** | .120** | 4.007 |
| 45 – 64 Years of Age | 1.281** | .214** | 6.704 |
| Over 65 Years of Age | 1.316** | .161** | 5.706 |
| *RACE* | | | |
| Black | -.453** | -.058** | -2.824 |
| Latino | -.291 | -.031 | -1.568 |
| Other (Non-white) Race | -.147 | -.012 | -.626 |
| Female | -.141 | -.027 | -1.367 |
| U.S. Born | .399* | .055* | 2.107 |
| *Institutional/Network Measures* | | | |
| Organizational Memberships-Social | .514** | .198** | 9.744 |
| Organizational Memberships-Political | .646** | .278** | 13.301 |
| Union Member | -.168 | -.026 | -1.316 |
| Church Attendance | .059 | .029 | 1.468 |
| Family, Friends, Co-Workers Vote Scale | .221** | .079** | 3.808 |
| Discuss Politics Scale | .170** | .195** | 8.152 |
| Recently Contacted to Participate | 1.230** | .202** | 9.913 |
| Homeowner | .276* | .052* | 2.371 |
| Length of Time at Present Address | .076* | .057* | 2.521 |
| Cited Neighborhood Problem | .336** | .062** | 2.959 |
| **Constant** | -1.722** | -4.389 | |

*t-value significant at the .05 level
R2=.470
**t-value significant at the .01 level
Adj. R2=.456
N=1,563
[a]See Notes a-f from Table 6A.

Specifically, the coefficient for black is now statistically significant, with participation differing for blacks relative to whites by .45 political acts (see Table 6B). Race now appears to have a negative independent effect on participation even after organizational and mobilization factors believed by some to mitigate the effect of race on participation are taken into account.

**TABLE 6C**
**NEW YORK STATE SURVEY**
**INFLUENCES ON POLITICAL PARTICIPATION[a]**

| | *Citizens Only* Unstandardized Coefficients | Standardized Coefficients | t-Values |
|---|---|---|---|
| *Socioeconomic Measures[b]* | | | |
| *EDUCATION* | | | |
| High School Graduate | .155 | .025 | .703 |
| Some College or Trade School | .499* | .084* | 2.233 |
| College Graduate | .566* | .098* | 2.480 |
| Graduate or Professional Degree | .006 | .000 | .017 |
| *INCOME* | | | |
| Annual Income $20,001 to $50,000 | .220 | .042 | 1.542 |
| Annual Income Over $50,000 | .021 | .004 | .126 |
| *AGE* | | | |
| 25 – 29 Years of Age | .126 | .014 | .572 |
| 30 – 34 Years of Age | .416 | .048 | 1.934 |
| 35 – 44 Years of Age | .711** | .113** | 3.812 |
| 45 – 64 Years of Age | 1.184** | .198** | 6.248 |
| Over 65 Years of Age | 1.160** | .142** | 5.044 |
| *RACE* | | | |
| Black | -.495** | -.063** | -3.098 |
| Latino | -.296 | -.032 | -1.609 |
| Other (Non-white) Race | -.124 | -.010 | -.540 |
| Female | -.162 | -.031 | -1.592 |
| U.S. Born | .334[b] | .046 | 1.789 |
| *Institutional/Network Measures* | | | |
| Organizational Memberships-Social | .514** | .199** | 9.893 |
| Organizational Memberships-Political | .643** | .277** | 13.433 |
| Union Member | -.138 | -.021 | -1.100 |
| Church Attendance | .028 | .014 | .692 |
| Family, Friends, Co-Workers | | | |
| Vote Scale | .193** | .069** | 3.352 |
| Discuss Politics Scale | .148** | .170** | 7.121 |
| Recently Contacted to Participate | 1.152** | .189** | 9.384 |
| Homeowner | .305** | .058** | 2.646 |
| Length of Time at Present Address | .056 | .042 | 1.841 |
| Cited Neighborhood Problem | .342** | .063** | 3.059 |
| *Attitudinal Measures* | | | |
| Partisan Strength | .845** | .130** | 6.463 |
| Interest in Politics | .054 | .010 | .464 |
| Political Efficacy Scale | .103** | .071** | 3.083 |
| **Constant** | -1.686** | | -4.282 |

*t-value significant at the .05 level
R2=.489
**t-value significant at the .01 level
Adj. R2=.474
N=1,563
[a]See Notes a-f from Table 6A.
[b]t-value significant at the .07 level

**TABLE 7A**
**NEW YORK STATE SURVEY**
**PREDICTORS OF VOTING**[a]

| | *Citizens Only* Voting in 1994 Gubernatorial | | Voting in 1996 Presidential | |
|---|---|---|---|---|
| | B | S.E. | B | S.E. |
| *Socioeconomic Measures*[b] | | | | |
| *EDUCATION*[c] | | | | |
| High School Graduate | .7532** | .2708 | .8632** | .2567 |
| Some College orTrade School | 1.1492** | .2761 | 1.2370** | .2620 |
| College Graduate | 1.6526** | .2842 | 1.8225** | .2765 |
| Graduate or Professional Degree | .7343 | .4089 | 1.9217** | .5070 |
| INCOME[d] | | | | |
| Annual Income $20,001 to $50,000 | .1766 | .1765 | .3693* | .1745 |
| Annual Income Over $50,000 | .6128** | .2063 | .8095** | .2112 |
| *AGE*[e] | | | | |
| 25 – 29 Years of Age | .8226** | .2561 | .7971** | .2568 |
| 30 – 34 Years of Age | 1.1461** | .2525 | .8821** | .2522 |
| 35 – 44 Years of Age | 1.8039** | .2255 | 1.3126** | .2196 |
| 45 – 64 Years of Age | 2.7098** | .2391 | 2.0159** | .2315 |
| Over 65 Years of Age | 3.4800** | .3433 | 2.6652** | .3279 |
| *RACE*[f] | | | | |
| Black | -.0567 | .1938 | .2230 | .2031 |
| Latino | -.0783 | .2268 | .1714 | .2328 |
| Other (Non-white)Race | -.1469 | .2839 | -.2215 | .2880 |
| Female | -.2745* | .1324 | .1457 | .1359 |
| U.S. Born | 1.2418** | .2276 | .8476** | .2366 |
| **Constant** | -3.1628** | .4182 | -2.5702** | .4063 |
| Total cases: | | 1,534 | | 1,554 |
| -2 log likelihood: | | 1,496.099 | | 1,408.484 |
| Predicted correctly: | | 76.79% | | 78.70% |

*t-value significant at the .05 level
**t-value significant at the .01 level
[a]Logistic regression.
[b]Dichotomized variables for missing cases for the education, income, and age categories are not reported.
[c]Base category="Less Than High School"
[d]Base category="Annual Income Less Than $20,000"
[e]Base category="18 – 24 Years of Age"
[f]Base category="White"

The third iteration of our participation model includes several attitudinal variables known to affect participation (see Table 6C). Overall, these measures do not significantly improve the model (the explained variance increases from 46% to 47%), nor do they further mediate the effect of nativity on participation. Partisan strength, however, stands out as an important predictor of participation, increasing the average number of political acts respondents engage in by four fifths of an act when we control for socioeconomic status and our organizational and network measures.

To examine voting behavior more precisely, we used logistic regression techniques to analyze self-reported voting in 1994 and 1996.[29] Table

**TABLE 7B**
**New York State Survey**
**Predictors of Voting**[a]

| *Citizens Only* | Voting in 1994 Gubernatorial | | Voting in 1996 Presidential | |
|---|---|---|---|---|
| | B | S.E. | B | S.E. |
| *Socioeconomic Measures* | | | | |
| *EDUCATION* | | | | |
| High School Graduate | .6073* | .3000 | .8014** | .2863 |
| Some College or Trade School | .9902** | .3072 | 1.2034** | .2936 |
| College Graduate | 1.4295** | .3159 | 1.6527** | .3056 |
| Graduate or Professional Degree | -.2163 | .4614 | 1.2794* | .5476 |
| *INCOME* | | | | |
| Annual Income $20,001 to $50,000 | -.0608 | .1943 | .2972 | .1929 |
| Annual Income Over $50,000 | .1203 | .2347 | .5758* | .2373 |
| AGE | | | | |
| 25 – 29 Years of Age | 1.0431** | .2858 | .9050** | .2828 |
| 30 – 34 Years of Age | 1.2650** | .2777 | .8488** | .2760 |
| 35 – 44 Years of Age | 1.7789** | .2506 | 1.2279** | .2423 |
| 45 – 64 Years of Age | 2.6329** | .2643 | 1.8141** | .2546 |
| Over 65 Years of Age | 3.3000** | .3700 | 2.4365** | .3561 |
| *RACE* | | | | |
| Black | -.3888 | .2155 | -.1866 | .2236 |
| Latino | -.3349 | .2505 | -.0895 | .2574 |
| Other (Non-white) Race | -.2353 | .3103 | -.2568 | .3202 |
| Female | -.3889** | .1459 | .1308 | .1487 |
| U.S. Born | 1.1152** | .2480 | .6162* | .2612 |
| *Institutional/Network Measures* | | | | |
| Organizational Memberships-Social | .2274** | .0799 | .0373 | .0825 |
| Organizational Memberships-Political | .2882** | .0813 | .2229* | .0893 |
| Family, Friends, Co-Workers Vote Scale | .4952** | .0776 | .5441** | .0783 |
| Recently Contacted to Participate | .2301 | .1870 | .4442* | .2077 |
| Homeowner | .6059** | .1511 | .2255 | .1570 |
| *Attitudinal Measures* | | | | |
| Partisan Strength | 1.5757** | .2238 | 2.1282** | .3026 |
| **Constant** | -4.4964** | .4873 | -3.7628** | .4719 |
| Total cases: | | 1,534 | | 1,554 |
| -2 log likelihood: | | 1,283.545 | | 1,204.041 |
| Predicted correctly: | | 80.51% | | 80.95% |

*t-value significant at the .05 level
**t-value significant at the .01 level
[a]See Notes a-f from Table 7A.

7A represents the basic socioeconomic model, including nativity, while Table 7B incorporates selected institutional affiliation, network and attitudinal variables associated with political participation (see Table 6C).

As Tables 7A and 7B suggest, nativity is an important predictor of voting. The strength of the coefficient for nativity remains statistically significant but is diminished by about half in both models for voting in 1996,

[29]Non-citizens were excluded from the analysis.

**TABLE 8**
**NEW YORK STATE SURVEY**
**INFLUENCES ON POLITICAL PARTICIPATION**[a]

| | *Citizens Only* Unstandardized Coefficients | Standardized Coefficients | t-Values |
|---|---|---|---|
| *Socioeconomic Measures* | | | |
| *EDUCATION* | | | |
| High School Graduate | -.310 | -.045 | -.297 |
| Some College or Trade School | -.606 | -.106 | -.614 |
| College Graduate | .355 | .067 | .369 |
| Graduate or Professional Degree | -.778 | -.081 | -.641 |
| *INCOME* | | | |
| Annual Income $20,001 to $50,000 | .791 | .156 | 1.210 |
| Annual Income Over $50,000" | .804 | .152 | 1.104 |
| AGE | | | |
| 25 – 29 Years of Age | -1.035 | -.102 | -1.076 |
| 30 – 34 Years of Age | -1.129 | -.138 | -1.361 |
| 35 – 44 Years of Age | -.516 | -.092 | -.735 |
| 45 – 64 Years of Age | .451 | .080 | .589 |
| Over 65 Years of Age | -.945 | -.098 | -.768 |
| *RACE* | | | |
| Black | -.057 | -.010 | -.104 |
| Latino | -.827 | -.124 | -1.256 |
| Other (Non-white) Race | -.487 | -.080 | -.848 |
| Years Living in U.S. | .014 | .092 | .807 |
| *Institutional/Network Measures* | | | |
| Organizational Memberships-Social | .427* | .195* | 2.294 |
| Organizational Memberships-Political | 1.390** | .447** | 5.370 |
| Union Member | -.175 | -.030 | -.371 |
| Recently Contacted to Participate | .607 | .106 | 1.225 |
| *Attitudinal Measures* | | | |
| Partisan Strength | 1.429* | .222* | 2.566 |
| **Constant** | 1.480 | | 1.291 |

*t-value significant at the .05 level
R2=.489
**t-value significant at the .01 level
Adj. R2=.350
N=123
[a]See Notes a-f from Table 6A.

compared to voting in 1994. This suggests the importance of factoring in election-specific variables when examining the voting patterns of naturalized citizens, and we tentatively conclude that the source of citizenship matters less for predicting voting in a presidential election than in a statewide election. This may be because national issues appear more relevant than state-level issues to the foreign born.

## *Naturalized Citizens*

Our multivariate analysis suggests that when we control for important variables associated with political participation, nativity has an independent and statistically significant effect on participation in New York State. What predicts participation (or, conversely, non-participation) for the foreign born citizen? To explore this question we used OLS regression techniques to model the political participation behavior of naturalized citizens in our sample. We included basic socioeconomic measures used in our general models, but because of the much smaller size of the naturalized citizen sample, we reduced the number of additional predictor variables, including only those which appear to have the biggest influence on participation. The results are reported in Table 8.

None of the socioeconomic variables in the model – education, income, age, or race – are statistically significant determinants of political participation. Notably, the length of time in the U.S. appears to have little impact on rates of political participation when socioeconomic status and organizational affiliation are controlled. Organizational memberships, particularly memberships in politically engaged organizations, and partisan strength exhibit strong and significant influences on participation. The latter two effects raise the level of participation by nearly half (1.4 participatory acts) the average level of participation (3.2 participatory acts).

These results are intriguing but the small sample size means they must be interpreted cautiously. Although they are not statistically significant, the signs of several of the socioeconomic variables have now reversed, leading to implausible interpretations of the data; for example, that naturalized citizens with high school and trade school education and those with professional degrees participate less than those lacking a high school degree. Further research on the political participation of the foreign born and bigger samples are needed. The role of organizational membership, partisan acquisition and strength, and other mobilizing forces should play a central role in this research.

## *CONCLUSION*

A century ago, a sustained surge in immigration from Europe fundamentally changed the social landscape of the United States. Today, a second unprecedented flow of immigrants, this time from Latin America, Asia, and the Caribbean, is further diversifying the nation, and will profoundly change the social composition of the United States into the new century. What does this mean for American democracy? To what extent are immigrants being incorporated into the political system? What are the factors that impede or promote their participation in the political life of the country? Political incorporation has been somewhat neglected in the scholarly literature on political participation and immigration, with more attention paid to the impact of large scale immigration on U.S. labor markets and social policy making than to issues of political inclusion and exclusion. However, just as the new immigration is reviving the old debate over assimilation for sociologists, it is also renewing the question of pluralism and the openness of the American political system for political scientists.

In an examination of recent patterns of political behavior among immigrants in New York State, we found that nativity has an independent, direct influence on political participation, particularly on registering to vote and voting. In general, foreign birth moderately depresses political participation, even when socioeconomic status is controlled. These findings support the general hypothesis of the assimilation model that immigrants become progressively more incorporated into the political system over generations. Some qualifications are in order, however. Naturalized citizens were somewhat less likely to be registered to vote, and much less likely than native born citizens to have voted in the 1994 statewide elections in New York State, but their turnout rates in the federal election of 1996 were similar to those reported by native born citizens. This suggests the importance of factoring in election-specific variables when studying turnout rates among foreign born citizens.

Unfortunately, our small sample did not permit the comparison of racial and ethnic groups among the foreign born that would have enabled us to detect the segmented political assimilation of different groups. To the extent that we could examine the influence of race on political participation we found mixed results. Controlling only for socioeconomic status and nativity, we found that race was not a statistically significant predictor of political participation. When mobilization variables are also factored in, the coefficient for black race is negative and significant, but these findings do not hold in our more focused analysis of voting. The variability in the findings on the impact of race when socioeconomic variables, nativity, and other predictors of participation are controlled suggests that segmented assimilation's engagement with the racial order, at least with respect to the political process, is more complex than we assumed.

In terms of explaining the lower participation of the foreign born, membership in organizations and inclusion in networks that are politically engaged emerged as important factors influencing levels of political participation. In general, the foreign born do not appear to be less connected to voluntary organizations and networks fostering participation than the U.S.

born. However, the foreign born are less involved in organizations they perceive to be engaged in politics, a variable we found to be consistently related to higher levels of political participation. These mobilization-related variables were more important than socioeconomic status, confirming the priority given to civic life in understanding political participation, as emphasized in the work of Verba, Scholzman and Brady, and Putnam.

Our research suggests that membership in specifically political organizations plays an important role in mobilizing both foreign born and native born citizens to participate in politics. Most likely, participation in these organizations, and the process of becoming a citizen itself, are factors shaping the political attitudes and preferences of their members. Further research should focus on understanding how political institutions and actors promote or impede the participation of immigrants in politics and on identifying effective strategies for including these new constituencies.

## *REFERENCES*

Alba, R. and V. Nee
1997 "Rethinking Assimilation Theory for a New Era of Immigration." *International Migration Review*, 31(4):826-874.

Bonilla-Silva, E.
1997 "Rethinking Racism: Towards a Structural Interpretation." *American Sociological Review*, 63(3):465-480.

Brackman, H. and S. P. Erie
1994 "Beyond Politics by Other Means: Empowerment Strategies for Los Angeles." In *The Bubbling Cauldron: Race, Ethnicity and the Urban Crisis*. Ed. M. P. Smith and J. R. Feagin. Minneapolis, MN: University of Minnesota Press. Pp. 282-303.

Brody, R. A.
1978 "The Puzzle of Political Participation in America." In *The New American Political System*. Ed. A. King. Washington, DC: American Enterprise Institute. Pp. 287-324.

Burner, D.
1975 *The Politics of Provincialism: The Democratic Party in Transition, 1918-1932*. New York: W. W. Norton & Company, Inc.

Burnham, W. D.
1982 *The Current Crisis in American Politics*. New York: Oxford University Press.

———
1970 *Critical Elections and the Mainsprings of American Politics*. New York: W. W. Norton & Company, Inc.

———
1965 "The Changing Shape of the American Political Universe." *American Political Science Review*, 59(1):7-28.

Camarota, S. A.
1999 *Immigrants in the United States: A Snapshot of America's Foreign Born Population*. Washington, DC: Center for Immigration Studies.

Campbell, A., P. E. Converse, W. Miller, and D. Stokes
1960 *The American Voter*. New York: John Wiley.

Converse, P. E.
1972 "Change in the American Electorate." In *The Human Meaning of Social Change*. Ed. A. Campbell and P. E. Converse. New York: Russell Sage Foundation.

Conway, M. M.
1985 *Political Participation in the United States*. Washington, DC: Congressional Quarterly Press.

Dahl, R.
1961 *Who Governs? Democracy and Power in an American City*. New Haven: Yale University Press.

DeSipio, L.
1998 *The New Urban Citizen: Political Participation and Political Attitudes of the Newly Naturalized*. Paper presented at the American Political Science Association Annual Meeting, Boston.

DeWind, J. and P. Kasinitz
1997 "Everything Old is New Again? Process and Theories of Immigrant Incorporation." *International Migration Review*, 31(4):1096-1111.

Erie, S. P.
1988 *Rainbow's End: Irish Americans and the Dilemmas of Urban Machine Politics, 1840-1985*. Berkeley, University of California Press.

Fix, M. E. and J. S. Passel
1994 *Immigration and Immigrants: Setting the Record Straight*. Washington, DC: The Urban Institute Press.

Fuchs, E. R., L. C. Minnite, and R. Y. Shapiro
1999 *Political Capital and Political Participation*. Columbia University School of International and Public Affairs Working Paper Number 3.

Gamm, G. H.
1986 *The Making of New Deal Democrats: Voting Behavior and Realignment in Boston, 1920-1940*. Chicago: University of Chicago Press.

Gans, H.
1992 "Second-generation Decline: Scenarios for the Economic and Ethnic Futures of the Post-1965 American Immigrants." *Ethnic and Racial Studies*, 15(2):173-193.

Glick-Schiller, N., L. Basch and C. Szanton Blanc
1992 "Transnationalism: A New Analytic Framework for Understanding Migration." In *Towards a Transnational Perspective on Migration: Race, Class, Ethnicity and Nationalism Reconsidered*. Ed. N. Glick-Schiller, L. Basch and C. Szanton Blanc. New York: *New York Academy of Sciences*.

Gordon, M.
1964 *Assimilation in American Life: The Role of Race, Religion, and National Origins*. New York: Oxford University Press.

Haslip-Viera, G.
1996 "The Evolution of the Latino Community in New York City: Early Nineteenth Century." In *Latinos in New York; Communities in Transition*. Ed. G. Haslip-Viera and S. L. Baver. Notre Dame: University of Notre Dame. Pp. 3-29.

Hernandez, R. and F. Rivera-Batiz
1997 "Dominican New Yorkers: A Socioeconomic Profile, 1997." *Dominican Research Monographs*: The CUNY Dominican Studies Institute.

Hirschman, C.
1983 "The Melting Pot Reconsidered." *Annual Review of Sociology*, 9:397-423.

Ignatiev, N.
1995 *How the Irish Became White*. New York: Routledge.

Jones-Correa, M.
1998 *Between Two Nations; The Political Predicament of Latinos in New York City*. Ithaca: Cornell University Press.

Kleppner, P.
1982 *Who Voted? The Dynamics of Electoral Turnout*. New York: Praeger.

Kleppner, P. and S. C. Baker
1980 "The Impact of Voter Registration Requirements on Electoral Turnout, 1900-1916." *Journal of Political and Military Sociology*, 8(2):205-226.

Ladd, E. C., Jr.
1970 *American Political Parties; Social Change and Political Response*. New York: W. W. Norton & Company, Inc.

Lien, P.
1998 *Who Votes in Multiracial America? An Analysis of Voting Registration and Turnout by Race and Ethnicity, 1990-1996*. Paper presented at the Annual Meeting of the American Political Science Association, Boston.

Master, B.
1997 "A New Political Strategy for American Unions." *Working U.S.A.*, Pp. 16-28.

McNickle, C.
1993 *To Be Mayor of New York: Ethnic Politics in the City*. New York: Columbia University Press.

Miranda, L. A., Jr. and D. Muzzio
1997 *Hispanic New Yorkers on Nueva York. Fifth Annual Survey*. New York: Hispanic Federation of New York City.

Mollenkopf, J., T. Ross and D. Olson
1999 *Immigrant Political Participation in New York and Los Angeles. Paper commissioned for the Negotiating Difference Project*. The International Center for Migration, Ethnicity and Citizenship. New York.

New York City Department of City Planning
1994 *Puerto Rican New Yorkers in 1990*. DCP 94-09. New York.

Passel, J. S. and R. L. Clark
1998 *Immigrants in New York: Their Legal Status, Incomes, and Taxes*. Washington, DC: The Urban Institute Press.

Perlmann, J. and R. Waldinger
1997 "Second Generation Decline? Children of Immigrants, Past and Present – A Reconsideration." *International Migration Review*, 31(4):893-922.

Piven, F. F. and R. A. Cloward
1988 *Why Americans Don't Vote*. New York: Pantheon.

Portes, A. and R. L. Bach
1985 *Latin Journey: Cuban and Mexican Immigrants in the United States*. Berkeley, University of California.

Portes, A. and R. G. Rumbaut
1996 *Immigrant America: A Portrait*. Berkeley: University of California Press.

Portes, A. and M. Zhou
1993 "The New Second Generation: Segmented Assimilation and Its Variants." *The Annals of the American Academy of Political and Social Science*, 530:74-97.

Poston, D. L., Jr., S. A. Camarota, L. F. Bouvier, G. Jin-Kai Li and H. Dan
1998 *Remaking the Political Landscape: How Immigration Redistributes Seats in the House of Representatives*. Washington, DC: Center for Immigration Studies.

Putnam, R.
1995a "Tuning In, Tuning Out: The Strange Disappearance of Social Capital in America." *PS: Political Science and Politics*, 28:664-683.

———
1995b "Bowling Alone: America's Declining Social Capital." *Journal of Democracy*, 6:65-78.

Raskin, J. B.
1993 "Legal Aliens, Local Citizens: The Historical, Constitutional and Theoretical Meanings of Alien Suffrage." *University of Pennsylvania Law Review*, 141(4):1391+.

Roediger, D. R.
1991 *The Wages of Whiteness; Race and the Making of the American Working Class*. New York: Verso Press.

Rosenstone, S. J. and J. M. Hansen
1993 *Mobilization, Participation, and Democracy in America*. New York: Macmillan Publishing Company.

Rusk, J. G.
1974 *Comment: The American Electoral Universe: Speculation and Evidence*. American Political Science Review, 68(3):1028-1049.

Saxton, A.
1990 *The Rise and Fall of the White Republic: Class Politics and Mass Culture in Nineteenth Century America*. New York: Verso.

Schattschneider, E. E.
1975 *The Semi-sovereign People: A Realist's View of Democracy in America. Hinsdale, IL*: The Dryden Press.

Shaffer, S. D.
1981 "A Multivariate Explanation of Decreasing Turnout in Presidential Elections, 1960-1976." *American Journal of Political Science*, 25(1):68-95.

Shefter, M.
1994 *Political Parties and the State: The American Historical Experience*. Princeton: Princeton University Press.

Teixeira, R. A.
1992 *The Disappearing American Voter*. Washington, DC: The Brookings Institution.

———
1987 *Why Americans Don't Vote: Turnout Decline in the United States, 1960-1984*. Westport, CT: Greenwood Press.

Tuckel, P. and R. Maisel
1994 "Voter Turnout among European Immigrants to the United States." *Journal of Interdisciplinary History*, XXIV(3):407-430.

U.S. Department of Commerce, Bureau of the Census
1998 *Current Population Survey: Annual Demographic File, 1998*. [Computer file]. ICPSR version. Washington, DC: U.S. Department of Commerce, Bureau of the Census [producer]. Ann Arbor, MI: Inter-University Consortium for Political and Social Research [distributor].

———
1997 *Current Population Survey: Voter Supplement File, 1996*. [Computer file]. ICPSR version. Washington, DC: U.S. Department of Commerce, Bureau of the Census [producer]. Ann Arbor, MI: Inter-University Consortium for Political and Social Research [distributor].

Verba, S. and N. H. Nie
1972 *Participation in America: Political Democracy and Social Equality*. Chicago: University of Chicago Press.

Verba, S., K. Lehman Schlozman and H. E. Brady
1995 *Voice and Equality; Civic Voluntarism in American Politics*. Cambridge: Harvard University Press.

Ware, A.
1995 *The Breakdown of Democratic Party Organization, 1940-1980*. New York: Oxford University Press.

Waters, M. C. and K. Eschbach
1995 "Immigration and Ethnic and Racial Inequality in the United States." *Annual Review of Sociology*, 21:419-446.

Wattenberg, M. P.
1990 *The Decline of American Political Parties: 1952-1988*. Cambridge, MA: Harvard University Press.

Wolfinger, R.
1965 "The Development and Persistence of Ethnic Voting." *American Political Science Review*, 59(4):896-908.

Wolfinger, R. and S. Rosenstone
1980 *Who Votes?* New Haven, CT: Yale University Press.

Yancey, W. L., E. P. Ericksen and R. N. Julani
1976 "Emergent Ethnicity: A Review and Reformulation." *American Sociological Review,* 41(3):391-403.

16

# Transformations: The Post-Immigrant Generation in an Age of Diversity[1]

RUBÉN G. RUMBAUT
*Michigan State University*

> "The problem of the children is the problem of the State. As we mold the children of the toiling masses in our cities, so we shape the destiny of the State which they will rule in their turn, taking the reins from our hands... The child is a creature of environment, of opportunity, as children are

[1]I gratefully acknowledge the support provided to the Children of Immigrants Longitudinal Study (CILS) by research grants from the Andrew W. Mellon, Russell Sage, Spencer, and National Science Foundations to Alejandro Portes and Rubén G. Rumbaut, principal investigators. The CILS project was carried out in Southern California and South Florida during the 1990s. An earlier version of this paper was presented at the annual meeting of the Eastern Sociological Society, March 1998.

> everywhere... The problems that seemed so perplexing in the light of freshly-formed prejudices against this or that immigrant, yield to this simple solution that discovers all alarm to have been groundless. Yesterday it was the swarthy Italian, today the Russian Jew, that excited our distrust. Tomorrow it may be the Arab or the Greek. All alike they have taken, or are taking, their places in the ranks of our social phalanx, pushing upward from the bottom with steady effort, as I believe they will continue to do... And in the general advance the children, thus firmly grasped, are seen to be a powerful moving force."
> Jacob A. Riis, *The Children of The Poor* (1892), pp. 1-8.

## THE NEW IMMIGRATION

It has become a commonplace to observe that the United States is once again being profoundly transformed by the process of absorbing a "new" immigration that began about four decades ago and that seems unlikely to abate for the foreseeable future. Central to that transformation are the modes of incorporation of today's immigrants – and more consequentially still, as Jacob Riis vividly saw more than a century ago, of their offspring. Immigrant children and U.S.-born children of immigrants constitute the fastest growing segment of the U.S. child population. The 1990 census showed that they already accounted for 15 percent of all American children under 18 years of age at that time, including about 60 percent of all children classified as Hispanic and an overwhelming 90 percent of all Asian-American children (Zhou, 1997). By 1997, based on my analysis of the Current Population Surveys,[2] they accounted for 20 percent of all American children, a proportion that has continued to grow as a result of both immigration and natural increase. Specifically, the 1990 census counted some 2 million foreign-born children under 18, and another 6 million U.S.-born children under 18 living with immigrant parents (Oropesa and Landale, 1997). But between 1990 and 1997 the immigrant population of the U.S. increased from 20 to 27 million, and the number of their children grew commensurately: by 1997, CPS data showed there were 3 million foreign-born children under 18, and over 10 million U.S.-born children under 18 living with at least one foreign-born parent.

[2]To obtain more reliable estimates of the immigrant-stock population of the U.S., the March 1997 Current Population Survey data file was augmented by unduplicated cases from the March 1996 CPS (U.S. Bureau of the Census, Annual Demographic Files). For this analysis, "first generation" refers to the foreign-born population, and "second generation" to U.S.-born persons with at least one foreign-born parent. This definition does *not* include U.S. citizens who were born, as were their parents, in Puerto Rico or other U.S. territories, and who are thus not immigrants or children of immigrants.

Indeed, by 1997 the "immigrant-stock" population of the United States had grown to about 55 million people – that is, the first generation of foreign-born persons (26.8 million) and the second generation of U.S.-born persons with at least one foreign-born parent (27.8 million). That figure – one fifth of the national total (20.5%) – did not include 2.8 million others residing in the 50 states who were born (as were their parents) in Puerto Rico or other U.S. territories, nor the even larger number who resided in Puerto Rico and the other territories. Furthermore, net immigration to the U.S. (legal and illegal) has been adding an estimated one million more per year to the foreign-born population. Thus, the 2000 census – the results of which are not yet available – is likely to have counted a foreign-born population of some 30 million persons and a second generation of about 30 million more.

These groups are heavily concentrated in areas of settlement. Fully one third of the 55 million people who made up the immigrant-stock population of the U.S. in 1997 resided in California alone, and another third resided in Florida, Texas, and the New York-New Jersey region. The concentrations were denser still within metropolitan areas in these states (*cf.* Farley, 1996:151-207; Portes and Rumbaut, 1996; Rumbaut, 1994a). For example, in 1997, 62 percent of Los Angeles County's 9.5 million people were of immigrant stock, as were 54 percent of the residents of adjacent Orange County and 43 percent of San Diego's, so that the megalopolitan corridor stretching from San Diego to Los Angeles alone contained 17.2 percent of the country's foreign-stock population. New York City and the New Jersey metropolitan areas on the other side of the Hudson River combined for another 16.5 percent of the country's first and second generations. The Bay Area in California – encompassing San Francisco, Oakland and San José – absorbed 4.3 percent of the national immigrant-stock total; the corridor stretching from Miami to Ft. Lauderdale and Palm Beach contained another 4.8 percent. Nearly three fourths (72%) of metropolitan Miami's population was either foreign-born or of foreign parentage (the highest proportion in the U.S.).

Of the 27 million foreign-born in 1997, fully 60 percent had arrived since 1980, while an overwhelming 90 percent had immigrated to the U.S. since 1960. Of those post-1960 "new immigrants," the majority (52%) had come from Latin America and the Caribbean, with Mexico alone accounting for 28 percent of the total. Another 29 percent had come from Asia and the Middle East; the Filipinos, Chinese, and Indochinese (Vietnamese, Laotians and Cambodians) alone accounted for 15 percent of the total, or as much as all of those born in Europe and Canada combined. (Africa and Oceania made up most of the remaining 4%.) This "new immigration" is thus, by definition, of very recent vintage. Its main cause has been conventionally credited to (or blamed on) the changes to U.S. immigration law passed in 1965. But it is worth noting that while the 1965 Act did open the gates to previously excluded Asian (and African) immigration, the law had little to do with the dominant flows from the Americas, including Mexico – the 1965 Act actually sought to restrict the flows from the Western Hemisphere – or with the huge refugee resettlement programs that were a legacy of the Indochina War specifically and of the Cold War more generally.

Immigration, as always, is principally the province of the young. Of the more than 24 million immigrants in the U.S. who had come since 1960, 40 percent arrived as children under the age of 18 (what I long ago termed the "1.5 generation" to distinguish them from both the "first generation" who immigrated as adults and the U.S.-born "second generation"), and another 40 percent arrived as young adults between the ages of 18 and 34. Only one in ten immigrated after the age of 40. And of the 28 million who formed the U.S.-born "second generation" (defined as those with at least one foreign-born parent), about 40 percent were children under 18 in 1997, and another 16 percent were young adults 18 to 34 – mostly the offspring of the new immigrants from Asia, Latin America and the Caribbean. (About a third, however, were over 55 years old – born before World War II to parents who had immigrated to the U.S., mostly from Europe, in the early 20th century, and who form the remnants of what is now the "old" second generation.)

The rapid growth of immigration to the United States has been followed by an intensified debate about the new immigrants and their impact on American society in an age of both unprecedented diversity and widening inequality. Yet less noticed has been the fact that a new generation of Americans raised in immigrant families has been coming of age – transforming their adoptive society even as they themselves are becoming transformed into the newest Americans. Over time, its members will decisively shape the character of their ethnic communities and of the localities where they concentrate (Portes, 1996; Portes and Rumbaut, 1996, 2001). Hence, it is the children of today's immigrants – a post-immigrant generation oriented not to their parents' immigrant pasts but to their own American futures – who represent the most lasting legacy of the new mass immigration to the United States.

**TABLE 1**
**SIZE AND LOCATION (IN FLORIDA OR CALIFORNIA) OF THE CILS SAMPLE, BY NATIONAL ORIGIN OF RESPONDENTS**

| National Origin | Miami/ Ft. Lauderdale (N) | San Diego (N) | Total Sample (N) |
|---|---|---|---|
| Latin America: | | | |
| Cuba | 1,224 | 2 | 1,226 |
| Mexico | 28 | 727 | 755 |
| Nicaragua | 340 | 4 | 344 |
| Colombia | 223 | 4 | 227 |
| Dominican Republic | 100 | 4 | 104 |
| Other Latin America | 311 | 55 | 366 |
| Haiti and West Indies: | | | |
| Haiti | 177 | 1 | 178 |
| Jamaica, West Indies | 253 | 19 | 272 |
| Asia: | | | |
| Philippines | 11 | 808 | 819 |
| Vietnam | 8 | 362 | 370 |
| Laos (Lao) | 1 | 154 | 155 |
| Laos (Hmong) | 0 | 53 | 53 |
| Cambodia | 1 | 94 | 95 |
| Chinese | 23 | 49 | 72 |
| Other Asia | 22 | 78 | 100 |
| All Other Countries[1] | 120 | 6 | 126 |
| TOTAL | 2,842 | 2,420 | 5,262 |

[1] Of those, 88 are of European or Canadian origin, 38 hail from the Middle East or Africa.

## *THE CHILDREN OF IMMIGRANTS LONGITUDINAL STUDY*

This paper summarizes some of the results of the Children of Immigrants Longitudinal Study (CILS), a multifaceted investigation of the educational performance and social, cultural and psychological adaptation of children of immigrants.[3] It is the largest study of its kind to date in the U.S. Since late 1991, the study has followed the progress of a sizable sample of teenage youths representing 77 nationalities in two key areas of immigrant settlement in the United States: Southern California (San Diego) and South Florida (the Miami and Fort Lauderdale areas). The original survey, conducted in Spring 1992 ("T1"), interviewed 5,262 students enrolled in the 8th and 9th grades in three school districts: the San Diego Unified School District (N=2,420), and the Dade and Broward County Unified School Districts (N=2,296 and 339, respectively). Also in the sample were 207 stu-

[3]A full analysis of CILS findings will be available in two forthcoming volumes: Portes and Rumbaut (2001) and Rumbaut and Portes (2001).

dents enrolled in two private bilingual schools in the Miami area. The sample was drawn in the junior high grades, a level at which dropout rates are still relatively rare, to avoid the potential bias of differential dropout rates between ethnic groups at the senior high school level. For purposes of the study, students were eligible to enter the sample if they were U.S.-born but had at least one immigrant (foreign-born) parent, or if they themselves were foreign-born and had come to the U.S. at an early age (most before age ten).

The resulting baseline sample was evenly balanced between males and females, and between foreign-born and U.S.-born children of immigrants – that is, respectively, between the 1.5 generation and the second generation. As Table 1 shows, the principal nationalities represented in the San Diego CILS sample are Mexicans, Filipinos, Vietnamese, Laotians, Cambodians, and smaller groups of other children of immigrants from Asia (mostly Chinese, Japanese, Korean, and Indian) and Latin America. In the South Florida CILS sample, the principal national-origin groups consist of Cubans, Haitians, Jamaicans, Colombians, Nicaraguans, Dominicans, and others from Latin America and the Caribbean. These groups are representative of the principal types of immigrants in contemporary American society – including immigrant laborers, professionals, entrepreneurs, and refugees with sharply contrasting socioeconomic origins, migration histories, and contexts of exit and of reception (*see* Rumbaut, 1994a; Portes and Rumbaut, 1996). It is worth noting that although the 27 million immigrants in the U.S. in 1997 came from over 150 different countries, about 40 percent came from only four: Mexico, the Philippines, Cuba, and Vietnam. Children of immigrants from those same four countries make up 60 percent of the CILS sample.

Three years later, in 1995-96 ("T2"), a second survey of the same group of children of immigrants was conducted – this time supplemented by in-depth interviews with a stratified sample of their parents. The purpose of this follow-up effort, which succeeded in re-interviewing 82 percent of the baseline sample, was to ascertain changes over time in their family situation, school achievement, educational and occupational aspirations, language use and preferences, ethnic identities, experiences and expectations of discrimination, and psychosocial adjustment. By this time the youths, who were originally interviewed in junior high when most were 14 or 15 years old, had reached the final year of senior high school and were embarking on their transitions to adulthood. This paper focuses on changes observed over time in language, identity, ambition, and achievement, and on some implications for American society of these transformations of the post-immigrant generation in an age of diversity.

## *SOCIOECONOMIC CHARACTERISTICS OF THE IMMIGRANT FAMILIES*

Table 2 sketches a socioeconomic profile of the families in the CILS sample, broken down by the major national-origin groups. There are very large differences in the parents' level of educational attainment. Few Mexican and Indochinese fathers and mothers had college degrees, well below the 1990 U.S. norm of 20 percent for adults 25 and over, whereas 41 percent of Filipino mothers had college degrees, well above national norms. The contrast is made even sharper by looking at the proportion of parents with less than a high school education – that is, less than what their children have now already achieved. Most of the more recently arrived foreign-born children from Mexico, Haiti, Vietnam, Laos and Cambodia have fathers and mothers who never completed secondary-level schooling.

Rates of labor force participation vary widely by nationality for both fathers and mothers as well. Refugee parents from Laos and Cambodia, and to a lesser extent those from Vietnam, had the lowest rates of labor force participation by far, indicative of their eligibility for and use of public assistance, whereas most of the other groups had rates that exceeded national norms. Cubans, Jamaicans, Filipinos and the "Other Asians" were most likely to have one or both parents working as professionals. Over half (56%) of the sample lived in families who owned their homes in 1992 (T1); three years later (T2) that proportion had edged up to 62 percent. But there was a huge gap between ethnic groups, ranging at T2 from a low of 4 percent among Hmong families from Laos and 8 percent of the Cambodians to over 80 percent of the Filipinos who were homeowners.

There are also significant differences in family structure among these groups. All of the Asian-origin nationalities had high proportions of intact families (over 75% of these children live with both natural parents at home), followed by the Latin American families (over 60%), while fewer than 50 percent of the Haitians and West Indians lived in intact families. However, within these families the quality of parent-child relationships varied significantly. Growing up in immigrant families is often marked by linguistic and other acculturative gaps between parents and children that can exacerbate intergenerational conflicts, cause the children to feel embarrassed rather than proud of their parents as they try to fit in with

**TABLE 2**

**Family Socioeconomic Status, Family Structure, and Quality of Family Relationships of Children of Immigrants in Southern California and South Florida (CILS Sample), in 1992 (T1) and 1995 (T2)**

| Characteristics by National Origin and Time of Survey | Time | Mexico | Cuba | Other Latin America | Haiti | Jamaica, W. Indies | Filipino | Vietnam | Laos, Cambodia | Other Asia | Total |
|---|---|---|---|---|---|---|---|---|---|---|---|
| *Socioeconomic Status:* | | | | | | | | | | | |
| Father: | T1 | | | | | | | | | | |
| % College graduate | | 7.7 | 26.3 | 31.2 | 11.1 | 24.9 | 29.1 | 15.5 | 7.8 | 42.5 | 23.1 |
| % Less than high school | | 64.8 | 37.6 | 31.2 | 57.8 | 42.3 | 15.7 | 59.7 | 72.8 | 20.6 | 40.7 |
| % Not in labor force | | 18.9 | 15.7 | 19.5 | 27.4 | 27.9 | 17.3 | 42.3 | 72.1 | 12.5 | 23.8 |
| Mother: | T1 | | | | | | | | | | |
| % College graduate | | 4.3 | 22.0 | 23.3 | 10.4 | 28.9 | 40.5 | 9.4 | 3.5 | 26.3 | 20.9 |
| % Less than high school | | 72.5 | 28.1 | 30.8 | 58.5 | 21.9 | 19.6 | 67.1 | 83.0 | 25.6 | 40.6 |
| % Not in labor force | | 43.4 | 28.4 | 26.5 | 24.4 | 16.4 | 12.2 | 56.5 | 80.9 | 34.0 | 32.5 |
| Home ownership: | | | | | | | | | | | |
| % Family owns home | T1 | 35.4 | 70.1 | 49.3 | 67.4 | 66.2 | 77.2 | 35.8 | 17.3 | 75.0 | 56.1 |
| % Family owns home | T2 | 43.9 | 72.0 | 59.2 | 77.0 | 71.6 | 81.8 | 36.5 | 22.6 | 80.6 | 61.7 |
| Family: | | | | | | | | | | | |
| *Family Structure:* | T1 | | | | | | | | | | |
| % Intact family (both natural parents at home) | | 64.4 | 62.2 | 63.9 | 49.6 | 47.3 | 81.5 | 77.1 | 73.9 | 78.4 | 67.5 |
| % Step family | | 12.2 | 13.4 | 14.3 | 18.5 | 17.4 | 8.4 | 4.8 | 5.7 | 6.3 | 11.5 |
| % Single parent | | 19.9 | 21.2 | 20.0 | 28.1 | 32.8 | 8.3 | 14.5 | 18.7 | 13.8 | 18.4 |
| % Other | | 3.5 | 3.2 | 1.8 | 3.7 | 2.5 | 1.8 | 3.5 | 1.8 | 1.9 | 2.6 |
| Parent-Child Conflict:* | T1 | | | | | | | | | | |
| % Low conflict | | 67.7 | 71.4 | 70.0 | 56.9 | 61.5 | 62.7 | 57.9 | 53.7 | 69.6 | 65.9 |
| % Medium conflict | | 25.2 | 24.9 | 25.1 | 34.6 | 33.5 | 30.9 | 34.8 | 40.6 | 22.8 | 28.4 |
| % High conflict | | 7.1 | 3.7 | 5.0 | 8.5 | 5.0 | 6.4 | 7.3 | 5.7 | 7.6 | 5.7 |
| Family Cohesion:* | T2 | | | | | | | | | | |
| % Low | | 28.1 | 30.9 | 29.1 | 53.0 | 34.3 | 33.9 | 41.6 | 32.5 | 31.9 | 32.5 |
| % Medium | | 33.2 | 32.5 | 30.7 | 24.2 | 35.9 | 37.5 | 30.5 | 37.5 | 33.1 | 33.2 |
| % High | | 38.7 | 36.6 | 40.2 | 22.7 | 29.8 | 28.6 | 27.9 | 30.0 | 35.0 | 34.3 |

* For details on the composition of the scales measuring parent-child conflict and family cohesion, *see* Rumbaut 1994b; Portes and Rumbaut, 2001.

native peers, or lead to role reversals, as children assume adult roles prematurely by dint of circumstance. As Table 2 shows, there were sharp differences in the degree of conflict and cohesiveness among the various national-origin groups, with all of the Latin Americans reporting higher family cohesiveness and the Haitian sample reflecting the highest degree of parent-child conflict.

## *LANGUAGE SHIFTS IN THE SECOND GENERATION*

For immigrant and second-generation youth, language is at the core of the process of acculturation, and it is also often a source of tension in their relationship with their immigrant parents. For the society that receives them, a perennial controversy in public debates on immigration concerns the role of so-called "bilingual education" and perceived threats to the continuing predominance of English as the common national language. Such concerns have been reflected in popular initiatives such as Proposition 227 in California – dubbed "English for the Children" – and Proposition 203 in Arizona, which were approved by the voters in 1998 and 2000, respectively. They aim to eliminate the states' bilingual programs and require that all public school instruction be conducted in English. CILS data on language use, preference and proficiency over time provide some illuminating information in this regard.

Over 90 percent of these children of immigrants lived in homes in which a language other than English was spoken. But as seen in Table 3, at T1 already 73 percent of the total sample preferred to speak English instead of their parents' native tongue, including 64 percent of the foreign-born youth and 81 percent of the U.S.-born. By T2, the proportion who preferred English had swelled to 88 percent, including 83 percent of the foreign-born and 93 percent of the U.S.-born. Even among the most mother-tongue-retentive group – the Mexican-origin youth living in San Diego, a city on the Mexican border with a large Spanish-speaking immigrant population and a wide range of Spanish-language radio and TV stations – the force of linguistic assimilation was incontrovertible. While at T1 only a third (32%) of the Mexico-born children preferred English, by T2 that preference had doubled to 61 percent; and while just over half (53%) of the U.S.-born Mexican-Americans in San Diego preferred English at T1, that proportion had jumped to four-fifths (79%) three years later. Among Cuban-origin youth in Miami, the shift was even sharper: 95 percent of both the foreign-born and the native-born preferred English by T2.

**TABLE 3**
**Language Preference and Proficiency Among Children of Immigrants in Southern California and South Florida (CILS Sample), in 1992 (T1) and 1995 T2)**

| Characteristics by National Origin and Time of Survey | Time | Mexico | Cuba | Other Latin America | Jamaica, Haiti | W. Indies | Filipino | Vietnam | Laos, Cambodia | Other Asia | Total |
|---|---|---|---|---|---|---|---|---|---|---|---|
| Primary Language Spoken at Home: | T1 | | | | | | | | | | |
| % English | | 2.5 | 3.2 | 2.7 | 3.0 | 61.7 | 5.6 | 0.3 | 0.0 | 13.3 | 6.1 |
| % Non-English | | 97.5 | 96.8 | 97.3 | 97.0 | 38.3 | 94.4 | 99.7 | 100.0 | 86.7 | 93.9 |
| English Language: | | | | | | | | | | | |
| % Prefers English | T1 | 45.7 | 83.1 | 73.9 | 83.7 | 75.6 | 89.4 | 51.6 | 59.4 | 77.5 | 72.6 |
| % Speaks it "very well" | T1 | 61.2 | 90.3 | 81.6 | 87.4 | 92.0 | 85.9 | 54.2 | 42.0 | 78.8 | 77.3 |
| | T2 | 62.4 | 88.9 | 83.6 | 86.7 | 94.0 | 88.4 | 50.6 | 43.8 | 77.5 | 77.9 |
| % Reads it "very well" | T1 | 55.3 | 82.7 | 74.4 | 81.5 | 90.0 | 87.2 | 50.0 | 34.6 | 75.6 | 72.4 |
| | T2 | 62.4 | 88.9 | 83.6 | 86.7 | 94.0 | 88.4 | 50.6 | 43.8 | 77.5 | 77.9 |
| Non-English Language: | | | | | | | | | | | |
| % Speaks it "very well" | T1 | 55.9 | 33.2 | 41.3 | 21.6 | 14.1 | 11.4 | 36.9 | 40.4 | 25.6 | 33.5 |
| | T2 | 59.4 | 37.5 | 42.8 | 25.9 | 9.5 | 10.5 | 33.2 | 38.5 | 23.8 | 34.5 |
| % Reads it "very well" | T1 | 41.7 | 24.1 | 30.4 | 9.6 | 14.9 | 9.4 | 14.2 | 4.6 | 10.0 | 21.8 |
| | T2 | 48.2 | 30.5 | 33.7 | 8.1 | 10.0 | 8.3 | 13.5 | 5.3 | 10.6 | 24.4 |

A main reason for this rapid language shift in use and preference has to do with their increasing fluency in English (both spoken and written) relative to their level of fluency in the mother tongue. Over three-fourths of the total sample at both T1 and T2 reported speaking English "very well," compared to only about a third who reported an equivalent level of spoken fluency in the non-English language. Even among the foreign born, those who spoke English very well surpassed by 69 percent to 41 percent those who spoke the mother tongue just as well. And the differences in reading fluency were much sharper still: those who could read English "very well" tripled the proportion of those who could read a non-English language very well (78% to 24%). The ability to maintain a sound level of literacy in a language – particularly in languages with entirely different alphabets and rules of syntax and grammar, such as many of the Asian languages brought by immigrants to California – is nearly impossible to achieve in the absence of schools that teach it, and of a community that values it and in which it can be regularly practiced.

As a consequence, the bilingualism of these children of immigrants becomes increasingly uneven and unstable. The CILS data document the rapidity with which English triumphs and foreign languages atrophy in the United States – even in a border city like San Diego with the busiest international border crossing in the world, or in Miami, the metropolitan area with the highest percentage of foreign-born in the country – as the second generation not only comes to speak, read and write it fluently, but prefers it overwhelmingly over their parents' native tongue. It bears adding that these results have occurred while the youths were still residing as dependents in their parents' home, where the non-English mother tongue retains primacy; once they leave the parental fold to lead independent lives of their own, the degree of English language dominance and non-English language atrophy is almost certain to accelerate, all the more among those living outside dense immigrant enclaves.

This pattern of rapid linguistic assimilation is constant across nationalities and socioeconomic levels and suggests that, over time, the use of and fluency in foreign languages will inevitably decline. The findings instead suggest that the linguistic outcomes for the third generation – the grandchildren of the present wave of immigrants – will be no different than what has been the age-old pattern in American history: the grandchildren will most likely grow up speaking English only. It is for this reason that the United States has been called a "language graveyard." Thus, while the public debate over English remains contentious, what is being eliminated rapidly instead are these children's ability to maintain fluency in the language of their immigrant parents, a significant loss of scarce and valuable bilingual resources not only for the individual but for the United States in an increasingly global economy.

The rise of "global cities" in the international economy has triggered a growing need for professionals and managers able to conduct business in more than one language (Portes and Hao, 1998). Among American cities, New York and Los Angeles are prime examples of global cities and fluency in a number of languages is much in demand there – as well as in Miami, which has become the administrative and marketing center of the nation's Latin American trade (Portes and Stepick, 1993). Yet business leaders in Miami have complained about the dearth of fluent Spanish bilinguals among the children of Latin immigrants – and a University of Miami study sponsored by the local Chamber of Commerce argued that young Hispanic Americans are leaving school with such insufficient Spanish-language skills that Miami's position as an international marketplace is at risk (Fradd, 1996). Although, as seen in the CILS data, many children of Cuban and other Latin immigrants do retain some ability in the language, their Spanish is not fluent enough to be able to conduct business transactions – a situation that recently led a local businesswoman to put the matter this way: "We have 600,000 Hispanics here and we cannot find qualified people to write a letter in Spanish" (Mears, 1997; *see also* Navarro, 1996).

## *IDENTITY SHIFTS IN THE SECOND GENERATION*

The way that adolescents see themselves is significant. Self-identities and ethnic loyalties can often influence patterns of behavior and outlook independent of the status of the families or the types of schools that children attend. In both CILS surveys, an identical open-ended question was asked to ascertain the respondent's ethnic self-identity. Four main types of ethnic identities became apparent: 1) an unhyphenated "American" identity; 2) a hyphenated-American identity; 3) a national-origin identity (*e.g.*, Filipino, Cuban, Jamaican); and 4) a pan-ethnic minority group identity (*e.g.*, Hispanic, Latino, Chicano, Asian, Black). In 1992, as Table 4 shows, a fourth of the sample (27%) identified by national origin; the largest proportion (41%) chose a hyphenated-American identification; 11 percent identified as plain "American;" and 17 percent selected pan-ethnic minority identities. Whether the youth was born in the U.S. or not made a great

**TABLE 4**

**Ethnic Self-Identity, Discrimination, and Perceptions of American Society Among Children of Immigrants in Southern California and South Florida (CILS Sample), in 1992 (T1) and 1995 (T2)**

| Characteristics by National Origin and Time of Survey | Time | Mexico | Cuba | Other Latin America | Jamaica, Haiti | W. Indies | Filipino | Vietnam | Laos, Cambodia | Other Asia | Total |
|---|---|---|---|---|---|---|---|---|---|---|---|
| *Ethnic Self-Identity:* | | | | | | | | | | | |
| % "American" | T1 | 2.3 | 22.1 | 15.9 | 13.3 | 17.9 | 3.3 | 3.9 | 2.1 | 13.8 | 11.3 |
| % Hyphenated-American | T1 | 30.9 | 53.7 | 20.2 | 38.5 | 27.4 | 59.5 | 47.7 | 33.9 | 46.3 | 41.1 |
| % National origin | T1 | 17.7 | 14.9 | 26.7 | 31.1 | 42.3 | 30.1 | 41.6 | 54.8 | 30.6 | 27.3 |
| % Racial/panethnic | T1 | 46.7 | 8.4 | 34.2 | 11.9 | 6.5 | 2.2 | 0.3 | 1.8 | 1.3 | 16.6 |
| % Mixed ethnicity, other | T1 | 2.3 | 0.9 | 3.0 | 5.2 | 6.0 | 4.8 | 6.5 | 7.4 | 8.1 | 3.7 |
| *Discrimination:* | | | | | | | | | | | |
| % Experienced discrimination | T1 | 62.5 | 35.3 | 48.0 | 62.7 | 69.5 | 63.9 | 66.3 | 65.0 | 59.7 | 54.3 |
| % Expects discrimination | T1 | 34.5 | 19.1 | 24.3 | 48.9 | 58.5 | 38.1 | 35.3 | 42.6 | 30.2 | 31.6 |
| | T2 | 38.4 | 21.8 | 26.4 | 63.8 | 55.6 | 44.2 | 38.4 | 43.1 | 34.4 | 35.0 |
| *Perceptions of U.S.:* | | | | | | | | | | | |
| % U.S. is best country to live in | T1 | 55.3 | 71.7 | 51.4 | 36.3 | 32.8 | 63.3 | 67.0 | 68.2 | 68.8 | 60.2 |
| | T2 | 64.5 | 80.7 | 69.2 | 53.7 | 49.7 | 75.7 | 79.4 | 68.6 | 66.9 | 71.5 |
| % Prefers American ways | T1 | 27.2 | 47.0 | 37.2 | 40.7 | 37.3 | 53.0 | 39.8 | 32.5 | 56.9 | 41.5 |
| | T2 | 24.9 | 40.5 | 34.7 | 46.7 | 40.3 | 53.9 | 38.4 | 39.2 | 49.4 | 39.7 |

deal of difference in the type of identity selected: at T1, the foreign-born were four times more likely to identify by national origin (43%) than were the U.S.-born (11%); conversely, the U.S.-born were much more likely to identify as American or hyphenated-American than were the foreign-born. Those findings at T1 suggested an assimilative trend from one generation to another (*see* Rumbaut, 1994b, for an analysis of T1 outcomes), possibly paralleling the pattern of language shift seen above.

But the results of the 1995 survey (conducted in the months after the passage of Proposition 187 in California) turned conventional expectations on their head. In Southern California, there was a rapid decline of both the plain "American" (cut to less than 2%) and hyphenated-American (dropping from 43% to 30%) self-identities. Instead, the biggest gainer by far in terms of the self-image of these youths was the foreign nationality identity, chosen by 32 percent at T1 but by 48 percent at T2. This shift took place among both the foreign-born and the U.S.-born, most notably among the youth of Mexican and Filipino descent – the two largest immigrant groups in the U.S. – an apparent backlash during a period (1992-96) of growing anti-immigrant sentiment and at times overt immigrant-bashing in the country, above all in California. Pan-ethnic identities remained at 16 percent at T2, but that figure conceals a steep decline among Mexican-origin youth in "Hispanic" and "Chicano" self-identities, and a sharp upswing in the proportion of youths now identifying pan-ethnically as "Asian" or "Asian American," especially among the smallest groups. In South Florida, the biggest gains overall were in pan-ethnic identities such as "Hispanic" and "Black," doubling from 17 percent at T1 to 38 percent at T2, mainly among all the Latin Americans and the Jamaicans, while the percent identifying by national origin remained unchanged at about a fifth. A plain American identity dropped sharply from 19 percent to less than 4 percent, and hyphenated-American identities fell to 30 percent overall. The Haitians were a notable exception in Florida: resembling the California pattern, the proportion selecting a denationalized pan-ethnic identity decreased, while the proportions identifying as "Haitian" and "Haitian-American" increased notably.

Change over time, in any event, has not been toward assimilative mainstream identities (with or without a hyphen), but rather toward a reaffirmation of the immigrant identity for some groups (the Mexicans and Filipinos in California, the Haitians and Nicaraguans in Florida), and toward racial or pan-ethnic minority group identities for almost all others, as these youths become increasingly aware of the ethnic and racial categories in which they are persistently classified by mainstream society – and this among a sample of children of immigrants only 13 percent of whom self-report racially as "white."[4] In both of these variants, the results point to the rise of a "reactive ethnicity" (Portes and Rumbaut, 1996, 2001) and to a growing identification with U.S. minority groups that, if sustained, may portend potentially significant political alignments and commitments in their adult years.

## *DISCRIMINATION AND VIEWS OF THE UNITED STATES*

The process of growing ethnic awareness among the children of immigrants in the CILS sample is especially evident in their experiences and expectations of racial and ethnic discrimination (*see* Table 4). Reports of being discriminated against increased from 54 percent to 62 percent of the sample in the last survey. Virtually every group reported more such experiences of unfair treatment as they grew older, with the highest proportions found among the children of Afro-Caribbean and Asian immigrants, followed by Mexicans and other Latin Americans, and the lowest proportions among the Cuban youth in Miami.

Among those reporting discrimination, their own race or nationality was overwhelmingly perceived to account for what triggers unfair treatment from others. Such experiences tend to be associated over time with a higher incidence of depressive symptoms, and with the development of a more pessimistic stance about their chances to reduce discriminatory treatment through higher educational achievement. In both surveys the students were asked to agree or disagree with the statement, "No matter how much education I get, people will still discriminate against me." At T1, 32 percent of the sample agreed with that assessment; by T2, the proportion agreeing was 35 percent, including substantial majorities of black immigrants from the West Indies (57%) and Haiti (64%).

Still, it is important as well to underscore the fact that despite their growing awareness of the realities of American racism and nativism, most of the youth in the sample (almost two-thirds) continued to affirm a con-

[4]The CILS survey asked the youth to report their "race" according to a fixed response format, which included a "multiracial" option as well as "other" (in which case they were asked to specify). Fewer than half adhered to the standard categories of white (13%), black (7%), and Asian (26%), while another 12 percent chose "multiracial." But about half of the Cubans and other Latin Americans, and a fourth of the Mexicans, specified "Hispanic" as their race, while about half of the Mexicans and a fourth of the Filipinos listed their nationality as their race – underscoring the socially constructed character of these perceptions.

fident belief in the promise of equal opportunity through educational achievement. Even more tellingly, 60 percent of these youths agreed in the T1 survey that "there is no better country to live in than the United States," and that endorsement grew to 72 percent three years later – despite a growing anti-immigrant mood in the country during that period. The groups *most* likely to endorse that view were the children of political exiles who found a favorable context of reception in the U.S.: the Cubans and the Vietnamese. The groups *least* likely to agree with that statement were those who have most felt the weight of racial discrimination: the children of immigrants from Haiti, Jamaica and the West Indies.

## *EDUCATIONAL AMBITIONS*

These children of immigrants are ambitious, as evidenced by the results shown in Table 5. When they were in the 8th and 9th grades, 67 percent *aspired* to advanced degrees and another 24 percent would not be satisfied with less than a college degree. Three years later, as the high school years came to a close, these proportions stayed exactly the same – showing the remarkable stability over time of these aspirations. But aspirations (what people desire) and expectations (what they think will actually happen) are not the same thing. The students were also asked for a "realistic" assessment of their chances of achieving those aspirations. At T1, 42 percent "realistically" *expected* to earn advanced degrees and another 37 percent would not be satisfied with less than a college degree; at T2, these proportions too stayed virtually the same – 44 percent now "realistically" expected to earn advanced degrees and another 38 percent expected to graduate from college – again showing the resilience over time of these more realistic expectations. The proportion of those who, based on a realistic assessment, believed that they would not reach as far as a college degree dropped slightly from 21 percent at T1 to 18 percent at T2.

Given the modest family origins and material resources of many of these children, their aspirations and expectations may be disproportionate with what many will be able to achieve in the end; that remains an open empirical question (one that we will seek to answer when we return to the field to reinterview the full CILS sample in 2001-02, when they will be nearing their mid-twenties). But ambition and a sense of purpose clearly matter. The research literature shows that high expectations are necessary for subsequent achievement. While most of these youths aim high, the least ambitious expectations were exhibited by the Mexicans, Cambodians

**TABLE 5**

**EDUCATIONAL ASPIRATIONS, EXPECTATIONS, AND PLANS OF CHILDREN OF IMMIGRANTS, THEIR PARENTS AND THEIR CLOSE FRIENDS IN SOUTHERN CALIFORNIA AND SOUTH FLORIDA (CILS SAMPLE), IN 1992 (T1) AND 1995 (T2)**

| Characteristics by National Origin and Time of Survey | Time | Mexico | Cuba | Other Latin America | Jamaica, Haiti | W. Indies | Filipino | Vietnam | Laos, Cambodia | Other Asia | Total |
|---|---|---|---|---|---|---|---|---|---|---|---|
| *Educational Aspirations:* | | | | | | | | | | | |
| % Advanced Degree | T1 | 50.9 | 72.4 | 72.4 | 73.7 | 73.1 | 73.1 | 61.2 | 46.2 | 73.8 | 67.0 |
| | T2 | 48.4 | 72.0 | 69.5 | 67.4 | 75.1 | 71.6 | 68.7 | 51.6 | 74.4 | 66.6 |
| % College Degree | T1 | 26.0 | 22.4 | 22.8 | 21.8 | 23.4 | 22.4 | 27.7 | 31.2 | 23.8 | 24.1 |
| | T2 | 29.5 | 21.7 | 22.0 | 20.7 | 17.9 | 22.4 | 23.2 | 30.4 | 21.9 | 23.5 |
| % Less than college | T1 | 23.1 | 5.2 | 4.7 | 4.5 | 3.5 | 4.4 | 11.1 | 22.6 | 2.5 | 8.9 |
| | T2 | 22.0 | 6.2 | 8.5 | 11.9 | 7.0 | 6.0 | 8.1 | 18.0 | 3.8 | 9.9 |
| *Educational Expectations:* | | | | | | | | | | | |
| % Advanced Degree | T1 | 30.0 | 51.3 | 45.6 | 52.6 | 51.2 | 40.5 | 39.7 | 19.9 | 50.0 | 42.3 |
| | T2 | 24.9 | 51.3 | 46.3 | 55.6 | 55.2 | 44.7 | 48.1 | 19.4 | 65.0 | 43.9 |
| % College Degree | T1 | 33.5 | 34.6 | 36.4 | 32.3 | 36.3 | 42.9 | 39.7 | 35.0 | 41.3 | 36.9 |
| | T2 | 39.0 | 37.1 | 38.7 | 25.6 | 28.4 | 41.5 | 38.4 | 49.8 | 26.3 | 38.2 |
| % Less than College | T1 | 36.5 | 14.1 | 18.1 | 15.0 | 12.4 | 16.6 | 20.5 | 45.1 | 8.8 | 20.8 |
| | T2 | 36.1 | 11.6 | 15.0 | 18.8 | 16.4 | 13.9 | 13.5 | 30.7 | 8.8 | 17.9 |
| *Parents' Expectations for Child:* | T2 | | | | | | | | | | |
| % Advanced Degree | | 51.4 | 67.5 | 71.5 | 66.9 | 70.0 | 64.4 | 67.2 | 56.1 | 69.4 | 64.9 |
| % College Degree | | 33.1 | 26.5 | 24.4 | 23.3 | 23.5 | 31.5 | 23.2 | 30.6 | 29.4 | 27.8 |
| % Less than College | | 15.5 | 6.0 | 4.0 | 9.8 | 6.5 | 4.0 | 9.6 | 13.3 | 1.3 | 7.3 |
| *Plans of R's Close Friends:* | | | | | | | | | | | |
| % Plan to attend 4-year college: | | T2 | | | | | | | | | |
| None | | 16.9 | 6.9 | 7.3 | 7.5 | 5.1 | 4.0 | 4.2 | 8.9 | 1.9 | 7.6 |
| Some | | 55.8 | 46.4 | 52.9 | 43.3 | 37.8 | 43.8 | 46.8 | 48.4 | 38.1 | 47.9 |
| Many or most | | 27.3 | 46.7 | 39.8 | 49.3 | 57.1 | 52.2 | 49.0 | 42.7 | 60.0 | 44.5 |
| % Dropped out of school: | T2 | | | | | | | | | | |
| None | | 48.1 | 50.4 | 43.2 | 60.9 | 58.1 | 60.5 | 63.3 | 53.4 | 76.9 | 53.3 |
| Some | | 44.0 | 46.1 | 49.7 | 34.6 | 39.4 | 37.6 | 33.8 | 43.1 | 21.3 | 42.3 |
| Many or most | | 7.9 | 3.4 | 7.1 | 4.5 | 2.5 | 1.9 | 2.9 | 3.6 | 1.9 | 4.4 |

**TABLE 6**
**Time Spent on School Work and Television by Children of Immigrants in Southern California and South Florida (CILS Sample), in 1992 (T1) and 1995 (T2)**

| Characteristics by National Origin and Time of Survey | Time | Mexico | Cuba | Latin America | Jamaica, Haiti | W. Indies | Filipino | Vietnam | Laos, Cambodia | Other Asia | Total |
|---|---|---|---|---|---|---|---|---|---|---|---|
| Homework and TV: | | | | | | | | | | | |
| *Homework hours daily:* | | | | | | | | | | | |
| % Under 1 hour | T1 | 29.6 | 31.3 | 29.8 | 11.3 | 21.0 | 11.3 | 10.1 | 11.3 | 11.3 | 22.5 |
| % 1 to 3 hours | | 59.2 | 54.4 | 54.6 | 59.4 | 48.5 | 59.6 | 58.1 | 60.8 | 61.9 | 56.9 |
| % Over 3 hours | | 11.2 | 14.3 | 15.6 | 29.3 | 30.5 | 29.2 | 31.8 | 27.9 | 26.9 | 20.6 |
| % Under 1 hour | T2 | 22.0 | 31.3 | 25.4 | 14.2 | 17.7 | 8.9 | 8.4 | 10.2 | 13.1 | 19.9 |
| % 1 to 3 hours | | 61.9 | 51.2 | 54.6 | 60.4 | 52.0 | 55.7 | 49.0 | 62.2 | 43.8 | 54.8 |
| % Over 3 hours | | 16.1 | 17.4 | 20.0 | 25.4 | 30.3 | 35.4 | 42.5 | 27.6 | 43.1 | 25.2 |
| *TV-watching hours daily:* | | | | | | | | | | | |
| % Under 2 hours | T1 | 34.9 | 27.6 | 28.7 | 20.1 | 24.5 | 26.4 | 40.3 | 38.9 | 45.3 | 30.6 |
| % 2 to 4 hours | | 37.4 | 35.7 | 34.0 | 26.1 | 33.5 | 43.1 | 41.6 | 41.3 | 32.7 | 37.2 |
| % Over 4 hours | | 27.7 | 36.7 | 37.3 | 53.7 | 42.0 | 30.5 | 18.0 | 19.8 | 22.0 | 32.2 |
| % Under 2 hours | T2 | 52.3 | 50.8 | 48.1 | 33.6 | 33.3 | 48.7 | 55.3 | 53.4 | 61.9 | 49.7 |
| % 2 to 4 hours | | 31.9 | 31.9 | 31.1 | 29.1 | 36.4 | 34.0 | 30.1 | 34.3 | 25.6 | 32.0 |
| % Over 4 hours | | 15.7 | 17.3 | 20.8 | 37.3 | 30.3 | 17.3 | 14.6 | 12.4 | 12.5 | 18.3 |

and Laotians. Thus, there were major differences in aspirations and expectations by family socioeconomic status, and this gap was not reduced over time. Children from better off families have predictably higher and more secure plans for the future.

Regarding their educational futures, our CILS respondents felt that their parents expected them to achieve at a higher level than the children themselves did. Indeed, for many immigrants that is precisely the purpose of bringing their children to the United States. At T2, while 44 percent of the students expected to attain an advanced degree, 65 percent of their parents did so; and while 18 percent of the children expected to stop short of a college degree, only 7 percent of the parents held such a low expectation. Parental expectations in turn are highly correlated with students' school performance.[5]

In contrast to the perceived parental pressure to achieve are the plans of the students' close friends – and again the types of peer groups in which the students are embedded vary in part by family socioeconomic status. As the bottom panel of Table 5 shows, the sharpest contrast in these friendship networks is seen between the Jamaicans, Filipinos and Other Asians (most of whose friends intend to attend 4-year colleges and universities) and the Mexican students (only a quarter of whom have friends who plan on attending 4-year colleges, and about 8% of whom reported at T2 that most of their close friends had already dropped out of school). These social circles can exercise a powerful influence in either reinforcing or undercutting children's high aspirations and confidence in reaching them.

Still, the children of immigrants in this sample almost universally value the importance of a good education. Out of a variety of choices given in the T2 survey, 90 percent ranked a good education as "very

[5]Kao and Tienda (1995), using the National Educational Longitudinal Study (NELS:88) data set with a sample of about 25,000 8th graders, found that the children of immigrants had higher educational aspirations than the children of native-born parents; tellingly, moreover, immigrant parents held *higher* aspirations for their children than did their own children, whereas native-born parents had *lower* aspirations for their children than did their own children. In this connection, it is worth noting two phenomena that may be interrelated: 1) divorced parents have lower expectations for their children's academic achievement than do non-divorced parents (*c.f.* Thomson, Alexander, and Entwisle, 1988); and 2) with some significant exceptions (such as the Dominicans, Jamaicans, and Haitians), children of immigrants are generally more likely to live in intact families than are the children of the native-born, with divorce rates assimilating to native norms and increasing from the first to the second and third generations (*cf.* Jensen and Chitose, 1994; Landale and Oropesa, 1995; Rumbaut, 1994a, 1997a, 1997b).

important" (more than any other value), and another 85 percent deemed becoming an expert in one's field "very important," while less than half as many (41%) equally valued "having lots of money."[6] And these values and aspirations are generally backed up behaviorally by persistent effort: as Table 6 shows, the majority of these children of immigrants invest a substantial amount of time on daily school homework. Although wide variations are seen among the different national origin groups, at both T1 and T2 about 80 percent of the CILS sample reported spending more than an hour each day on homework, and over 40 percent spent over two hours daily on homework, well above the national U.S. average of less than an hour a day (Rumbaut, 1995, 1997a). The Asian-origin groups invested the most time on homework, while the Latin Americans invested the least.

## *EDUCATIONAL PERFORMANCE*

A key question raised by this study is whether the level of educational achievement exhibited by these children of immigrants matched, exceeded, or fell below the grade 9-12 average for the respective school districts overall – and hence how the immigrants' children compared to the children of non-immigrants. We can address this question directly with district-wide and CILS results from San Diego and Miami-Dade, focusing first on an issue of central public policy concern: school dropouts. A precise comparison of official dropout rates is possible, since the respective school systems are the same source of information for both populations and define the dropout measure equivalently. Specifically, we report here the multi-year (or longitudinal) dropout rate for grades 9-12, which measures the percentage of students enrolled in the 9th grade who dropped out of school before finishing high school four years later.

A first major finding is that, in both school districts on both coasts, a significantly greater proportion of students district-wide drop out of school than do the youth from immigrant families. The multi-year dropout rate for grades 9-12 in the Miami-Dade public schools was 17.6

[6]These value preferences stand in stark contrast to those of entering college freshmen in U.S. colleges in 1997. The annual UCLA nationwide poll, taken at the start of the Fall 1997 semester, found that 75 percent of freshmen chose being "very well off financially" as an essential goal, while only 41 percent chose "developing a meaningful philosophy of life" – value preferences which have switched places over the past three decades. In 1968, the survey results were the exact opposite, with only 41 percent of entering freshmen then selecting material affluence as an essential goal and 83 percent citing the importance of developing a meaningful philosophy of life. *See* Bronner (1998).

FIGURE 1 DROPOUT RATES OF CILS RESPONDENTS FROM MIAMI AND SAN DIEGO PUBLIC HIGH SCHOOLS BY 1996, BY ETHNO-NATIONAL ORIGIN

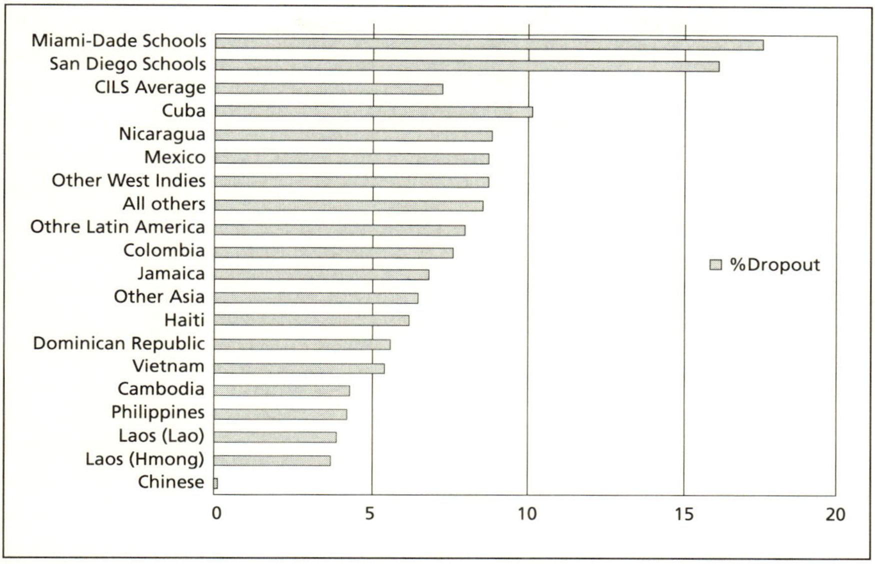


FIGURE 2. MEAN ACADEMIC GRADE POINT OF CILS RESPONDENTS, 1995, BY ETHNO-NATIONAL ORIGIN

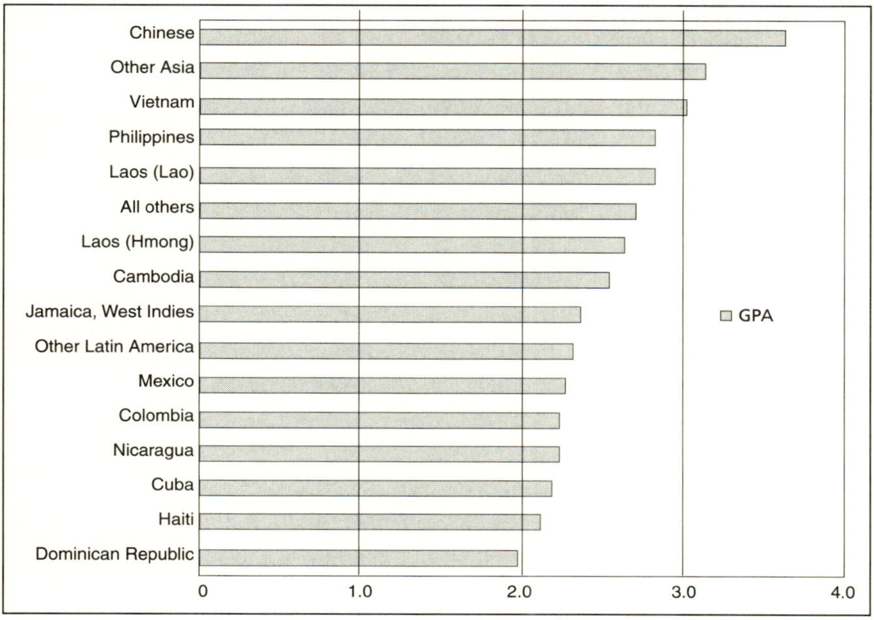

percent, or about double the rate of 8.9 percent for the entire original CILS sample of children of immigrants there – that is, of the 2,296 Miami-Dade public school students who were originally interviewed in 1992 in the 8th and 9th grades, 8.9 percent were officially determined to have dropped out of school at any point by 1996. On the other coast, the differential was even greater: the multi-year dropout rate for grades 9-12 in the San Diego schools was 16.2 percent, nearly triple the rate of 5.7 percent for the CILS sample there – that is, of the 2,420 students who were originally interviewed in 1992 in the 8th and 9th grades, only 5.7 percent were officially determined to have dropped out of school at any point by 1996.

The CILS dropout rates were also noticeably lower than the district-wide rates for preponderantly native non-Hispanic white high school students (13.6% in Miami-Dade, and 10.5% in San Diego). Lower dropout rates for children of immigrants were seen for both males and females, and for every racial-ethnic category. In Miami-Dade, the highest dropout rate in the district was found among non-Hispanic black students (20.2%), but the rate among Haitian, Jamaican and other West Indian children of immigrants was only 7.5 percent. In San Diego, among the students from immigrant families, the highest dropout rate was 8.7 percent for students of Latin American origin (including a rate of 8.8% among Mexican-origin youth), but even that rate was noticeably lower than the 26.5 percent district norm for all Hispanics, and slightly lower than the rate for non-Hispanic whites. Finally, while in both school systems the lowest dropout rates district-wide were registered by Asian-origin students (*most* of whom tend to come from immigrant families), on both coasts the Asian youth in the CILS sample (*all* of whom are children of immigrants) had lower rates still. These findings, coming from two of the nation's largest school districts most affected by mass immigration, are remarkably consistent.

Another key measure of school performance, academic grade point averages (GPAs), was examined comparatively with district-wide data from San Diego City Schools, broken down by grade level (9-12), compared against the GPAs earned in grades 9-12 in those same schools by the entire original CILS sample during 1992-95. The results showed that at every grade level the children of immigrants outperformed the district norms, although the gap narrowed over time and grade level. Only 29 percent of all 9th graders in the district had GPAs above 3.0 (top students with As and Bs in their academic classes), compared to a much higher 44 percent of the 9th graders from immigrant families; and while 36 percent of

9th graders district-wide had low GPAs under 2.0 (less than a C on average), only half as many (18%) of the children of immigrants performed as poorly. Those differentials declined over time by grade level, so that the advantage by the 12th grade was reduced to a few percentage points in favor of the children of immigrants. That narrowing of the GPA gap appears to be due primarily to the fact that, as noted above, a greater proportion of students district-wide drop out of school than do the youth from immigrant families.

However, while there are clearly significant overall differences between the children of immigrants and of natives taken as a whole, there are also very large differences among the children of immigrants themselves. In particular, as shown in Figures 1 and 2, we found wide disparities by national origin in both educational outcomes – GPAs and dropout rates. These results in turn portend a significant ethnic segmentation of the socioeconomic trajectories of these youths as they make their transition into the adult labor force.

As Figures 1 and 2 make clear, the Chinese finished high school with by far the highest GPAs and the lowest dropout rates in the study. They also reported very ambitious educational goals that matched those of other Asian-origin high-status immigrant groups (especially those from India, followed by the Japanese and Koreans). Exhibiting above average performance were the Vietnamese and the Filipinos, followed by Laotians and Cambodians – although, as seen earlier, the latter two groups also exhibited the lowest educational expectations for the future. The Jamaicans and other West Indians had lower GPAs, and the Haitians much lower still, yet nonetheless those Afro-Caribbean groups reported well above average ambitions.

Overall, the poorest performance was registered by Latin American youth, with the lowest GPAs in the sample found among the Dominicans, and, unexpectedly, the highest dropout rates among Cuban youth in Miami public schools (10.1%), followed by Mexican-origin youth in San Diego (8.8%). The dropout rate for the Cuban youth is particularly surprising, given the paradox that they are a highly assimilated group of longer residence in the U.S. than most among the "new immigration," of average to above average socioeconomic backgrounds, who have experienced less discrimination than any other group in the CILS sample, and who uniquely form a majority group in a dense and diversified immigrant enclave (over half of all Cubans in the U.S. are concentrated in the Miami metropolitan area alone). Among those of Latin American origin, Mexican,

Dominican, and Central American children showed the lowest educational expectations, while the Cubans (notwithstanding their lower GPAs and higher dropout rates) and South Americans were the most ambitious, reflecting the socioeconomic status of their parents. These results are striking, and raise yet another question: what explains them?

## *PREDICTORS OF ACHIEVEMENT AND AMBITION*

What set of factors was found to be most predictive of the children of immigrants' educational achievement and ambitions? With cross-sectional data, the fact that most of the variables we have reviewed thus far are highly correlated makes difficult a causal interpretation. But the CILS longitudinal data afford an opportunity to examine the effect of variables measured at T1 (1992) when these young people were in junior high, upon selected outcomes three to four years later at T2 (1995-96), around the end of senior high. The temporal ordering of these variables is thus unambiguous.

Specifically, we analyze three different outcomes (dependent variables) measured in 1995-96. Two are indicators of educational achievement reported by the school system: the latest GPA achieved, and having officially dropped out of school at any point since T1. The third outcome examined here is our measure of the highest educational expectations reported at T2 – *i.e.*, the most ambitious who responded in the T2 survey that they "realistically" expected to earn an advanced degree.

The selected predictors (independent variables), all measured in 1992, include national origin, gender, age, length of residence in the United States (a proxy for acculturation), parental socioeconomic status (a standardized composite measure of father's and mother's education and occupation, and home ownership), family structure, parent-child conflict (measured by a 3-item scale), English proficiency (a 4-item index of the student's ability to speak, understand, read and write in English), school homework hours per day, TV-watching hours per day, educational expectations reported at T1, ethnic self-identity, and self-esteem at T1 (measured with the 10-item Rosenberg global self-esteem scale; *see* Rumbaut, 1994b). Multivariate analyses controlling for all of these predictors simultaneously are presented in Table 7. We rely on OLS multiple linear regression for the analysis of GPAs (a continuous variable), and logistic regression for the analysis of dropping out and of the highest educational expectations (dichotomous variables). In each analysis two models are presented: the

**TABLE 7**

**T1 (1992) Predictors of T2 (1995-96) Educational Achievement and Ambition Outcomes: OLS and Logistic Regressions on GPAs, Educational Expectations, and Dropouts (CILS Longitudinal Sample)**

| | T2 (1995-96) Outcomes | | | | | |
|---|---|---|---|---|---|---|
| | GPA[1] | | Ambition[2] | | Dropout[3] | |
| T1 (1992) Predictors | Model I | Model II | Model I | Model II | Model I | Model II |
| Gender (1=female, 0=male) | 9.6 *** | 10.5 *** | 51.5 *** | 46.6 *** | -0.2 NS | -0.1 NS |
| Age (years) | -3.9 *** | -3.3 ** | -5.2 * | -6.4 * | 3.7 * | 3.3• |
| Years in U.S. (4=all my life) | -5.2 *** | -2.2 * | -7.9 ** | -7.8 ** | 0.1 NS | -0.9 NS |
| Parent socioeconomic status[4] | 5.3 *** | 7.6 *** | 149.0 *** | 93.9 *** | 0.6 NS | -0.9 NS |
| Intact family (1=yes, 0=no) | 9.6 *** | 6.2 *** | 0.8 NS | 3.7 * | -27.9 *** | -18.1 *** |
| Parent-child conflict index[5] | -2.8 *** | -4.1 *** | -10.5 ** | -10.1 ** | 0.5 NS | 0.5 NS |
| Homework hours per day | 15.2 *** | 11.7 *** | 59.0 *** | 65.9 *** | -5.4 * | -1.3 NS |
| TV hours per day | -7.5 *** | -5.6 *** | -14.3 *** | -19.4 *** | 0.3 NS | 0.0 NS |
| English proficiency index[6] | -1.4 NS | 0.6 NS | 15.6 *** | 11.8 ** | -0.0 NS | -0.1 NS |
| Educational expectations[7] | 9.8 *** | 11.8 *** | - | - | -3.8 * | -5.9 ** |
| Self-esteem[8] | 4.0 *** | 5.9 *** | 51.9 *** | 41.8 *** | -5.0 * | -6.3 ** |
| Panethnic identity[9] | -6.8 *** | -3.8 *** | -6.9 ** | -5.2 * | 0.5 NS | -0.0 NS |
| Vietnamese | - | 12.4 *** | - | 1.8 NS | - | -2.2 NS |
| Laotians and Cambodians | - | 8.8 *** | - | -25.4 *** | - | -7.6 ** |
| Filipinos | - | 9.6 *** | - | -19.5 *** | - | -6.1 * |
| Mexicans | - | 3.1 ** | - | -15.8 *** | - | -0.0 NS |
| Cubans | - | -5.9 *** | - | 0.3 NS | - | 5.1 * |
| Haitians | - | -3.1 ** | - | 3.2• | - | -0.3 NS |
| *Constant* | 10.2 *** | 7.5 *** | 6.1 * | 2.6 NS | -5.2 * | -3.2• |
| Adjusted R2 | .186 | .246 | - | - | - | - |
| Model Chi Square | - | - | 590.3 | 669.9 | 64.6 | 93.8 |
| (degrees of freedom) | | | (11) | (17) | (12) | (18) |

1 Figures are *t-ratios* from OLS multiple linear regressions of selected T1 predictors on T2 academic grade point average.
2 Figures are *Wald* statistics from logistic regressions (the sign of the logistic regression coefficient is added), indicating the strength and direction of the effect of selected T1 predictors on the T2 expectation of earning an advanced degree.
3 Figures are *Wald* statistics from logistic regressions (the sign of the logistic regression coefficient is added), indicating the strength and direction of the association between selected T1 predictors and having dropped out of school by T2.
4 Standardized composite index of father's and mother's education, occupational prestige, and home ownership.
5 Mean of three-item parent-child conflict scale, scored 1 to 4.
6 Mean of four-item scale (self-reported ability to speak, understand, read, and write English), scored 1 to 4.
7 "Realistically" expected, at T1, to go on to earn an advanced degree (=3), a college degree (=2), or less than college (=1).
8 Mean of ten-item Rosenberg self-esteem scale, scored 1 to 4.
9 Self-identified as "Hispanic," "Latino," "Chicano," "Black," or "Asian" at T1.

Significance levels: *** p < .0001 ** p < .01 * p < .05 • p < .10 NS = Not Significant

Note: The results on dropouts are for the CILS sample in both the San Diego and Miami-Dade County public schools only (N=4,716); they do not include Broward County public schools or two private schools in the Miami area.

first model introduces all of the predictor variables except nationality; then we enter a set of national-origin indicators to examine the extent to which ethnicity makes an additional contribution to achievement or not. The statistics shown in Table 7 permit a comparison of the relative strength and significance of the effect of each predictor on the respective outcome. The results may be briefly highlighted as follows:

## *Gender, Age, and Length of Residence in the U.S.*

Even after controlling for all other variables in these models, gender strongly affects grades and ambitions, with females exhibiting superior performance compared to male students, as well as having a significant edge in educational expectations. Gender makes no difference in terms of dropping out of school. Younger age is associated with better outcomes in all these models, although the effect is weak. More significantly, even with all other predictors controlled for, length of time in the United States – a proxy for degree of acculturation – retains a *negative* influence on academic grade point averages and on high educational expectations for the future. It does not, however, affect the likelihood of dropping out of school. This finding reinforces other research (*e.g.*, Rumbaut and Ima, 1988) which has indicated that the level of school engagement and of school work discipline tend to dissipate with increasing Americanization and over time in the United States, resulting in lower academic marks.

However, with length of residence in the U.S. controlled, as Table 7 also shows, the index of English proficiency is positively and significantly associated with high educational ambitions. While English fluency has no significant effect on grades or dropping out or school, it makes a difference to the student's realistic expectation of being able to achieve an advanced degree. In other analyses (not shown here) of only the CILS sample in San Diego, we also found that students who had been classified as LEP (Limited English Proficient) at T1 remained significantly associated with lower academic attainment by T2. On the other hand, FEP (Fluent English Proficient) students achieved higher GPAs and had lower dropout rates than both LEP and English-only students, confirming previous research pointing to the positive link of fluent bilingualism with cognitive achievement.

## *The Family – Resources and Vulnerabilities*

Children who come from intact families with both natural parents present at home clearly do much better – that is, they have higher GPAs, higher educational ambitions, and much lower dropout rates – than children being raised in stepfamilies or single-parent homes. In fact, an intact family had by far the strongest (negative) effect on dropping out of school than any other predictor in the models tested. The effect on GPAs and especially on ambition is even more pronounced in families with lower levels of parent-child conflict. The greater the stability of the family, both structurally *and* emotionally (in terms of the quality of parent-child interactions), the greater the educational achievement and expectations. Low-conflict intact families exhibit the best outcomes across the board; high-conflict non-intact families fare worst.

In addition, the socioeconomic status of the parents had strong positive effects on grades and ambitions for the future (it had by far the strongest effect of any other predictor on the children's expectations of achieving an advanced degree), but it washed out of the equation predicting the odds of dropping out of school. It is scarcely surprising that youths whose parents have a college education and higher status occupations perform much better in terms of achieving high grades, and in aspiring to advanced degrees, than do those whose parents have lesser levels of education or who work in low-wage jobs or are not in the labor force. Overall, a more cohesive, stable, and resourceful home environment leads to higher educational achievement – and in these respects too, children of immigrants are no different from the native-born.

## *Work Discipline and Future Goals in Early Adolescence*

The students who had dedicated more hours to school work in junior high at T1 did significantly better in terms of educational achievement three years later – a clear illustration of the positive long-term effects of the early inculcation of disciplined work habits and of school engagement. They were also much more likely to expect to earn an advanced degree. That work ethic is part of the reason for the superior school performance found among these children of immigrants relative to district-wide norms. Conversely, students who spent a large number of hours in front of the television by age 14 were more prone to get poor grades in subsequent years and to report lower aspirations (though it had no effect on dropping out of school). The generally negative effect of television on children's academic performance is illustrated by these findings.

Educational and occupational goals and values in early adolescence are themselves closely associated with remaining in school and with better educational performance. As Table 7 shows, high educational expectations at T1 were strongly and positively associated with high GPAs and ambitions at T2, and were significantly and negatively associated with dropping out of high school, net of other factors. Taken together, these results show that, even among student from low socioeconomic backgrounds, and for both males and females, work discipline and a clear sense of future goals pay off in achievement dividends.

### *Self-Esteem and Pan-Ethnic Self-identities*

Other subjective factors also shaped performance outcomes. The self-esteem score at T1 remained significantly associated with all of these outcomes across the board: the higher the self-esteem score at T1, the better the students' school performance three years later (in both higher GPAs and lower odds of dropping out), and the greater their educational ambitions. And pan-ethnic self-identities (*e.g.*, Chicano, Latino) selected by age 14 or 15 in junior high were linked three years later with lower GPAs and lower aspirations. No such effects were observed for any of the other types of ethnic self-identities reported at T1. That finding lends some support to analyses that have pointed to the defensive development in the adolescent years of "oppositional" or "adversarial" identities which, while protective of self-esteem, disparage doing well in school as "acting white" and as a betrayal of ethnic loyalty (*see* the papers collected in Gibson and Ogbu, 1991; Portes, 1996; Rumbaut and Cornelius, 1995; *cf.* Waters, 1996).

## *CONCLUSION*

The results described above illuminate the adaptive challenges that children of immigrants confront in their transitions – and transformations – to an American adulthood. Mostly from Asia, Latin America and the Caribbean, they face diverse circumstances that can significantly add to the developmental stressors of adolescence, and exhibit wide variations among national origin groups in their vulnerabilities and resources, and in their patterns of acculturation, ambition, and achievement. The findings show that there is no single assimilation path but rather a variety of paths which, depending on the mix of circumstances, may lead to upward or downward assimilation to different sectors of American society. As previously noted, the very large differences by national origin in all educational outcomes examined through the end of high school may presage a significant ethnic segmentation of their future social and economic trajectories. Still, all things considered, the overall picture that emerges from our study thus far is one of resilient ambition and noteworthy achievement. Whether that can be sustained as these youths make their entry into the world of work and careers in a restructured U.S. economy, as they form new families of their own, and as they seek to carve out a meaningful place in the society of which they are the newest members, remain as yet unanswered questions. They are the questions that will guide our work as we return to the field to locate and survey once more the original sample.

## *REFERENCES*

Bronner, E.
1998 "College Freshmen Aiming for High Marks in Income." *New York Times,* January 12.

Farley, R.
1996 *The New American Reality: Who We Are, How We Got Here, and Where We Are Going.* New York: Russell Sage Foundation.

Fradd, S. H.
1996 *The Economic Impact of Spanish-Language Proficiency in Metropolitan Miami.* Miami: School of Education, University of Miami.

Jensen, L. and Y. Chitose
1994 "Today's Second Generation: Evidence from the 1990 Census." *International Migration Review,* 28(4):714-735.

Kao, G. and M. Tienda
1995 "Optimism and Achievement: The Educational Performance of Immigrant Youth." *Social Science Quarterly,* 76:1-19.

Landale, N. S. and R. S. Oropesa
1995 "Immigrant Children and the Children of Immigrants: Inter- and Intra-Ethnic Group Differences in the United States." Population Research Group (PRG) Research Paper 95-2. East Lansing, MI: Institute for Public Policy and Social Research, Michigan State University.

Mears, T.
1997 "Miami Hispanics Losing Their Spanish." *Boston Globe,* October 5.

Navarro, M.
1996 "Bilingual Parents Dismayed by English's Pull on Children." *New York Times,* August 31.

Oropesa, R. S. and N. S. Landale
1997 "In Search of the New Second Generation: Alternative Strategies for Identifying Second Generation Children and Understanding Their Acquisition of English." *Sociological Perspectives,* 40(3):427-455.

Portes, A., ed.
1996 *The New Second Generation.* New York: Russell Sage Foundation.

Portes, A. and L. Hao
1998 "E Pluribus Unum: Bilingualism and Language Loss in the Second Generation." *Sociology of Education,* 71:269-294.

Portes, A. and R. G. Rumbaut
2001 *Legacies: The Story of the Immigrant Second Generation.* Berkeley and New York: University of California Press and Russell Sage Foundation. [in press]

———
1996 *Immigrant America: A Portrait.* 2nd edition. Berkeley: University of California Press.

Portes, A. and A. Stepick
1993 *City on the Edge: The Transformation of Miami.* Berkeley: University of California Press.

Riis, J. A.
1892 *The Children of The Poor.* New York: Charles Scribner's Sons.

Rumbaut, R. G.
1997a "Ties that Bind: Immigration and Immigrant Families in the United States." In *Immigration and the Family: Research and Policy on U.S. Immigrants.* Ed. A. Booth, A. C. Crouter, and N. S. Landale. Mahwah, NJ: Lawrence Erlbaum Associates. Pp. 3-46.

———
1997b "Assimilation and Its Discontents: Between Rhetoric and Reality." *International Migration Review,* 31(4):923-960.

———
1995 "The New Californians: Comparative Research Findings on the Educational Progress of Immigrant Children." In *California's Immigrant Children: Theory, Research, and Implications for Educational Policy.* Ed. R. G. Rumbaut and W. Cornelius. La Jolla: Center for U.S.-Mexican Studies, University of California, San Diego.

———
1994a "Origins and Destinies: Immigration to the United States Since World War II." *Sociological Forum,* 9(4):583-621.

———
1994b "The Crucible Within: Ethnic Identity, Self-Esteem, and Segmented Assimilation Among Children of Immigrants." *International Migration Review,* 28(4):748-794.

Rumbaut, R. G. and W. Cornelius, eds.
1995 *California's Immigrant Children: Theory, Research, and Implications for Educational Policy.* La Jolla: Center for U.S.-Mexican Studies, University of California, San Diego.

Rumbaut, R. G. and K. Ima
1988 *The Adaptation of Southeast Asian Refugee Youth: A Comparative Study.* Two volumes. Washington, DC: U.S. Office of Refugee Resettlement.

Rumbaut, R. G. and A. Portes, eds.
2001 *Ethnicities: Children of Immigrants in America.* Berkeley and New York: University of California Press and Russell Sage Foundation. [in press]

Thompson, M. S. , K. L. Alexander, and D. R. Entwisle
1988 "Household Composition, Parental Expectations, and School Achievement." *Social Forces,* 67:424-451.

Waters, M.

1996 "Ethnic and Racial Identities of Second-Generation Black Immigrants in New York City." In *The New Second Generation.* Ed. A. Portes. New York: Russell Sage Foundation. Pp. 171-196.

Zhou, M.

1997 "Growing Up American: The Challenge Confronting Immigrant Children and Children of Immigrants." *Annual Review of Sociology,* 23:63-95.

# APPENDIX I

# CMS Twenty Second National Legal Conference on Immigration and Refugee Policy

*Hyatt Regency Hotel, Washington, DC*
March 30–26, 1999

**THURSDAY, MARCH 30, 2000**

7:45 a.m. – 8:45 a.m. FINAL REGISTRATION
8:45 a.m. – 9:30 a.m.
*Welcome:* Lydio F. Tomasi, *CMS Executive Director*
*Opening Remarks:* "The Immigration Agenda: A View from Congress"
Congressman Howard L. Berman (D-CA)

---

9:30 a.m. – 10:45 a.m.: SESSION I **Columbia Room B**

---

**REFORM OF THE 1996 IMMIGRATION LAWS**

*Chair:* Austin T. Fragomen, Jr.,
*Fragomen, Del Rey, Bernsen & Loewy, New York*

1. The Administration View
   Owen B. Cooper, *INS General Counsel*
2. The Impact of the 1996 Criminal Alien Provisions
   Nancy Morawetz, *New York University Law School*
3. Due Process Provisions of IIRIRA
   Carol Leslie Wolchok, *American Bar Association*
4. How to Fix Some Untoward IIRIRA Provisions
   Angela Kelly, *National Immigration Forum*

*Comment:* Donald Keener, Deputy Director for Appellate Litigation,
U.S. Department of State

10:45 a.m. – 11:00 a.m. Coffee/Tea Break

| 11:00 a.m. – 12:30 p.m. | SESSION II | **Columbia Room B** |
|---|---|---|

**EMPLOYMENT MIGRATION INTO THE UNITED STATES**

*Chair:* Adolfo Mata, *Migrant Health Program, DHHS*

1. Temporary Workers
Lindsay Lowell, *Institute for the Study of International Migration, Georgetown University*
2. Labor Shortage Complaints at the Top and Bottom of the Labor Market: Similarities/Differences in Argument, Data and Policy Proposals
Philip L. Martin, *University of California, Davis*
The Movement of Bringing in Unskilled Labor into the U.S.
Rick Swartz, *President, Rick Swartz and Associates, Washington, DC*
4. The View from Congress
Lynn Frendt Shotwell, *American Council on International Personnel*

*Comment:* Bruce Goldstein, *Farmworker Justice Fund*

12:30 p.m. – 2:00 p.m. AWARDS LUNCHEON PROGRAM **Ticonderoga Room**

*Presiding:* Marion Dawson Carr, *Dearfield Associates and CMS Board of Trustees*

*Invocation:* Msgr. William P. Fay
*United States Catholic Conference*

*Keynote Speaker and Award Recipient:* Senator Spencer Abraham (R-MI),
*Chairman, U.S. Senate Subcommittee on Immigration*

| 2:00 p.m. – 3:30 p.m. | SESSION III | **Columbia Room B** |
|---|---|---|

**INS RESTRUCTURING**

*Chair:* Thomas W. Hussey, *Director, Office of Immigration Litigation, U.S. Department of Justice*

1. Framing the Issue
T. Alexander Aleinikoff, Georgetown University Law Center
2. An Update from Capitol Hill
Lora Reis, *Counsel, House Subcommittee on Immigration and Claims*

3. The Administration View
Fred G. Gordon, *Acting Director, INS Office of Restructuring*

3:30 p.m. – 3:45 p.m. Coffee/Tea Break

3:45 p.m . – 5:45 p.m. SESSION IV **Columbia Room B**

**INS PROCESSING: ENTRY, APPLICATIONS, CITIZENSHIP**

*Chair:* Gideon Aronoff, HIAS, Washington, D.C.

1. INS Citizenship Processing and Backlogs
Michael Pearson, *INS, Executive Associate Commissioner of Field Operations*
2. Translating INS Regulations into Service
Fujie Ohata, *Director, INS Service Center*
3. Impact of INS Processing on the Community
Donald Kerwin, *CLINIC, Washington, DC*
4. Legal Implications
Margaret Catillaz, *AILA President-Elect*

6:30 p.m. – 8:30 p.m. **Reception at the US Capitol**
Co-Sponsored by the American Immigration Lawyers Association

9:00 a.m. – 10:30 a.m. SESSION V **Columbia Room B**

**HUMAN RIGHTS OF MIGRANTS: REFUGEE PROTECTION GENDER-BASED VIOLENCE AND TRAFFICKING**

*Chair:* Mark Franken, *Migration and Refugee Services, USCC*

1. Combating Human Smuggling by Enlisting the Victims: A Modest Proposal
Arthur C. Helton, *Council on Foreign Relations*
2. Gender Asylum and Violence Against Women Act
Deborah Anker, *Harvard University*
3. States and Trafficking
James Puleo, *Director of the Bureau of Narcotics and Law Enforcement, U.S. Department of State*

10:30 a.m. – 10:45 am. Coffee/Tea Break

| 10:45 a.m. – 12:30 p.m. | SESSION VI | **Columbia Room B** |
|---|---|---|

INTEGRATION OF IMMIGRANTS AND THEIR DESCENDANTS

*Chair:* Charles B. Keely, *Georgetown University*

1. Data on the Second Generation
2. Language Acquisition and Language Politics in the U.S.
   Gillian Stevens, *University of Illinois, Urbana*
3. Political Incorporation of New Immigrants
   Lorraine C. Minnite, *Barnard College, Columbia University*

*Discussant:* Michael Le May, *California State University, San Bernardino*

**ASYLUM PROCESSING AND DUE PROCESS**

*Chair:* Mark Franken,
*Executive Director, Migration and Refugee Services, USCC*

*Panelists:*
1. David A. Martin, *Virginia School of Law*
2. Carol L. Wolchok, Esq., *American Bar Associaton*
3. Karen Koning AbuZayd, *UNHCR (U.S. and Caribbean)*

6:30 P.M. – 8:30 P.M. **RECEPTION AT CASA ITALIANA**
595 Third Street, NW, Washington, D.C. 20001
(Walking Distance from the Hyatt Regency Hotel)
**Remarks by Congressional Legislators**
Hot Hors D'oeuvres
Imported Wines

**FRIDAY, MARCH 26,**

| 9:00 a.m. – 10:30 p.m. | SESSION V | **Columbia B** |
|---|---|---|

**IMMIGRATION POLICYMAKING:**
**MULTILATERAL AGREEMENTS AND CONSULTATIONS**

*Chair:* Charles B. Keely, *Georgetown University*

*Panelists:*
1. Mark Elliot, *Bureau of Population, Refugees and Migrants, Dept. of State*
2. Susan Gzesh, *University of Chicago*
3. Gary P. Freeman, University of Texas, Austin

10:30 a.m. – 10:45 a.m. Coffee/Tea Break

| 10:45 a.m. – 12.45 p.m. | SESSION VI | **Columbia B** |
|---|---|---|

IMMIGRATION LAW ENFORCEMENT:
COMPARISON OF DOCUMENTATION AND CONTROL

*Chair:* Jeanne Butterfield,

*Executive Director, American Immigration Lawyers Association*

*Panelists:*
1. Robert Bach, *Associate Commissioner, INS*
2. Stephen Legomsky, *Washington University School of Law*
3. Patrick Weil, *CEPIC, Paris*
4. Dr. Christian Klos, *Ministry of the Interior, Germany*

# APPENDIX II

# Program Organizing Committee

| | |
|---|---|
| Chairman | Lydio F. Tomasi, *Executive Director, Center for Migration Studies of New York, Inc.* |
| Members | Austin T. Fragomen, Jr., *Fragomen, Del Rey & Bernsen, New York*<br>Anna Isgro, *CMS Washington, DC Representative*<br>Charles B. Keely, *Georgetown University*<br>Mark J. Miller, *University of Delaware* |

ADVISORY COMMITTEE

| | |
|---|---|
| Alexander Aleinikoff | *Georgetown University Law School* |
| Deborah Anker | *Harvard University Law School* |
| Thomas J. Archdeacon | *University of Wisconsin* |
| Frank D. Bean | *University of Texas* |
| Vernon Briggs | *Cornell University* |
| Jeanne Butterfield | *American Immigration Lawyers Association* |
| Jorge Bustamante | *El Colegio de la Frontera Norte Tijuana* |
| Fernando Chang-Muy | *UNHCR Branch Office, Washington, D.C.* |
| Muzaffar Chishti | *ILGWU, New York* |
| Barry Chiswick | *University of Illinois* |
| Luca Dall'Oglio | *I.O.M., Washington, D.C.* |
| Ralston Deffenbaugh | *Lutheran Immigration & Refugee Service, New York* |
| Bishop N. DiMarzio | *Bishop of Camden, N.J.* |
| Mark Franken | *USCC Migration and Refugee Services, Washington, D.C.* |
| Lawrence H. Fuchs | *Brandeis University* |
| Leonard Glickman | *HIAS, New York* |
| Guy S. Goodwin-Gill | *International Journal of Refugee Law, Ottawa* |
| Mark Handelman | *New York Association for New Americans* |
| Arthur C. Helton | *Council on Foreign Relations, New York* |
| Francesco Isgro | *U.S. Department of Justice, Washington, D.C.* |
| Stephen H. Legomsky | *Washington University School of Law* |
| Arnold H. Leibowitz | *Washington, D.C.* |
| Michael LeMay | *California State University, San Bernardino* |
| David Martin | *University of Virginia School of Law* |
| Philip L. Martin | *University of California, Davis* |
| David Martin | *University of Virginia School of Law* |
| Philip L. Martin | *University of California, Davis* |
| Susan Martin | *Institute for the Study of International Migration, Georgetown University Law Center* |
| Demetrios Papademetriou | *Carnegie Endowment for International Peace* |
| Richard Parkins | *Episcopal Migration Ministries, New York* |
| William Sage | *Immigration and Refugee Program, CWS, New York* |

| | |
|---|---|
| Peter A. Schey | *Center for Human Rights and Constitutional Law, Los Angeles* |
| Paul W. Schmidt | *Board of Immigration Appeals, Washington, D.C.* |
| Peter H. Schuck | *Yale Law School* |
| Frank Sharry | *National Immigration, Refugee & Citizenship Forum* |
| Marta Tienda | *Population Research Center, University of Chicago* |
| Michael Teitelbaum | *Alfred P. Sloan Foundation, New York* |
| Aristide Zolberg | *New School for Social Research, New York* |

# INDEX

C



D